# KURSK 1943

# KURSK 1943

## HITLER'S BITTER HARVEST

ANTHONY TUCKER-JONES

In my opinion the Battle of Kursk Salient was the turning point in the Great Patriotic War. It was decisive in determining the defeat of Hitlerite Germany and the ultimate triumph of our Soviet Army, our ideology, and our Communist Party.

Nikita Khrushchev

First published 2018

The History Press
The Mill, Brimscombe Port
Stroud, Gloucestershire, GL5 2QG
www.thehistorypress.co.uk

British Library Cataloguing in Publication Data.
A catalogue record for this book is available from the British Library.

ISBN 978 0 7509 8448 5

Typesetting and origination by The History Press
Printed and bound in Great Britain by TJ International Ltd

# CONTENTS

# INTRODUCTION

# 'DRIPPING WITH FRAGRANT JUICES'

That summer a warm wind blew across the Russian steppe, nurturing the land despite the ravages of war. It was welcome recompense after the bitter winter of 1942–43. In the Kursk region the state farms found themselves in the midst of a vast fortress. The crops were supplemented by a much deadlier harvest, millions of mines sown with one intent: to kill Nazis.

It was high summer, putting some in a poetic mood. 'If you like fancy phrases, you could say that the countryside was in full bloom, dripping with fragrant juices,' recalled Political Commissar Nikita Khrushchev when he first arrived in the Kursk salient.[1] He had seen the sappers toiling in the summer heat and been briefed on the Red Army's extensive preparations.

Soviet leader Joseph Stalin sent him to act as political advisor to Lieutenant General Vatutin, commander of the Voronezh Front, holding the southern shoulder of the salient. Khrushchev was glad to be at Kursk, away from the awful killing fields of Stalingrad; it gave him fresh purpose and helped him forget his recent painful news. This was what any father dreads – the loss of a child. Earlier in the year Khrushchev stood phone in hand in a state of anguish, his fighter pilot son was missing presumed dead. At the end of 1942 and early 1943 Nikita Khrushchev was riding high following his involvement in the defence of Stalingrad. The Red Army's stunning victory was a turning point, making up for the disastrous previous two years of conflict. For Khrushchev his failure to retake Kharkov in 1942 had been expunged.

Nikita's relationship with Stalin was rocky, but he was a born survivor and he took great pride in his role at Stalingrad. As the Communist Party boss for Ukraine he had overseen the disastrous attempts to liberate Kharkov – Stalingrad had been a punishment posting, a much better option than the firing squad. After his moment of triumph his son Leonid had been shot down. To add to his sense of woe they could not find Leonid's body, which led to dark mutterings that he had defected. To make matters worse Leonid's wife, Liuba, was accused of spying and arrested. Khrushchev and the rest of his family had been left feeling politically exposed.

Nikita was now being given another chance to redeem himself over the Kharkov debacle. Having toured Kursk he noted with great optimism:

> Our armies under Rokossovsky [commanding the Central Front on the northern shoulder of the salient] were supposed to start an offensive of their own on 20 July. We were sure we would be successful, that we would crush the Germans and push west to the Dnieper. We were all driven by a single desire – to break through the German lines and to liberate Kharkov.[2]

Khrushchev was a local, having been born in the village of Kalinovka in the Kursk region. Just for a moment he recalled his religious parents and the icons that had adorned the walls of the family home. It had been a simple life – it was not so simple any more.

Novelist Vasily Grossman, special correspondent for the *Red Star* military newspaper, was seated on the terrace of a dacha enjoying the company of old comrades. Although Jewish and a non-combatant, he still wore a uniform and was accepted by those around him for who he was. Besides, as a chronicler of the war against the Nazis he was very good at his job.

Grossman was also captivated by the natural beauty to be found in the Kursk salient. In early May 1943 he made a welcome reunion when he travelled to see General Chuikov's Stalingrad veterans, who were part of the reserve Steppe Front just behind Kursk. 'I've arrived at the 62nd Stalingrad Army. It is now stationed among the gardens that are beginning to blossom – a wonderful place with violets and bright green grass. It is peaceful. Larks are singing.'[3]

The atmosphere with Chuikov and his officers was not so peaceful. They were seething over their portrayal in a supposedly documentary film *Stalingrad* that was doing the rounds. Vasily, peering through his small circular wire-framed glasses, had hoped to hear of future battle plans, but instead had to listen to bitter griping. Chuikov felt that he and his men were seen as little more than sacrificial lambs while General Rokossovsky's forces received all the glory for smashing the Axis armies around Stalingrad.

Grossman resolved to visit Rokossovsky's headquarters to find out what was happening at Kursk. One of the perks of his job was that he was granted access wherever he went. His first port of call would be Rokossovsky's intelligence officers, they would tell him what was going on. Or so he hoped.

Another Stalingrad veteran was Mansur Abdulin, who found himself on a rattling train en route to the Voronezh Front with the 66th Guards Rifle Division. Stopping off at the village of Dobrinka he recalled, 'Even though in those days life was very hard, there was a festive mood in the streets, and everyone was sure that the war would soon be over.'[4] He arrived before the harvest and food was scarce, but he did not mind. He was just glad to be free of the terrible lice that had plagued him and his comrades at Stalingrad. They had driven him to such distraction that he had even considered throwing himself into a blazing tank to escape their constant biting torment. His division was to deploy to the north of a place called Prokhorovka inside the Kursk salient.

Second Lieutenant Evgeni Bessonov was beginning to think that the fighting was passing him by. He was a Moscow lad born and bred. When war had broken out he and his mate were on their way to the cinema. Within days he had volunteered to help dig anti-tank defences in the Bryansk region until sent back to Moscow. During that time he had been bombed several times by the Luftwaffe. Although the bombs had fallen far away he and his fellow workers had run 'like rabbits'. He had been conscripted in the summer of 1941 and sent to military academy, but frustratingly had seen no further action. He was assigned to a reserve rifle brigade that took no part in the counteroffensive at Stalingrad. By the spring of 1943 he was languishing at Kuchino just outside Moscow as part of the officer reserve. 'We did almost nothing there,' he lamented, 'and tried to get sent to the front as quickly as possible.'[5]

The Soviet High Command though had plans for Bessonov and his brother officers. They were to be sent to the Bryansk Front facing the Nazi salient at Orel, which formed the northern shoulder around the Soviet defences at Kursk. Bessonov was destined to join the 49th Mechanised Brigade, which was part of the 4th Tank Army. Bessonov endured an arduous trip there: 'We started our journey from Moscow by train, then we hitchhiked and then even had to walk.'[6]

Someone else, like Khrushchev and Grossman, who was glad to be in the Kursk region and free of the horrors of Stalingrad was Lieutenant Antonina Lebedeva. Known to her friends as Tonya, she had arrived at the Bryansk Front in the spring of 1943 with the 65th Guards Fighter Aviation Regiment. Although her unit was predominantly male, she was not the only woman as she was joined by Klavdiya Blinova.

Lebedeva studied at Moscow State University, developed a passion for flying and joined a local club. At the outbreak of the war she signed up with the Red Air Force to become a fighter pilot. She had fought in defence of Saratov and then Stalingrad. Lebedeva was almost killed on 10 January 1943 when she tangled with two enemy fighters. Although she shot one down, her aircraft was badly damaged and while still under attack managed to make an emergency wheels-up landing.

Much further north in the Kremlin, aircraft designer Alexander Yakovlev was having a very bad day. He and other aircraft industry representatives had been summoned by Stalin because a problem with his Yak-9 fighter was holding up an 'important operation'. The boss was furious, he had been briefed that poor quality paints and lacquers had been used on the wooden airframes. 'You're being made a fool of, your plane is being sabotaged and you just stand by,' said Stalin coldly to the assembled aviation experts.[7] During Stalingrad the Yak had exhibited a very nasty habit of catching fire, in addition the coatings were not protecting the aircraft from the unforgiving Russian weather.

There was tension in the room and everyone stared nervously at their shoes. 'Our whole fighter plane force is out of commission,' raged Stalin. 'There have been a dozen cases of the skin separating from the wing. The pilots are afraid to fly. How has this come about?' He was reacting to reports that the fighters gathered for the Kursk operation were now non-airworthy after being left exposed. They were coming unglued.

Alongside Yakovlev, Pyotr Dement'ev, Deputy Commissar for Aircraft Production, bore the brunt of Stalin's gathering fury. Yakovlev witnessed 'Dement'ev stood there, completely flushed, nervously twirling a piece of the ill-fated covering in his fingers.'

Yakovlev was aware of the major military preparations in the Orel–Kursk area, but felt it would take up to two months to repair all the aircraft affected. Suddenly Dement'ev, in a state of sheer panic, announced the work would be done within two weeks. For a second you could have heard a pin drop; Dement'ev had committed himself and his colleagues to an impossible deadline. Flabbergasted, Yakovlev could do nothing but concede: 'I swear that in the shortest possible time the defect will be corrected.' Stalin seemed mollified.

Under ideal conditions the aircraft would be recalled and the problem rectified in the factory, but these were not ideal times. After frantic phone calls to the main fighter factories, special repair brigades were rapidly despatched to Kursk to commence immediate field repairs. It would be a race against time before Stalin's 'important operation' commenced.

Seated in his office in the affluent Berlin district of Zehlendorf, Colonel Günther d'Alquen put down the latest copy of *The Black Corps*, the official newspaper of the Waffen-SS. Producing a weekly was no great hardship. His other job though was slightly more demanding as he was also responsible for the paper's war correspondents or SS-Kriegsberichter.[8] Reichsführer-SS Heinrich Himmler had got word that his SS Panzer Corps was to be involved in Operation Citadel, the army's big push this summer. Himmler had been delighted that it had retrieved the situation at Kharkov earlier in the year and had flown out personally to congratulate the men of Das Reich's Tiger tank unit. The Reichsführer liked to be followed around by a Waffen-SS cine cameraman and d'Alquen's photographers had been on hand to record the moment. Himmler was now determined he would get his share of the glory this time around as well.

D'Alquen's illustrious predecessor, the writer Kurt Eggers, was a hard act to follow. He had served with a Panzer company before becoming editor of *The Black Corps* and commander of the SS-Kriegsberichter Battalion. Eggers was soon thirsting for combat again and had joined the 5th SS Panzergrenadier Division *Wiking*, a unit formed from foreign volunteers fighting on the Eastern Front. He had only just come back from the Caucasus and as far as d'Alquen was concerned Eggers was going to get himself killed. His wife, Traute Kaiser, and four children would not thank him for that. Prancing around the battlefield was no place for an intellectual, after all Eggers was a poet and playwright not a real Panzertruppen.

D'Alquen now had under his command combat reporters attached to all the major Waffen-SS units.[9] Typically his men were not drawn from the SS training schools at Bad Tölz in Bavaria and Braunschweig but from the media, from Germany's thriving cinema, newspaper and radio industries. In the early days the reporters had been embedded out of harm's way with headquarters, these days they were in the thick of it.

His men had recorded the SS Panzer Corps triumphantly rolling back into Kharkov in March 1943 and this had greatly pleased the Reichsführer.

Himmler's office had been on the line, he had given explicit instructions that his reporters and photographers were to give significant coverage to the two premier SS Panzergrenadier divisions. Again he was particularly interested in the Tiger tanks. D'Alquen was not entirely sure why so much fuss was being made about the Tiger, but he ensured that the relevant orders were passed down to his company and platoon commanders. It would be a busy summer for his SS–Kriegsberichter.

General Wolfgang Thomale put down the phone and rubbed his chin. Since the start of the year good news had been in short supply. The Nazi-controlled media had put a brave face on the loss of an entire army at Stalingrad. The press and radio had been full of heroic resistance, ultimate sacrifice on the Volga, blah, blah, but you could not just shrug off the loss of a quarter of a million men like it was of no consequence – especially when it affected so many families. Behind closed doors people were beginning to ask what was going on.

Unhappily, Wolfgang knew exactly what was going on. Their Führer, Adolf Hitler, had set his heart on a place that Germany and indeed the rest of the world had never heard of – Kursk. Wolfgang had been in the presence of the Führer on a number of occasions and struggled to understand his leader's logic. Especially when by Hitler's own admission the thought of Kursk made him sick to the stomach.

Hitler's new powerful Panther tank was supposed to be the answer to all their prayers, but six months after production had started it was still being a bloody headache and had not yet even seen combat. Hitler, fed up of constantly delaying his ambitious plans, wanted it ready for the summer at all costs. Thomale had just been on the phone to the factory director. It was still not good news. The factories were supposed to be cranking out 200 Panther tanks a month, rising to 600; by now there should have been enough to equip at least three whole tank divisions. However, the first pre-production models that had appeared in late 1942 proved a complete disaster. Some 250 tanks should have been delivered by mid-May 1943, but this had not happened either. Now the director was promising 324 Panthers by the end of the month. Thomale knew the man was just saying what everyone wanted to hear, delivering was another matter.

Wolfgang Thomale, as Chief of Staff to General Heinz Guderian, was worried about his boss. The latter, in his role as head of all the Panzer forces, was constantly crossing swords with the Führer. Guderian was in a wholly unique and privileged position as he operated outside the armed forces chain of command. He answered directly to Hitler and no one else.

This obviously made Guderian many enemies amongst Hitler's inner circle. Besides his responsibility for overseeing the myriad of armoured forces and their facilities, Guderian liked to keep well informed about the strategic situation. It was this strategic awareness that had got him in trouble in 1941, when he vehemently argued the army should dig in for the winter on the Eastern Front. Hitler thought otherwise and saw Guderian's position as flagrant insubordination. Since his new appointment Guderian had created his own command that neatly sidestepped all the very senior generals surrounding Hitler.

Wolfgang was well aware of his boss's impetuous and hot-tempered nature. Nonetheless, Guderian was a shrewd and experienced operator. During May 1943 he had regularly lobbied Hitler not to launch a summer offensive at Kursk. Thomale had attended these meetings and was alarmed at the prospect of Guderian getting sacked again. He was also seeing the reports coming from Major Meinrad Lauchert down at Grafenwöhr regarding the troublesome Panther. This was proving to be Guderian's Achilles heel.

Guderian was not a happy man at the best of times, but 1 June 1943 was proving to be a particularly irksome day. He had flown to the Grafenwöhr training base in Bavaria to see Lauchert and his two Panzer battalion commanders. He knew what they wanted and that was to grumble yet again about the Panther. Early in the year the mechanics and fitters from the manufacturers had done everything they could at the Erlangen training ground near Grafenwöhr to resolve the teething problems. There were serious issues with the engine, transmission and steering.

Some bright spark had decided that the Panther should be waterproofed and the engine compartment was lined with rubber. The overheating resulted in engine fires. The exasperated crews could not understand why, after so much combat experience with the other Panzers, the designers could not get it right this time round. The only thing they really liked was the very powerful gun.

In April the Panthers had been unceremoniously sent back to the factory and the crews shipped off to France. They had only just returned to Erlangen when Guderian arrived. After his visit he flew on to Berlin and was aghast to discover that Hitler had got it in his head to send their new tanks to Greece to guard against a British landing in the Peloponnese. What madness was this; it was akin to Hitler's insistence the previous year on wasting the then new Tiger tank by sending it to fight at Leningrad and in Tunisia. It had been expended in penny packets and swiftly captured by the Allies. It was quickly pointed out that the Panther could not cope with the local Greek bridges and narrow mountain tracks.

'I spent 15 June worrying about our problem child, the Panther,' recalled Guderian. 'The track suspension and the drive were not right and the optics were also not yet satisfactory. On the next day I told Hitler of my reasons for not wishing to see the Panthers sent into action in the East. They were simply not yet ready to go to the front.'[10] Three days later Guderian arrived back at Grafenwöhr to listen to a litany of woe. Aside from the ongoing technical problems, not least was that crew training remained inadequate and many of them lacked battle experience.

It mattered little as Guderian had been overruled and the Panthers ordered east. All Guderian could do was commiserate with Lauchert. He told Thomale that the Panther was to fight at Kursk whether he liked it or not. If it failed to perform then it would be on Guderian to explain why.

At the beginning of April 1943 General von Mellenthin, Chief of Staff of 48th Panzer Corps, went on much-needed leave hoping to spend a brief spell at home. Instead he found himself in the Masurian Lakes region of East Prussia on the way to the fortress of Lötzen (now the Polish town of Giżycko). This was the headquarters of the Army High Command and he had been summoned by General Zeitzler, Chief of the Army General Staff. The nearby Boyen fortress was also home to Reinhard Gehlen's Eastern Front military intelligence organisation.

He smiled to himself, knowing how much his corps commander, Otto von Knobelsdorff, would have hated this trip. It was a not unpleasant flight as the hilly and picturesque lake land contained several thousand lakes that sparkled in the sunlight. During the First World War it had been the scene of two battles with the Russians.

Mellenthin assumed he was to brief Zeitzler on the combat readiness of his corps after the fighting in the Kharkov area. In addition to this though, Mellenthin learned of 'a great offensive in which we were destined to play a very significant part'.[11] Mellenthin was enthused by Zeitzler's plan:

> As part of the 4th Panzer Army, the 48th Panzer Corps was to be the spearhead of the main drive from the south. I welcomed the idea, for our hardened and experienced Panzer divisions had suffered little in the recent thrust on Kharkov, and were fit and ready for another battle as soon as the state of the ground would permit us to move. Moreover, at this stage the Russian defences around Kursk were by no means adequate to resist a determined attack.[12]

Mellenthin appreciated the utility of an operation with a limited objective. However, he left the meeting feeling deflated after Zeitzler informed him that Hitler was postponing the offensive until a full brigade of Panthers was ready for action. Mellenthin knew that time was simply not on their side. Intelligence indicated that the Red Army had not yet recovered from its mauling at Kharkov and was still making good its losses. 'A delay of one or two months,' observed Mellenthin, 'would make our task far more formidable.'[13]

Meantime, General Hermann Balck was feeling rather pleased with himself. His new temporary command, the *Grossdeutschland*, was shaping up rather well all things considered. It had started life as a motorised infantry unit, but earlier in the year had been converted to a Panzergrenadier division. That meant it would get tanks, but not just any old tanks. Someone further up the food chain had decided it would have almost the same organisation as Himmler's elite SS Panzer divisions. That meant it would get the latest Tigers and Panther tanks. It helped, of course, that Reich Propaganda Minister Dr Joseph Goebbels was *Grossdeutschland's* patron. After the fierce fighting around Rshev some of the men had even been summoned to Berlin to attend a reception hosted by the minister.

Despite the prospect of brand new tanks, the division's supporting assault gun battalion had been pulling its weight. In early April Captain Hanns Magold received the Knight's Cross for taking out five enemy tanks in a single engagement. The previous month his men had clocked up twenty-six enemy tanks and fifty anti-tank guns in the space of just under two weeks. The assault artillery detachment had also done well. Balck took pleasure in awarding its commander, Captain Peter Frantz, with the Oak Leaves to his Knight's Cross. A cameraman had dutifully recorded the occasion. The grinning crews in their helmets and short grey tunics had hoisted Frantz on to their shoulders. He was a man they had every confidence in.

Balck was a tough customer and had spent the last year commanding the 11th Panzer Division on the Eastern Front, which formed part of Knobelsdorff's 48th Panzer Corps. It had helped stabilise the situation after the disaster at Stalingrad, in particular thwarting the Red Army at Rostov. Just as Balck arrived, *Grossdeutschland* had received a whole battalion of Tigers. The division had got its hands on a few at the start of the year and by God they were awesome. The gun could chew its way through anything and tore open armour like a tin opener. The division was also to receive a battalion of brand new Panthers. Rumour had it that the division's tank regiment was to be boosted by another regiment made up entirely of Panthers. This would make it the most powerful division in the army and a force to be reckoned with.

There had been some light relief for Balck and his officers. When the call had come down from corps headquarters, Balck and Colonel Graf Strachwitz, his Panzer commander, had been highly amused by the request. Apparently Mellenthin had been so impressed by the Tiger he wanted to learn to drive one. They could hardly refuse.

Balck was grateful that the surviving veterans had pulled together to help the new recruits. During 1942 *Grossdeutschland* had been through the meat grinder and lost more than 10,000 men. Twice it had almost collapsed. Balck had helped get the division combat ready once more before he was posted. The new lads were itching for a fight, the veterans less so. He was due to hand command back to the division's previous commander, General Walter 'Papa' Hörnlein, who would lead them in the coming summer operation. One of Balck's regrets was that he would not get to see the new Panther in action alongside the Tiger. Now that would be something to behold.

The train pulled into Salzburg's Liefering station amid the full pomp of a state visit. The band started to play the Italian national anthem. SS-Major Otto Günsche, one of Hitler's military adjutants, straightened his uniform and stood to attention just behind the Führer. All eyes swivelled as the train doors opened and out climbed Italian dictator Benito Mussolini. Günsche watched as the SS honour guard very smartly presented arms.

Pleasantries were exchanged between the leaders, then they and their entourages headed to the staff cars waiting in the car park. The cavalcade, with its pennants fluttering in the breeze, made its way to the former summer residence of the Archbishop of Salzburg. Günsche was impressed by Schloss Klessheim, the baroque palace built to the west of the city. It was an ideal location for international conferences. Hitler had chosen it largely because it was only an hour's drive from his Obersalzberg headquarters.

Günsche knew that Hitler would have to muster every diplomatic bone in his body to get through this visit and the subsequent ones by the leaders of Hungary and Romania. In the wake of Germany's humiliating defeat at Stalingrad, Hitler was having to put a brave face on things and soothe his anxious allies. In private he was still fuming and viewed their armies as 'a cowardly rabble'[14] who were responsible for Stalingrad.

Nonetheless, he was going to have to make a grand military gesture to convince them that Germany's military power was not waning. Günsche watched as the Führer promised 'a grandiose new offensive that confirmed certain victory'.[15] Mussolini departed believing they would win. He was delusional: having just lost one army in Russia, he was about to lose another one in Tunisia. Günsche hoped they could succeed, but he was well aware that Hitler had lied to the Italian leader and would lie to the other leaders. No one outside German circles was to know just how bad the situation was on the Eastern Front.

Hitler was putting a brave face on things. SS-Major Heinz Linge was a loyal servant to Hitler, but he was thoroughly alarmed at the sight of his Führer writhing around in agony. Hitler's health had deteriorated since Stalingrad and the pressures of the coming summer campaigning season seemed to be making him much worse. All this talk of Kursk upset Hitler's stomach and was making him ill. Linge called Dr Theodor Morell, who sounded vexed on the other end of the line. Morell instructed Linge to give the Führer his opium shot as that would calm him. The doctor added that he would attend Hitler after breakfast to give him his pick-me-up dose of stimulants. The Führer needed these as he was not sleeping and because of a list of other health problems.

Being Hitler's personal assistant and valet was a great honour and responsibility. Linge saw that Hitler's pained expression was mute testimony to the level of pain he was in. While the German public revered the Führer, his inner circle knew that he was ailing. Linge found the syringe, then helped Hitler remove his jacket and roll up his sleeve. Linge was concerned by the Führer's growing reliance on Morell and his drug cocktails. Germany's future rested in Hitler's hands and his ability to make rational decisions. Linge knew that to express such concerns would be an act of unthinkable disloyalty, but he was not convinced the drugs were helping.

On the high seas Arthur Oakeshott watched as a minesweeper came alongside the cruiser HMS *Scylla* while still under way and deliver eighty bedraggled survivors from a torpedoed merchant ship. Arthur was a Reuters special correspondent and, looking for adventure and a good story, had got himself assigned to the British Home Fleet. During the dark days of late 1942 Britain and America helped sustain the Red Army by sending tanks and fighter aircraft while Stalin's relocated weapons factories got back into full swing.

Arthur travelled with one of the Arctic convoys aboard HMS *Scylla*, the flagship of Rear Admiral Burnett. *Scylla* was known as 'a toothless terror' because she lacked heavy weaponry. However, she was bristling with anti-aircraft guns capable of giving Hitler's Luftwaffe a good hammering.

To his alarm he found himself involved in a desperate four-day battle with the Luftwaffe. When action stations sounded Arthur was soon staring at the bellies of Heinkel and Junkers bombers intent on sending the convoy to the bottom of the Barents Sea. Yeoman White, one of the crew, described it as the 'worst torpedo bombing attack of the war'.[16] The bombers were met by pom-pom anti-aircraft guns nicknamed 'Chicago pianos' and any other weapons the sailors could lay their hands on.

The first wave consisted of forty-two aircraft, followed by a second wave of twenty-five. During this battle Arthur even looked down on aircraft as they roared past almost at sea level. In response the gunners ricocheted tracer shells off the water and into the fuselage and cockpit. One bomber dropped its 'tin fish' in the direction of the *Scylla*. Her skipper, Captain Macintyre, turned the ship 'with the rapidity of a motorist swerving a car'. 'There were losses, but nothing like the Nazis hoped,' said Arthur.[17] The convoy got through.

This sacrifice helped the Red Army stay in the fight until early 1943. However, Stalin's ingratitude was to result in an almighty and very public row with the Allies. All Stalin wanted was for Britain and America to open a second front in France, instead they were busy planning the invasion of Sicily. He firmly believed this would not take the pressure off the Red Army and he could not wait another year.

In England, Captain John Cairncross wandered through the gates and nodded acknowledgement to the bored-looking guard. Cairncross's trousers felt uncomfortable as they were stuffed with secret documents.[18] He could not believe just how lax security was at Britain's top-secret intelligence facility, Bletchley Park. Its boffins were daily intercepting and decrypting German, Italian and Japanese coded signals, yet Bletchley was leaking like a sieve. Bizarrely and in contrast, when it came to petty pilfering of the cafeteria crockery and the length of tea breaks the authorities were positively draconian.[19]

Cairncross had decided that Churchill's government was not doing enough to help Stalin, so he had taken matters into his own hands. He was of the opinion that Bletchley ought to share its intelligence with all its allies – not just the Americans. A Scottish Marxist, Captain Cairncross, known as 'The Fiery Cross' at Trinity College, had been recruited by Soviet intelligence in the late 1930s.[20] He preferred to believe that the Soviet Union was a workers' utopia rather than a brutal totalitarian state. His early career in the Foreign Office and then the Treasury had made him a valuable source of information.

At Bletchley the captain worked in Hut 3 and he regularly scooped the processed decrypts from the floor and, adding them to his own translations, he then hid them in his trousers. Once at the local railway station he put them in a bag and travelled to London to meet 'Henry', his Soviet handler.[21] Curiously, Cairncross was never patted down by the guards, nor did he seem particularly surprised that he always managed to find useful stuff on the floor that would be of help to his foreign friends.

In particular he had valuable intelligence that showed Hitler was planning to pinch off the Kursk salient. Cairncross wanted to make contact with Anatoli Gorsky as soon as possible. What he did not know was that Leo Long, a militarily intelligence officer who worked in the War Office, was also leaking Bletchley intelligence on Kursk. He was doing this via Soviet mole Anthony Blunt, who worked for MI5.

Despite initial fears that it might be part of a deliberate British deception plan, Soviet military intelligence deemed the information to be 'very valuable'.[22]

In Geneva, Sándor Radó had just come from seeing Englishman Allan Foote. Radó and Foote's contact in Lucerne – known as 'Lucy' – had come through for them via German émigré Christian Schneider. The source was a German exile by the name of Rudolf Roessler, who was a committed anti-Nazi with extremely well-placed sympathisers in the German High Command and military intelligence. Radó had been informed of Herr Hitler's summer plans in some detail.

Radó, Foote and Schneider were spies working for Soviet Military intelligence. Radó and his network knew secrecy was everything. Although Switzerland was neutral, should the authorities discover spy rings operating in Geneva and Lucerne, they would arrest everyone. Schneider, code name 'Taylor', was Roessler's only point of contact. Roessler was a journalist and publisher who in the early 1930s had incurred the displeasure of the Nazis. He lived in fear of being handed over to Hitler's henchmen. By way of insurance he was also working for Swiss intelligence.

Having been contacted by Schneider, Radó had instructed Foote to radio Moscow – major German offensive at Kursk imminent. Schneider had reassured him more intelligence would be forthcoming regarding troop deployments and timetables. If Hitler thought he was going to take the initiative he had another thing coming. If he tried anything at Kursk he would reap a bitter harvest.

# PART ONE

# STALIN RESURGENT

# 1

# TRAINING AT SARATOV

The racket was deafening. There was the sound of hammering, drilling and riveting. Every now and then there was the clang of metal upon metal. The harsh electric lights were supplemented by the flash of welders. The elaborate girders holding up the enormous roof disappeared skyward, creating an industrial cathedral. Outside the factory building the trains rattled along the sidings day and night carrying tanks. The workers likewise toiled day and night, they were cold and hungry, but grumbling did no good. To complain was unpatriotic and subversive. Some worked for the love of the Motherland, others simply because they had to.

Whenever any *Red Star* or Party cameramen turned up it was all smiles and hearty waves. No one really wanted to see just how grim the conditions were in the defence factories relocated to the Urals. As well as the noise, they were cold and dirty. Much of the workforce were older men, women and youngsters. The men of fighting age had been conscripted. They had to endure sixteen-hour shifts with meagre rations to keep them going.

Each tank had up to a dozen workers bustling around it. They were dressed in overalls and caps. Subassembly took place in the other buildings until the tank hull and suspension had been complete. The body was then brought into the main production hall and lowered into the line by a gantry for the men to work on. The gantry was then used to swing the completed turret over the hull ready for installation. Once in place the twin circular turret access hatches were flung open for ease of access into the interior. Upright these made it look as if the tank had ears similar to those of a very famous American cartoon mouse.

Often young, apprehensive-looking tank crews would arrive at the factories to collect their new steeds. The T-34 tank was so durable you could drive it straight to the front, though the preferred method of transport was by train. The men had come from the tank training schools or were from decimated front-line units that were being rebuilt. The factory workers were amazed at what these young men did with their tanks, but there was no hiding the fact that they always needed more. The T-34 was a good tank but the Red Army's losses seemed unending.

Seventy-three-year-old Yevgeny Paton smiled at the sight of the production line, it had not always been such a hive of efficient activity. When he first arrived in Nizhny Tagil it had been chaos. Moving the T-34 tank factory from Kharkov along with his staff from his Electric Welding Institute in Kiev had not been easy. Similarly, moving elements of the Kharkov and Leningrad tank plants to Chelyabinsk had equally been a giant logistical headache.[1] Other tanks plants had been set up at Gorkyy, near Moscow, and at Stalingrad. After the loss of the latter to the Nazis, production had been moved to Sverdlovsk. In the early days machinery and workers had gone missing, trains had been rerouted or requisitioned. Nonetheless, saving the Red Army's tank factories had been nothing short of a miracle and ultimately nothing had stopped the mass migration eastwards. Chief tank designer Alexander Morozov, also from Kharkov, had played a part in this.

Morozov was grateful for what Paton had done for the Soviet Union's defence industries. They were now locked in a production war with Nazi Germany, which to win meant they had to produce everything faster and in greater quantities than the invaders. The armed forces needed aircraft, ammunition, artillery and tanks, as well as rifles and uniforms, in phenomenal quantities. Slowly but surely the Red Army's losses in men and equipment were being made good.

Just before the war Paton had gone to see Nikita Khrushchev to show him the fruits of his research. Khrushchev had seized upon his welding technology immediately and urged Stalin to implement it in factories and building sites. He also saw that it had a military application. 'Tell me, comrade Paton,' said Khrushchev, 'do you think your technique would work on tank steel?'[2] Paton thought it possible and was packed off to the Kharkov tank factory to work with Alexei Yepishev, who was the Ukrainian Communist Party representative there. Yevgeny had been made a commissioner to the Council of the People's Commissar's despite not being a member of the Communist Party.

The results of Yevgeny's work were soon apparent with the smooth welding finish on the turret of the first two versions of the T-34 tank, which was made from rolled plate armour. Some turrets though were also cast from moulds. The tank looked streamlined and modern, a worthy successor to the thousands of inadequate tanks the Nazis had destroyed on the road to Moscow.

When Hitler invaded, Khrushchev recalled, Paton 'moved with our armour works to the Urals when we had to evacuate our industry from Kharkov early in the war'.[3] In the summer of 1943 the Red Army needed yet more tanks and Yevgeny helped ensure that happened. 'Thanks to the improvements he introduced in our tank production,' said Khrushchev, 'tanks started coming off our assembly lines like pancakes off a griddle.'[4]

The new tanks were shipped as battle replacements to the front-line units and to the Saratov Tank School. Many of the other tank training schools had been overrun during the invasion. Despite the ever-growing number of Soviet-built armour, some units found themselves equipped with American- and British-supplied tanks. Morozov was now working on a new T-34 armed with a bigger gun, but it would not be ready until the end of the year.

Summer was coming and you did not need to be a rocket scientist to forecast a big battle was imminent. The season was always campaigning time. It did not matter if the Red Army or the Wehrmacht started it, there would be fighting one way or another. That meant more tanks than ever were needed as the Red Army stockpiled its equipment ready for some big push.

In London, Prime Minister Winston Churchill liked to think that he was partly responsible for this frenzied Soviet military build-up. Captain Jerry Roberts, a decoder at Bletchley Park, recalled Soviet scepticism: 'At first, they ignored British intelligence, but we managed to find ways to send very detailed reports to the Russians … Eventually the Russians put pressure on their factories to deliver as many tanks as possible to the Kursk area. The Russians were able to deliver huge numbers of tanks …'[5]

Paton was a hero of the Soviet Union; at home though he had a dark secret that had worried him for a long time. It put him and his family in very grave danger. He was fairly certain that the state knew about it, but to date had chosen not to act. Yevgeny was thankful that he had escaped Stalin's purges in the late 1930s. Hundreds if not thousands of engineers and designers had been consigned to the Gulag. Some had been released, others never heard of again. He was conscious now that his prominent profile with the war effort inevitably put the spotlight on him. He was anxious his past might catch up with him should he be denounced. His father had been a Tsarist consul at the time of the 1917 Revolution and Yevgeny had a Tsarist upbringing. This made him and his kin potential enemies of the people.

He decided if he could join the Communist Party it might at least afford him some protection. Paton resolved to put pen to paper and write to the Central Committee, saying:

> I believe I have recently made a significant contribution to the wartime defense of our country by helping in the production of tanks. Therefore I feel I have earned the moral right to address myself to the Party with a request that I be accepted into its ranks. I enclose an application for Party membership, and I ask the Central Committee for its endorsement.[6]

Paton felt that the letter on its own might not be enough, he needed help from a well-placed sponsor. Travelling to Moscow, he sought out Khrushchev and requested to see him. As luck would have it Stalin had summoned Khrushchev to the capital. Khrushchev willingly took Yevgeny's letter to Stalin. The issue could have gone one of two ways. Luckily for Yevgeny, Stalin issued a special decree allowing him to join the party immediately, waiving the normal two-year trial period. He was safe for the foreseeable future.

Even using Yegeny's welding technique, by 1943 production of the T-34 tank was deemed too slow and Morozov had been tasked the previous year with looking at ways of not only speeding up production but also improving the turret armour. The solution was a hexagonal cast turret that resulted in the Model 1943 T-34, although it had gone into production the previous year. Thanks to its turret hatches the Germans had dubbed it Mickey Mouse because it looked just like the cartoon character's ears.

Despite the enormous efforts made by the Soviet Union's industries in the wake of Hitler's invasion, even by early 1943 they were still struggling. In March that year, Deputy Supreme Commander Marshal Georgi Zhukov took part in a meeting 'to discuss fuel supplies for metal production and electricity generation and for the aircraft and tank works'. He was alarmed to find 'Their reports clearly revealed the grave situation that still persisted in industry'.[7]

Alexander Werth with *The Sunday Times* in Moscow observed:

Soviet armaments production did not reach a satisfactory level until the autumn of 1942. The evacuation of hundreds of plants from west to east in the autumn and winter of 1941 had resulted in an almost catastrophic drop in arms production, which largely accounted for the disappointing results in the Russian Moscow counter offensive in the winter of 1941–42 and the disasters of the summer of 1942.[8]

Monthly tank production was to average 2,000 in 1943, slightly less than the previous year. However, the production of light tanks was almost stopped in 1943, while at the beginning of 1942 it accounted for more than half the total. In 1943 Soviet weapons factories churned out 16,000 heavy and medium tanks, 3,500 light tanks and 4,000 mobile guns. This was eight and a half times more than in 1940 and almost four times more than in 1941. It was a remarkable feat.

In contrast, supplies from America were not as forthcoming as Stalin might have wished. Zhukov's meeting with Stalin in the Kremlin showed 'There were hold-ups in the aid under lend-lease from the USA.'[9] Stalin and his advisors did not like to admit it but British and American raw materials were playing an important role in helping rebuild their weapons factories and their armies. 'We received steel and aluminium from which we made guns, airplanes, and so on,' admitted Khrushchev. 'Our own industry was shattered and partly abandoned to the enemy.'[10]

This and other aid ironically caused great resentment in Moscow. 'The fact remains that the Allied raw materials enormously helped the Soviet war industries,' wrote Werth. However, he also noted, 'But this still does not dispose of the profound emotional problem created by the simple fact that the British and Americans were losing much fewer people.'[11] This sense of bitterness was to result in an almighty row with the Allies in the early part of that year. It was ill-timed in light of Stalin's developing plans for the summer.

The Red Army had endured a tough year during 1942. It suffered a severe defeat at Kharkov in May 1942 and, although it scored a remarkable victory at Stalingrad, it needed to recuperate. Replacement soldiers had to be increasingly drawn from the length and breadth of the Soviet Union. Infantry training instructor Lieutenant Evgeni Bessonov found that the quality of the replacements was often poor:

Most of the soldiers were 18 years old in 1943. They were not strong physically, mostly small and frail youngsters, so I tried to adjust the training programme to meet their physical and health capacity. Day and night we trained them for future battles.[12]

Language was also a problem. Amongst the recruits Bessonov received were middle-aged Azeri soldiers, some 30–35 years old. They required a translator as they could not understand orders given in Russian. However, Bessonov had no complaints about them as they proved to be tough fighters.

In particular, the Red Army needed to replenish its battered armoured units ready for the summer of 1943. Sensibly, tank training regiments were established at the main T-34 factories at Chelyabinsk, Nizhniy Tagil and Sverdlovsk. This was intended to greatly speed up getting combat replacements to the front. Nineteen-year-old Lieutenant Vasiliy Pavlovich Bryukhov received his initial tanker training at Kurgan and was commissioned in April 1943. The following month he joined his first crew at Chelyabinsk and was assigned to the 2nd Tank Corps just before Kursk. Bryukhov was lucky as Senior Sergeant Petr Kirichenko, deployed to the 159th Tank Brigade, was promoted after just a month of training.

Typically, if they survived, tank company commanders ranged from 22 to 27 years old, while platoon leaders averaged 19 to 21. The junior officers were normally recruited for their political loyalties as much as their level of education. They had usually been teenage members of the Communist Komsomol organisation and were high school graduates. The sergeants were little more than 18, while the senior sergeants were promoted where possible from surviving enlisted men.

On the whole the Soviet tank units attracted some of the best recruits because they were drawn from the towns and cities and were therefore better educated. SS-General Max Simon, who served with the 3rd SS Panzergrenadier Division *Totenkopf*, observed:

The Russian townsman, who is highly interested in technical matters, is just as well suited for the modern tank arm as the Russian peasant is for the infantry … It was amazing to see the primitive technical means with which the Russian crews kept their tanks ready for action and how they overcame all difficulties …

An added factor is that the Russian worker usually is a convinced communist, who, having enjoyed the blessings of 'his' revolution for decades, will fight fanatically as a class-conscious proletarian. Just as the

Red Infantryman is ready to die in his foxhole, the Soviet tank soldier will die in his tank, firing at the enemy to the last, even if he is alone in or behind enemy lines.[13]

To conduct basic training tank schools were also established at Kurgan, Ufa, Ulyanovsk and Saratov. Assigned to a tank-training battalion, the men got four to eight weeks of instruction. Unlike their German counterparts the crews were not expected to show much initiative and the classes were very simple. Cross-role training did not occur very often, which meant the crews could not stand in for each other. The driver was the only one able to move the tank, while the loader was restricted to his task and the radio operator could just about turn on the radio and change the frequency. Unit training was not any larger than platoon level. Many platoon leaders were unable to map read, which could prove fatal when they went into combat.

Unfortunately for the trainee crews, T-34s were not readily available for training even in 1943, as they tended to be sent straight to the front where they were needed the most. This meant the men did their basic training on obsolete tanks. While at Kurgan Lieutenant Bryukhov was instructed on old BT tanks armed with 45mm guns and he noted that 'Training at the base was very weak', culminating in an exercise called 'tank platoon in the offensive'.[14]

Afterwards the trainee crews were packed off to the training regiments near the T-34 factories, where they would be issued with a tank. These units could handle up to 2,000 men, who normally received another month of training. Again this was rudimentary, with the largest unit training being carried out at company level. Apart from advancing in line formation or as a wedge, little thought was given to more complex tactical procedures.

In trained hands the T-34 was quite agile and could run rings around the Panzers; in untrained hands it was a completely different matter.

Drivers were not taught to employ terrain to their benefit, such as using folds in the ground to fire and retire. Essentially tanks were cavalry and all they needed to do was charge toward the enemy. Many crews completed their training feeling they could have been better prepared.

A major drawback with the four-man crew of the T-34 was that the tank commander was also the gunner. This meant the commander had to direct his own tank, plus a platoon or company, if he was in charge, as well as find and engage enemy targets.[15] In the heat of battle such multi-tasking inevitably slowed the tank's rate of fire. The loader was also supposed to act as an observer, but usually did little more than ram shells into the breech.

Tank crews were only ever to abandon their tank under two circum-stances: the main gun had been damaged, or the tank was on fire.

The training regiments also ended up with the detritus from front-line units. This meant they were the focal point for survivors from destroyed tank formations, wounded tankers returning to duty and men reassigned from other branches of the army. This was a logical step, especially as the newer recruits could benefit from their experience, but sometimes it undermined morale. There would have been dark mutterings from the veterans that the newbies would have to learn on the job the hard way.

Some women were also recruited to tank units as Soviet manpower began to diminish. A few volunteered as tank drivers in early 1942, but in January of the following year a number were sent to the tank training regiments. They were posted as individual combat replacements, often to the more prestigious Guards tank brigades. Most served as drivers but a very few survived to become tank commanders. The T-34 required a lot of strength to drive, especially with the twin steering levers and the double declutching needed to change gear. Unfortunately for the drivers, they rarely escaped if the tank was hit.

Crews were not always harmonious, nor did they always stay together. Junior Lieutenant Sergei Burtsev found his first crew formed at Nizhniy Tagil had a broad spectrum of undesirable characters. His loader was edu-cationally subnormal and panicked so much the first time they fired the gun that he scrambled out of their tank and fled. The unhappy driver was a convicted criminal and the radio operator/bow machine-gunner was a restaurant waiter. They had nothing in common other than the desire not to die the minute they went into combat.

The tank factories were constantly short of workers and sometimes the new tankers could find themselves sidetracked on to the factory floor. When Bryukhov arrived at Chelyabinsk, to complete his training with the 6th Tank Training Regiment, he ended up spending two frustrating weeks manning a lathe. 'Nikolay and I were assigned to drilling apertures in engine cylinder blocks. Nikolay had completed a training course and was a qualified fourth-grade metal worker … Our work at the plant didn't last for long …'[16]

Once an assembled crew had been issued with their tank, they were gathered into a march company consisting of ten tanks. These would then drive to the nearest gunnery range, where they often got to fire off little more than three rounds and a drum of machine gun bullets.

After gunnery training was complete the tanks and their crews were then loaded on to a train and sent to the front as combat replacements. This, of course, was easier said than done because units were always on the move. Upon arrival the new crews did not have time to integrate with their unit properly and the old hands often shunned them as 'dead meat'.

Nor was getting the tanks to the front always straightforward, as Bryukhov relates:

> After Malyi Yaroslavets there was an air-raid, but no bombs hit the train. The train turned south. Later we stopped in a railway yard, and an order to disembark and unload was given. There was no unloading platforms. The drivers began to unload the tanks, crumpling the flat wagons, and were practically jumping down to the ground. Two tanks rolled upside down, but were quickly set on their tracks again. A representative of the 2nd Tank Corps was waiting for us and the battalion marched to the deployment area, where it joined the Corps' 99th Brigade.[17]

Aleksandr Slesarev from Smolensk had started life in the army as an artilleryman, but after showing promise in 1942 he was chosen for promotion. He was trained for almost a year before he took command of a tank as a lieutenant. Slesarev was posted to the 1st Guards Tank Army, one of five new tank armies formed in early 1943. Twenty-two-year-old Ivan Gusev, another tank lieutenant, wrote to his family in June 1943, 'Every hour is taken up with fussing over the machines. Sometimes you forget the time and date, you forget everything.'[18]

Slesarev was surprised by the conditions: 'Our food is first-class – and apart from that we get an extra ration because we're at the front. My work is interesting and I get to travel about.'[19] His reason for travelling was not so much to take part in scheduled exercises, but to help on collective farms and assist engineers rebuild hospitals and stores. Gusev, writing home, observed:

> You lie down to sleep in the evening, you feel a terrible exhaustion in your whole body, you know that you have carried out a great and difficult task, but your heart is full of gladness, a special kind of sensation, a sort of pride or internal satisfaction. These are the best moments of all.[20]

From the spring of 1942 the mauled Red Army began to reorganise, most notably with the creation of tank armies, tank corps and mechanised corps. It had learned the hard way what happened to its armoured regiments when they were divided up amongst the infantry divisions. Initially these new tank armies were mixed formations with three tank corps and two or three infantry divisions. This proved unsatisfactory because the infantry could not keep up with the tanks when they achieved a breakthrough. The tanks then found themselves operating on their own.

By the time of Stalingrad these mixed formations were abandoned with tank armies formed by two tank corps, one mechanised corps plus anti-tank and artillery support. Independent tank and mechanised corps as well as brigade level formations were also maintained that could be assigned when and where they were needed.

According to General Shtemenko, Stalin's Chief of Operations, 'The organisational structure of the tank forces became very flexible … This organisation corresponded to "manoeuvre warfare" then being waged by the Soviet forces on the field of battle.'[21] In essence the Red Army was learning how to harness Hitler's Blitzkrieg and turn it against the Wehrmacht. 'It assured the action of tanks together with infantry and the independent use of great tank formations working jointly with aircraft,' said Shtemenko.[22]

Stalin, after Stalingrad, was determined that the Red Army should build on its experiences. Following its previously abysmal performance, he was astute enough to appreciate that modern warfare was constantly evolving. Training was not enough, they needed to move with the times. At the beginning of May 1943 Stalin instructed, 'That all Red Army men – infantrymen, mortar gunners, artillerymen, tankmen, airmen, sappers, signallers, cavalrymen – indefatigably continue to perfect their fighting mastery …'[23] He also warned, 'To stand still in military matters means to lag behind, and, as is known, those who lag behind are beaten.'[24] His tankers took heed – it was time to beat the Panzers and avenge 1941.

# 2

# ABDULIN AND FRIENDS

Lieutenant Colonel Pantyukhov was sat in his field headquarters. Division had just been on the line – get your regiment down to Shopino as quickly as possible. Lieutenant Colonel Voronov, the division's political officer, had been in a panic. All the gains made in recent weeks were in danger of being lost. It was clearly an emergency as Pantyukhov's unit formed part of General Chistyakov's 21st Army, which had just been redeployed from the Stalingrad area in some haste. Word was that the Red Army's defence around Kharkov had completely collapsed. For five days the 25th Guards Rifle Division had desperately thrown themselves at the divisions of the advancing Waffen-SS. The terrible winter weather was improving, which favoured the Panzers.

On 16 March 1943 General Paul Hausser's SS Panzer Corps rolled back into newly liberated Kharkov. Then, just two days later, it fought northwards and retook Belgorod. Alarm bells began to ring with the Red Army's High Command. If Hausser maintained his attack he might cut his way through to Oboyan or the rail junction at Prokhorovka and on to Kursk, the regional capital. That would imperil the whole of the recently liberated salient. If the Germans got to Kursk then the Red Army would have to retreat or face potential encirclement.

Hitler was heartened by the victory at Kharkov and even managed to joke, 'A short while ago I still believed I would have a stroke if anyone were to bring me good news.'[1] Reichsmarschall Hermann Göring, in disgrace since Stalingrad, when he finally reappeared at Hitler's Wehrwolf forward headquarters at Vinnitsa in Ukraine, undeservedly gave General Zeitzler all the credit. 'Zeitzler,' he exclaimed, 'it is simply a miracle that you have managed to stabilise the front.'[2] Zeitzler positively glowed in response to the Reichsmarschall's fawning praise. He certainly wanted to stabilise the front, but it was none of his doing; Field Marshal Erich von Manstein was the man who had pulled the proverbial rabbit from the hat. Nonetheless, the reversal of Red Army fortunes must have further encouraged him to believe such a feat could be repeated but on a larger scale. Inadvertently, Manstein had helped put the Germans on the road to Kursk.

Kursk had fallen to the Werhmacht in the autumn of 1941 and not been liberated until February 1943, along with Belgorod and Oboyan. Before the war it had been home to around 120,000 people. In the fourteen months of occupation the Germans laid waste to the city and its surrounding province. The population was decimated through deportation, disease and starvation. The men of fighting age were in the Red Army, under arrest or dead. The remaining women and children and the elderly were left to eke out a miserable living. Some 200,000 people in the district were reliant on the state for food and fuel by the spring of 1943.

Almost 40,000 houses had been destroyed, while many abandoned buildings were stripped of wood when the fuel ran out during the winter. In the rubble lay unexploded mines and shells to catch the unwary. When the Germans withdrew, anything they could not carry away with them they destroyed. Even with the return of the Red Army, law and order remained a problem, violent crime such as robbery and rape was commonplace. Amongst the ruins lurked hungry armed gangs of criminals, deserters and orphaned teenagers. They stole anything they could lay their hands on. Perhaps the most tragic victims were the women who had children by German soldiers, willingly or otherwise. No one wanted German bastards and many were cruelly abandoned to their fate.

Despite the rich black soil, the Kursk region's agriculture was wrecked, with seed sowing at the beginning of 1943 set to be lower than 10 per cent of the levels achieved at the beginning of the war. Mines and unexploded ordnance made many state farms unsafe. 'The farmers looked emaciated,' recalled Mansur Abdulin, 'dressed in threadbare clothes with tattered boots on their feet.'[3]

After the liberation, troops of the Central Front were instructed to help the farmers transport feed, assist with lambing and sow their spring crops. However, this help was not to be at the detriment of their military duties. Similarly, the local civilians found themselves dragooned into militias ordered to dig trenches and clear German mines. At the same time, the NKVD internal security forces prowled round hunting for deserters. For many civilians they could console themselves that at least they were being oppressed by their own soldiers rather than foreign ones.

Over the next few days the Voronezh Front did everything it could to stop Manstein capitalising on his victory at Kharkov. Deputy Supreme Commander Zhukov urged Stalin and the Chief of the General Staff, General Vasilevsky, to commit all available reserves to stopping him. In response the 1st Tank, 21st and 64th Armies were rushed to the area.

With the Germans back in Belgorod it fell to Chistyakov's 21st Army to stop then pushing any further north. He instructed units of his 22nd and 23rd Rifle Corps to move into position and stand firm. The stop line north of Belgorod was at Shopino and along the Donets. Chistyakov called General Kozin, commander of the 52nd Rifle Division, and ordered him to head for Belgorod immediately. He in turn instructed his vanguard consisting of Lieutenant Colonel Pantyukhov's 155th Guards Rifle Regiment to move swiftly on Shopino and to ascertain the enemy's intentions.

Chistyakov's intelligence told him that the 1st SS Panzergrenadier Division *Leibstanbdarte Adolf Hitler* had pushed through Kharkov, with the 2nd SS *Das Reich* on its left and the 3rd SS *Totenkopf* on the right. If they maintained this deployment to the north-west of Belgorod it meant that Kozin would come up against the tanks of *Totenkopf*. When informed of this Kozin told Pantyukhov to give the Germans a bloody nose.

The men of Major General Max Simon's *Totenkopf* were perhaps being over-confident and ran straight into an ambush set up by Pantyukhov. German prisoners were taken and when interrogated revealed that the SS were indeed heading for Oboyan. Usually slapping, kicking and punching had the desired effect with even the most recalcitrant Nazi prisoner.

Pantyukhov learned that the SS had turned soft after spending three months in France. *Totenkopf* had only just come back to the Eastern Front after re-equipping as a Panzergrenadier division and receiving much-needed combat replacements. On its return the 3rd SS had not got off to a very good start as its commander, Lieutenant General Theodor Eicke, was killed during the opening stages of the Third Battle of Kharkov. Eicke, who had been with the division since 1941, was flying in his spotter plane when it was shot down on 26 February 1943.

Once the rest of Kozin's 52nd Division had taken up position, it was reinforced by the 67th Guards Rifle Division to the right and the 375th Rifle Division on the left. *Totenkopf* was caught off guard by this solidifying of Soviet defences. However, Kozin was soon forced to throw his other two regiments into action. Lieutenant Colonel Yudich and Lieutenant Colonel Babich, commanders of the 151st and 153rd, both distinguished themselves in the fighting north of Belgorod. They and many of their men were recommended for gallantry awards by an impressed Kozin.

While the Germans were held the rest of Chistyakov's 21st Army moved into position during 21 and 22 March setting up their defences. Just in case the Germans should break through, the 1st Tank Army was concentrated to the south of Oboyan. The 64th Army was also entrenched on the Seversky Donets. Nonetheless, more reinforcements were going to be needed if the SS were to be thrown back.

Following its successful recapture of Kharkov the 1st SS *Liebstandarte Adolf Hitler* Division received a surprise gift in the form of a cheque for more than 2 million Reichsmarks, to commemorate Hitler's birthday on 20 April. This had been raised by the Winter Relief Fund over the previous months and was to be spent on divisional welfare cases. Reichsführer-SS Himmler, determined to share in their glory, arrived in Kharkov on 23 April, having allowed a decent period for the city to be completely pacified. The Reischführer did not like to take any chances when it came to his personal safety.

He gathered the officers of his three SS divisions at the badly damaged university. There, in a rather self-congratulatory and menacing tone, he told them, 'We will never let that excellent weapon, the dread and terrible reputation which preceded us in the battle for Kharkov, fade, but will constantly add new meaning to it.'[4] They had indeed added to their 'dread and terrible reputation' by committing yet more war crimes in the city.

Over a two-day period SS troops murdered 800 wounded Soviet soldiers from the 69th Army. They had lain helpless in a military hospital on Trinkler Street. One woman desperately searching for her husband found him 'mutilated and covered in blood, lying on the floor between the beds. The head was bashed in, one eye had been knocked out, the arms were broken, and blood flowed from still gaping wounds.'[5] Others had tried to escape by jumping out of the windows, but had been gunned down.

Later a Soviet investigation determined the extent of the atrocities:

> ... during the occupation of Kharkov and the Kharkov region, the German command and Gestapo agents savagely exterminated, by means of poisoning with carbon monoxide in *Dushagubbi* (murder vans), shooting and hanging, tens of thousands of Soviet citizens, including women, old men, children, wounded Red Army men under

treatment in Kharkov hospitals, as well as arrested persons incarcerated in Gestapo prisons.[6]

While the people of Kharkov may have been cowed by the brutality of the SS, these atrocities did nothing to dampen their hatred of the Germans. Many recalled how when the invaders had first arrived in 1941 they had strung up resistance leaders from the city's public buildings. Around the city a network of spies went about gathering what intelligence they could ready for the time when the Red Army returned.

Private Mansur Abdulin and his comrades stood to attention under the trees near a village called Tipoly Kolodets. In front of them, General Aleksandr Rodimtsev was handing over a new ceremonial banner. Thanks to its brave performance at Stalingrad the 293rd Rifle Division was being reorganised as the 66th Guards Rifle Division. Abdulin's unit, under Captain Pavel Bilaonov, was redesignated the 193rd Guards Rifle Regiment. Bilaonov had injured a leg so stood leaning on crutches next to Rodimtsev.

'This was a great honour. Not many of my old comrades had lived to witness it,' said Abdulin. 'How many wonderful lads had been left lying in the ground between the Don and Volga?'[7] He watched as Rodimtsev, commander of the 32nd Guards Corps, presented the banner to the deputy regimental commander, who went down on one knee and kissed the fringe. There was a sense of anticipation: '… now we were impatient to receive the Guards badge.'[8] This recognition was also tempered by a sense of loss. 'I realised that almost all my old comrades had perished,' reflected Abdulin, 'and that for me the best reward was to be alive.'[9]

At Surok station Evgeni Bessonov was getting bored. After graduating in the summer of 1942 as a junior lieutenant he had been posted to a training regiment, which produced battlefield replacements for front-line units. He helped run the sniper course, acting as a platoon commander. During his time at military academy he had trained on mortars and was shocked by the ineptitude of the instructors: 'In general during the war our mortar crews were really bad shooters. Of course artillery units – mortar battalions and even regiments – were very well trained, but the infantry mortars were not so successful. Indeed they almost killed me once!'[10] He never finished his training on the 82mm mortar, nor did he ever fire live rounds.

At just 19, initially he was uncomfortable instructing men much older than himself. For a year he found little to alleviate the routine at Surok:

During the summer and autumn of 1942 I was twice sent as an escorting officer for marching companies to the combat units, first to Mozhaisk area, and the second time to Voronezh area. The task of the escorting officer was to deliver the company without losses in personnel (there were cases of escapes) ... In late May 1943 I was sent to the personnel section of the Moscow Military District.[11]

For the next two months he waited to go to war until finally orders came through sending him to join the Bryansk Front holding the line opposite German-occupied Orel.

Abdulin's retitled division formed part of General Zhadov's 5th Guards Army. This was one of six armies assigned to Colonel General Konev's Reserve Front, which was redesignated the Steppe Front. The 66th Guards and two other divisions were grouped under Rodimtsev's 32nd Corps. The 33rd Guards Rifle Corps included another four rifle divisions.

That summer Zhadov's command was deployed on the southern shoulder of the Kursk salient to the east of Oboyan to protect the left flank of the Voronezh Front and General Chistyakov's 6th Guards Army (formerly 21st Army). On Zhadov's other flank was Rotmistrov's 5th Guards Tank Army. Abdulin and his comrades had no way of knowing that they were to be involved in the bloody tank battle of Prokhorovka and Stalin's counter-offensive against the German-held Belgorod bulge.

Soviet soldiers rightly feared Hitler's Panzers; those who had miraculously survived the battles of 1941–42 knew the full terror of the Blitzkrieg. It was imperative that the Soviet rifle divisions be trained to withstand assault by tanks. Abdulin felt they were adequately prepared for the ordeal to come:

> The infantry had enough reliable anti-tank weapons: all the soldiers carried anti-tank grenades and there was an ample supply of Molotov cocktails ... Every day our T-34 tanks helped us practice. We would learn how to throw cocktail bottles, and the heavy percussion grenades. Such a grenade can explode in your hand if you accidently strike it against the side of the trench when throwing it. But if it hits a tank, the powerful blast could stop it dead.[12]

Abdulin knew that they faced serious trouble, adding, 'Because of the intensive exercises involving tanks, we realised that very soon we'd be taking part in some heavy fighting between large armoured forces.'

For infantrymen confronting tanks it was all about keeping your nerve, but when you had a 25- to 60-ton monster bearing down on you this was easier said than done.

Evgeni Bessonov also understood the importance of conducting anti-tank drills:

> We considered that removing 'tank fear' and training soldiers to knock tanks out with hand grenades was a crucial point in the training. We did a 'tank test-drive' for that purpose. Soldiers would sit in trenches, while a T-34 would roll over the trenches once or twice. Boys were happy to see that it was not that scary and they were happy to see how brave they were. We had a little combat training with live ammo in attack and defence.[13]

The forest was shrouded in darkness until a man lifted a flashlight to his wristwatch. It was time so he lifted the light and flashed it several times. Immediately two parallel rows of landing lights came on to reveal a narrow landing strip. For a moment the man thought he heard an engine, but then nothing. All of a sudden a two-seat biplane dropped on to the runway. It bounced several times, but stopped well before it reached the trees. On approach, to avoid drawing attention the pilot had killed the engine and glided down. It was some impressive flying.

From behind the pilot a Red Army officer hopped over the fuselage and ran across to the partisan commander. They shook hands and exchanged brief pleasantries. He had been sent to arrange the delivery of explosives and other supplies, as well as more men. Moscow had decided to put the partisan war on a more organised footing. A group of men hurried to the plane and under direction from the pilot turned the aircraft around. In moments the engine spluttered to life and the plane was airborne again heading for home. The lights went out and the men vanished into the forest.

Later, an explosion echoed down the Desna River valley. For a split second the 60ft high railway bridge shuddered in response to the shock-wave, then the double spans fell into the water. The Soviet saboteurs allowed themselves a brief cheer, then swiftly headed for the sanctuary of the nearby forest. There was no pursuit by the Germans as the bodies of the dead guard detachment lay strewn around the dropped bridge. A surprise attack from the east by 300 partisans had sealed their fate.

More than 1,000 partisans from three different units had targeted the Desna bridge near Vygonichi on 7 March 1943. One unit made a feint assault from the west to distract the guards. That same night another team attacked the relief line running from Krichev to Unecha. For a distance of some 60 miles they cut the line in ninety different places. The following week they also destroyed the Revna bridge near Sinzoertei.[14]

The Desna bridge was a vital link in the supply route to Kluge's Army Group Centre, taking up to twenty trains a day. Its destruction reduced rail traffic for several crucial weeks. Within five days German engineers built an improvised structure, but it could only safely take one freight wagon at a time rolled across by hand. After a week the new bridge could take an entire train but not the weight of a locomotive. This meant that the wagons had to be pushed on from one end and pulled off from the other.

Stalin may have been briefed on this daring operation; it was certainly publicised with the Soviet armed forces when the military newspaper *Red Star* covered the attack in its 9 April 1943 issue. Such propaganda pieces were designed to enhance the mysticism of the partisans in the public's eyes and encourage more such attacks.[15]

While Stalin's regular armed forces were doing all they could to prepare themselves, his irregular forces, the partisans, were also busy making life unpleasant for the Germans. The dense forests and impenetrable marshes in the Leningrad area, central Russia and Byelorussia hosted 80 per cent of all partisan activity. This was largely due to Ukraine's open countryside and nationalism ruling out any organised resistance. During 1942 officers and regular troops were sent to assist the partisan units (called Otryadi) in Leningrad, central Russia, and Byelorussia. Supplies were also air dropped to them and their raids became much more effective. By the end of the year there were around 130,000 partisans in control of large areas in the Germans' rear. However, in a stand up fight they were no match for the powerful Wehrmacht.

Before Zeitzler had ever seriously considered Operation Citadel, the attack on the Kursk salient, Stalin and his generals sought to disrupt Hitler's summer preparations. According to Soviet intelligence, partisans were a constant nuisance to the Germans. In particular they were regularly attacking fixed installations, severing lines of communication and hampering troop movements. The Soviets estimated that these activities were holding down 10 per cent of the Germans forces on the Eastern Front. Around 500,000 men from police and auxiliary units were tied up along with twenty-five army divisions trying to maintain security in the Germans' occupied areas.[16]

The inaccessible Pripet Marshes created a vast partisan haven that was impossible to pacify. Throughout the first half of 1943 the Germans conducted a whole series of anti-partisan operations designed to secure their lines of communication before the summer. This included action against irregular Soviet forces west of the Minsk–Slutsk road and in the area of the Novi–Borisov–Minsk railway in Byelorussia.[17] More important was Operation Marksman conducted further to the east, in an area north of Bryansk.[18]

A major choke point for German communications on the Eastern Front was at Bryansk. The town was the junction for three key railways and a highway. This made it an important staging post on the main line of communications to Orel to the east. Karachev, a third of the way along the line to Orel, was a pinch point. If Rokossovsky's Central Front should push north and Sokolovsky south to the town then the German Orel bulge would be completely cut off. To the south Poltava sat astride the main railway to Kharkov and Belgorod and was a key supply point for Army Group South. During the spring and early summer 1943 across the central sector attacks on the railways rose from 626 in April to 841 in June. During the latter attacks, of the 1,822 trains transiting the area 296 were derailed.[19]

Security for the garrison at Bryansk was a complete nightmare. The region was heavily forested, which provided sanctuary for three major partisan strongholds to the north and south, as well as to the west of the town. An area of some 4,000 square miles concealed up to 16,000 partisans. These forces regularly blew up roads and railways, and during 1942 sparked a series of brutal anti-partisan operations by the exasperated Germans. Although these reduced the number of attacks they failed to wipe out the partisan menace.

The Germans conducted Operation Robber Baron from 16 May to 6 June 1943 against the southern area, which involved six whole divisions, one of which was armoured. This killed and captured more than 4,000 partisans and more than 200 camps were destroyed. Almost 16,000 civilians were evacuated. Despite this success, as many as 4,000 partisans still remained at large. To make matters worse for the Germans, plans were under way for the partisans to commence in August a two-month campaign known as the 'Battle of the Rails'.

Although these partisan attacks showed that great swathes of territory behind German lines were bandit country, the build-up for Citadel went according to plan and the offensive was not delayed due to logistical problems. After the Desna attack German security forces ensured that the partisans did not achieve such a success again.

Hitler was furious that 'banditry in the East has assumed intolerable proportions, and threatens to become a serious danger to supplies for the front and to the economic exploitation of the country'.[20] Originally anticipating a swift victory in 1941, he had not planned for an army of occupation. When it became clear the war on the Eastern Front would be a protracted affair his solution was to form ill-equipped security divisions using middle-aged reservists. Deployed to guard vulnerable and extended lines of communication, these units were conspicuously understrength and had limited capabilities.

The level of resistance in the occupied territories became such that these security forces had to be reinforced by reserve divisions and even field training divisions. These were joined by various unsavoury local para-military police regiments as well as unarmed and armed Soviet auxiliaries. Many of these units became infamous for their wholesale brutality.

The escalating partisan attacks incensed Hitler, who had naively hoped to rule and exploit his conquests without hindrance. His response was to unleash his SS thugs. By the summer of 1942 Himmler was firmly in charge of pacifying the occupied territories. Hitler instructed, 'The Reichsführer-SS has the sole responsibility for combating banditry in the Reich Commissioner's territories ... The Chief of the Army General Staff is solely responsible for action against bandits in operational areas.'[21] It was a clear demarcation that made little difference to the partisans' struggle.

Hitler also promised 50,000 reinforcements from the Reserve Army to help with policing duties. In addition he instructed that 'completely reli-able' native units were 'to be maintained and extended' for anti-bandit operations. He rescinded this order on 23 June 1943 by saying there was to be no further extension of local volunteer units because many of them were ill-disciplined and untrustworthy. On the ground many local com-manders short of manpower ignored such orders.

Intelligence chief Colonel Gehlen, aware that the Germans needed to capitalise on anti-Soviet sentiment, tried to encourage a new strategy for the partisan war. He was deeply concerned that Hitler's approach to the problem was simply making matters worse:

Colonel Altenstadt (of the Quartermaster-General's Branch) and I drew up studies urging the necessity of psychological and political warfare in the east. We called for new methods of dealing with the partisan plague. The studies were highly praised, widely discussed and entirely without effect: on the contrary, Hitler personally issued orders for the ruthless liquidation of all partisans, regardless of whether they were willing to surrender or to desert to us or not, and these orders resulted in a further escalation of the partisan conflict, and a renewed embitterment of the population towards everything that was German.[22]

Meanwhile, Stalin and his generals after their victory at Stalingrad worked hard to ensure that the Red Army was fully ready for the summer. General Shtemenko and his colleagues built up their reserve forces once more:

> In the spring of 1943, by way of preparation for the Battle of Kursk, the Stavka [Soviet high command] and the General Staff carried out sweeping organisational measures. Infantry, air and artillery divisions were formed ... The scope of this work is indicated by the fact that by April 1943 the Stavka's reserves included ten armies, a number of tank, mechanised, and artillery corps, and control of the Reserve (later the Steppe) Front.[23]

Hitler had foolishly ignored warnings about the Red Army's massing reserves in 1942 and paid the price at Stalingrad. The following year he once again refused to acknowledge the Red Army's growing strength. He had picked a fight with a slumbering giant, whose manpower easily outnumbered Germany's.

# 3

# DIGGING FORTRESS KURSK

Following Stalingrad it was apparent that Hitler would have to scale back his ambitions, if not sit tight while the German armed forces recuperated.

Nonetheless, by the spring of 1943 Rokossovsky's Central Front and Vatutin's Voronezh Front – respectively deployed in the northern and southern areas of the Kursk salient – were acutely aware that attack was imminent. Regardless of the very good intelligence that was flowing into the Kremlin, common sense indicated that Hitler would at least want to capitalise on his success at Kharkov earlier in the year. Rokossovsky's Chief of Staff, Lieutenant General M.S. Malinin, and his officers examined all the intelligence and they could come to only one conclusion.

Malinin signalled the General Staff in Moscow:

> Taking into account the forces and means and, what is most important, the outcome of the offensives in 1941 and 1942, in the spring and summer period of 1943 an enemy offensive is to be expected solely in the Kursk and Voronezh operational direction … Consequently, the enemy may be expected to go over to the decisive offensive in the second half of May 1943.[1]

Just for good measure, Malinin recommended that both fronts each be reinforced with ten regiments of anti-tank guns and fighter aircraft. Rokossovsky was in agreement with this assessment and a few days later also reported to Moscow, concluding, 'The enemy is not yet ready to launch a big offensive. The offensive is not expected to begin earlier than 20 April, but most likely in early May.'[2]

While Field Marshal von Manstein was riding high with the Werhmacht after his success at Kharkov, Rokossovsky's star was likewise in the ascendancy with the Red Army. In the opening stages of the war he had rapidly been promoted from a corps commander to an army commander. His 16th Army had distinguished itself during the Battle of Smolensk and then during the battle for Moscow. The latter had proved the Red Army could withstand the full fury of Wehrmacht. During the Battle of Stalingrad Rokossovsky had commanded the Don Front, which had played a decisive role in the encirclement and destruction of the trapped German forces.

Zhukov liked Rokossovsky; he was a survivor and hard as nails. More importantly, he was a highly competent general. Before the war he had been a guest of Stalin's Gulag. During that time Viktor Suvorov recounts:

> Nine of his teeth were knocked out, three of his ribs were broken, his toes were hammered flat. He was sentenced to death and spent more than three months in the condemned cell. There is testimony, including his own, that twice, at least, he was subjected to mock shootings, being led to the place of execution at night, and made to stand at the edge of a grave as generals on his right and left were shot, while he was 'executed' with a blank cartridge fired at the nape of his neck.[3]

On the eve of Hitler's invasion Stalin had released him, saying, 'Take command of this mechanised corps prisoner, and we'll see about your death sentence later …'[4] Rokossovsky seems to have borne Stalin little malice and rose quickly through the ranks.

On 12 April 1943 Zhukov, in his role as deputy supreme commander, along with the Chief of the General Staff General Vasilevsky and his deputy A.I. Antonov, met with Stalin to discuss the situation on the Eastern Front. Vasilevsky found Stalin, for all his many faults, a relentless taskmaster. He kept a punishing routine:

> In every twenty-four-hour period the Chief of the General Staff had to give the Supreme Commander in Chief two oral reports on the situation at the front: one at twelve noon about events which had taken place during the night, and one at 9:00 or 10:00 p.m. about changes which had taken place during the day. The General Staff was obligated to report to Stalin immediately all serious developments or major events.[5]

Stalin also received a third briefing by telephone, normally at about 10 a.m., conducted by the chief of operations. Ironically Stalin, like Hitler, found that although he was a feared dictator his senior generals felt that they were entitled to direct access to him. They regularly attempted to avoid the chain of command by telephoning and demanding to speak to him personally.

After his discussions with Zhukov and the others Stalin concurred with the view that Hitler was most likely to strike at Kursk, but remained very concerned about the Moscow sector. The dark days of the winter of 1941–42, when Hitler had got to the very gates of the capital, still haunted Stalin. When it came to Kursk there was much discussion about whether to dig in, conduct a mobile defence or to pre-empt Hitler's offensive by attacking first. While no immediate decision was made, they all agreed that Kursk should be turned into a fortress.

Afterwards Zhukov wrote:

> When discussing the plan for the operations at the Supreme Command GHQ, we came to the conclusion that it was imperative to build up stable defences, well organised in depth on all the most important sectors, and above all, in the Kursk Bulge area. In this connection, the commanding officers at the fronts were given the necessary instructions.[6]

Hitler was not be permitted to conduct a Blitzkrieg as he had done in 1941–42, or be given freedom to manoeuvre. The order was issued to create fortress Kursk. Zhukov noted that they had taken the initial steps in what he called 'deliberate defence'. The Red Army would be able to ride out the Nazi storm and then choose the best moment for going over to the counteroffensive. It was decided to construct a multi-layered defence up to 50 miles deep that would be able to absorb Hitler's armoured fist. This would comprise three belts backed by the forces of a third front that would be held in reserve – Konev's Steppe Front.

The Soviet military chain of command leapt into action. The front commanders instructed their army commanders, who signalled their various Corps HQs, who in turn issued orders to the divisional commanders. It was not long before the sappers and infantry were furiously digging for victory. The sappers sowed the ground with anti-personnel and anti-tank mines as well as assorted home-made booby traps. On the Central Front alone Rokossovsky's men laid more than 400,000 mines. Miles and miles of barbed wire was also unrolled.

Mansur Abdulin found himself preparing defences:

> One day, after picking out our firing position, we began digging
> trenches. At last, we had some heavy rain, but we kept on working until
> it got dark ... We also made a dugout with a thick layer of earth over
> the roof. It was a dry and pretty comfortable dwelling. The field kitchen
> arrived and we had a hearty meal.[7]

Civilians in the region were likewise called on to do their bit. As
Zhukov recalled:

> The local population in the Kursk Bulge area gave great help to the
> logistical services and the forces there. Industrial enterprises in the
> areas near the front lines did repairs to tanks, aircraft, motor vehicles,
> and artillery and other equipment. They produced large amounts of
> army and hospital wear. The local inhabitants also did an enormous
> amount of work, constructing lines of defences and building and
> repairing roads.[8]

To the south the Voronezh Front under Vatutin, whose political officer
was Khrushchev, was tasked with holding the southern face of the salient.
They set about creating a complex maze of defences that would funnel in
and destroy the enemy. His command consisted of the 6th and 7th Guards
Armies, reorganised from the 21st and 64th Armies veterans of Stalingrad,
still under Chistyakov and Shumilov respectively. It also included
Chibisov's 38th and Moskalenko's 40th Armies. Behind Chistyakov held
in reserve was Katukov's 1st Tank Army, while behind Shumilov stood
Kruchenkin's 69th Army. In addition the front's reserves included three
corps, one of which was armoured, while in the air support was provided
by General Krasovski's 2nd Air Army.

Thirty-year-old infantry officer Georgi Gubkin arrived with his
4th Rifle Company at the Voronezh Front in late June. His unit formed
part of the 184th Rifle Division ordered to hold the chalk hills to the
east of a huge state farm called Chapeyev. Battalion commander
Melnichenko told Gubkin his task was to construct 3 miles of trenches
as well as create weapon pits for a six-gun anti-tank battery commanded
by Azim Makhmudov. Calling together his three platoon commanders,
including Junior Lieutenant Zaitsev, Gubkin issued his instructions to
commence their engineering works.

He was not impressed by the lack of enthusiasm his men showed for their digging. Many of the company's new combat replacements were a mixture of nationalities, with men from as far afield as Central Asia and Siberia. Gubkin had fought at Stalingrad so he appreciated the value of good cover, being in the open meant death. He shouted at them, telling them to remember: 'The soldier's Thirteenth Commandment. It is better to dig 10 metres of trenches than a 3-metre grave.'[9] This did not have the desired effect so he took off his tunic and shirt and began to dig alongside them. It was hard work and took them a week to prepare their defences, but Gubkin was pleased with the finished results.

In the north, Rokossovsky, with the same team that had led the Don Front at Stalingrad, commanded from north to west five armies consisting of the 48th, 13th, 70th, 65th and 60th under Generals Romanenko, Pukhov, Galanin, Batov and Chernyakhovsky. The 2nd Tank Army under Rodin was held in reserve. Air support came from General Rudenko's 16th Air Army. Each of Rokossovsky's armies created three defensive lines. The first was some 3½ miles deep. This consisted of minefields and anti-tank ditches, screening trenches and emplacements protected by sandbags and barbed wire. The emplacements contained anti-tank guns and artillery.

In planning the defence of fortress Kursk nothing was left to chance. Zhukov and the others decided to try something new by concentrating an entire reserve front behind Kursk. Should Hitler break through either Vatutin's or Rokossovsky's defences then his men would run headlong into Konev. Also, his presence meant the Red Army had much greater flexibility in moving and concentrating its reserves to developing danger points. At his disposal Konev had the 5th Guards, 27th, 47th and 53rd Armies, commanded by Generals Zhadov, Trofimenko, Korsun and Managarov, plus the 5th Guards Tank Army under Rotmistrov. Konev's reserve assets were also quite considerable, comprising two tank, one mechanised and three cavalry corps. In the air he was backed by Goryunov's 5th Air Army.

Konev's Steppe Front was similarly equipped with an abundance of artillery. Mansur Abdulin's 66th Guards Rifle Division formed part of Zhadov's 5th Guards Army and was in its second echelon to the north of Prokhorovka. He was simply amazed at the firepower available: 'Neither before nor since had I seen so much artillery. The commanders of artillery units, with their guns of different calibre, had a hard time finding positions from which they could fire without disturbing their neighbours.'[10]

While the Red Army fortified the Kursk salient it also ensured that the German bulges to the north and south were hemmed in by strong forces.

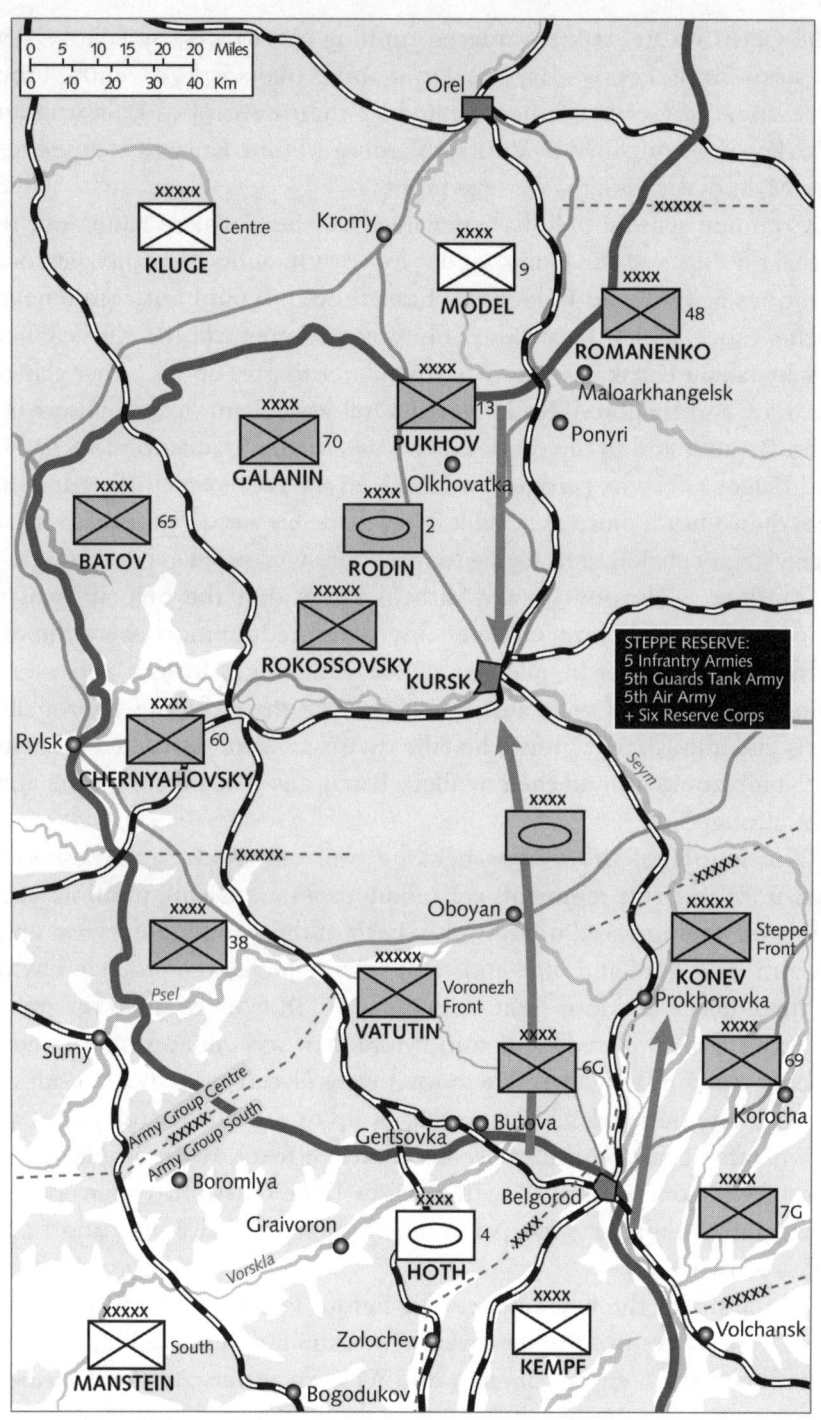

Soviet deployment around Kursk and Operation Citadel's proposed line of attack.

The German Orel bulge was faced running east to west by Sokolovsky's Western Front, Popov's Bryansk Front and Rokossovsky's Central Front. Likewise, the German bulge created by their control of Belgorod and Kharkov was contained by Vatutin's Voronezh Front, Konev's Steppe Front and Malinovsky's South-Western Front.

Common sense should have dictated that the Germans flatten out the Eastern Front and the Kursk salient by withdrawing from their exposed positions at Orel and Belgorod. Hitler though would not countenance such a move, which meant the only way to flatten out the Kursk salient was by taking Kursk. He was determined not to give up his earlier gains at Kharkov and Belgorod. To the north, Orel was reliant on the railway line from Bryansk and to the south Poltava was the main junction to Kharkov and Belgorod. Soviet partisans and the Red Air Force were ordered to disrupt these lines as much as possible. They made life a misery for the German Army's rear echelon units trying to make sure vital supplies got through.

Zhukov, Rokossovsky and Vatutin knew that the priority was to stop the German Panzers. The enemy armoured divisions were the one thing that must not be allowed to break through. To that end everything was dedicated to an anti-tank role, even the artillery, self-propelled guns and anti-aircraft guns. The rifle divisions were instructed to create anti-tank zones around their artillery battalions to supplement the anti-tank strongpoints.

The whole of the salient became one enormous anti-tank trap. The front-line rifle regiments created up to four anti-tank positions each, while the divisions had up to twelve. Each of these strongpoints had up to six anti-tank guns and nine anti-tank rifles, which were protected by up to three heavy and four light machine guns. In front of them the minefields were of an incredible density. More than 100 mines were planted in unequal rows 6–10m apart. These rows were placed 15–40m apart but not parallel. The minefields had a density of up to 1,500 anti-tank mines and 1,700 anti-personnel mines per kilometre of front. For example, on the Voronezh Front Shumilov's 25th Guards Rifle Corps had an average of 1,000 anti-tank mines sown per kilometre of its defensive front and 1.6km of barbed wire.

In the north the key defences lay before Ponyri, while to the south they were in front of Prokhorovka. When the time came Zhukov was to coordinate the Central, Bryansk and Western Fronts; Vasilevsky would take charge of the Voronezh Front. As a result, Zhukov spent a lot of time helping to prepare Rokossovsky's defences.

Their strongest anti-tank defences were built in front of Pukhov's 13th Army and on the flanks of Galanin's 70th and Romanenko's 48th Armies to the west and east respectively. Zhukov and Rokossovsky were concerned about Pukhov's ability to hold Ponyri so they greatly bolstered his firepower. The bulk of the Central Front's artillery units were deployed to the area. These were then bolstered by the 4th Artillery Corps, which brought with it another 700 guns and mortars. Zhukov claims he ended up with almost 100 guns and mortars per kilometre of front, with thirty anti-tank guns per kilometre.

Gun and mortar crews knew it was vital to get their emplacement just right. If you made it too small you spent all your time tripping over the paraphernalia of war and squeezing past each other. If it was too large it became an open killing ground that welcomed shrapnel. It had to be just the right size to provide optimum cover and a reasonable workspace. Inevitably, when you opened fire you often received counterbattery fire. It was then you had to hope the heaped sandbags warded off the scything hot pieces of metal that whizzed through the air.

Vatutin's defences consisted of almost sixteen guns per kilometre in front of Chistyakov's 6th Guards and Shulimov's 7th Guards Armies, which were either side of Belgorod. Just behind them was Kurchenkin with the 69th Army, which was guarding the approaches to Prokhorovka. Defending the air space over Kursk was the combined strength of the 2nd, 5th and 16th Air Armies, plus two fighter divisions from the anti-aircraft defence organisation. Integrated with them was an early warning system plus the anti-aircraft batteries.

This was not the end of the defensive plans for Kursk. Once these defences were held it was envisaged that a twin attack would be launched. Konev would move between the Voronezh and South-Western Fronts to conduct a counteroffensive via Belgorod and Kharkov to the Dnieper River. In the north the Bryansk and Western Fronts under Popov and Sokolovski would strike in the Orel area.

War correspondent Vasily Grossman and photographer Oleg Knorring drove to the Central Front in an open-top jeep amidst the gathering armies. The pair were old hands and had first visited the Central Front together in the dark days of 1941 covering the war for the military *Red Star* newspaper. Despite their uniforms, Vasily, in his round glasses, looked decidedly bookish, but Oleg was much more dashing. They had got to a spot about 130km north-east of Kursk and just under 100km south-east of Orel when Vasily recorded with some humour in his notebook:

We entered the village of Kuban in dust and smoke, amid the flow of thousands of vehicles. How can one possibly find one's friends in this terrible mess? Suddenly I saw a car with luxurious new tyres standing in a shed. I said prophetically: 'This car with incredible tyres belongs either to the Front Commander Rokossovsky, or to TASS correspondent Major Lipavsky.' We entered the house. A soldier was eating borscht at the table. 'Who's billeted in this house?' The soldier replied: 'Major Lipavsky, TASS correspondent.' Everyone looked at me. I had that feeling probably experienced by Newton when he discovered the law of gravity.[11]

On finding Rokossovsky's HQ he interviewed the commander's intelligence officers looking for a story. They were amazed that the Germans seemed to be wilfully ignoring the strength of fortress Kursk. 'A gigantic burden had fastened the Germans to the Orel axis,' wrote Vasily, 'although [Luftwaffe] pilots kept telling them how strong our defence was.'[12] Rokossovsky's HQ also let slip that Ponyri was where the action would be. Vasily decided that would be his next port of call.

As well as preparing defences, Soviet troops also undertook training and exercises. This was not universally popular. Officer Nikolai Belov, with one of the rifle divisions assigned to protect Maloarkhangelsk, grumbled, 'We've got to do some intense training. We'll have to work in earnest again now, and you can't protect yourself from the intensity of it.'[13] Belov found keeping himself and his men occupied beneficial, but he was unable to find a solution to the shortage of guns and other supplies that his unit was suffering from.

'The air is motionless and dry. All day long our regiment is involved in tactical exercises,' wrote Mansur Abdulin. 'I am now commander of the first and main mortar gun crew and assistant platoon commander. We train our new recruits, sharing our Stalingrad experiences, and also learn some of the things which we didn't have time for at the Tashkent Military School.'[14]

At the end of May the Luftwaffe started dropping leaflets urging the Soviet soldiers to surrender with a promise of good treatment. Belov was informed on 27 May that five riflemen had deserted. He was at a loss to explain their behaviour: 'It's hard to understand what brought that on. Evidently the general tiredness.'[15] Desertion proved a problem in the salient. Between February and July 1943 at least 8,000 soldiers went over to the Germans, the equivalent of an entire rifle division.

Meanwhile, General Antipenko arrived in the Kursk salient with an absolutely enormous job. He was responsible for organising the logistical support for Rokossovsky. Such a task required both a methodical man and an experienced staff officer. He had served as the chief of logistics for the 49th Army during the battle for Moscow and Zhukov thought highly of him. It fell to Antipenko to ensure that Rokossovsky's armies were supplied with all the shells, bullets, mines and rations they needed.

Coordinating this required a cool head, especially when the Luftwaffe and bad weather did everything possible to impede the delivery of supplies. Antipenko and his staff officers were reliant on General Khrulev's support organisation. Khrulev was the Red Army's quartermaster, holding the dual post of Chief of Rear Services and Transport. Antipenko and General Anisimov, his counterpart with Vatutin, needed to ensure that their armies had enough stockpiled to fight an initial defensive battle then go over to the counteroffensive without pause. If they got it wrong the Red Army could run out of steam halfway through either of these phases.

Scheduling train timetables became an obsession of Antipenko's. Well over 141,300 railway carloads of supplies were employed to ferry supplies to the front, including everything from tanks to aircraft. His staff officers had to liaise with the anti-aircraft regiments to ensure the trains included flat cars fitted with 37mm flak guns. The Red Air Force was also tasked to protect the railways and chase off any nosy Luftwaffe reconnaissance planes. The troops had to be moved smoothly and efficiently as well. This meant securing sufficient 'teplushka' rail cars. These were simply freight wagons with a wooden bar fixed across the door frame to prevent the men falling out when the door was slid back.

Ponyri was an important railhead as it sat astride the Kursk–Orel railway. The line then ran south to Prokhorovka and on to Belgorod. Both the junctions at Orel and Belgorod remained occupied by the Germans. Those lines outside the salient behind the gathering Soviet forces were reliant on trucks to move things up to the front lines. Antipenko's preparations did not go unhindered; the Luftwaffe's bombers hit the vital rail junction at Kursk on 2 and 3 June 1943. Despite being intercepted by Soviet fighters, they still managed to cause considerable damage.

Not only did Antipenko have to feed and clothe the Red Army, but he found the requirements of the hungry civilian population also put a strain on his logistical efforts. In April, 105,000 civilians were drafted in to help dig the Kursk defences. Two months later this number had tripled and not all of them were able to feed themselves. Field kitchens had to be set up and water brought to the workers toiling in the growing heat.

Zhukov was full of praise for Antipenko and Anisimov's achievements:

> Supplying more than 1.3 million soldiers, 3,600 tanks, 20,000 guns and 3,130 planes (including long-range bombers) for the Battle of Kursk required a tremendous amount of work. Despite the difficult conditions, the rear services handled their task brilliantly and ensured a steady flow of provisions during both the defensive phase of the battle and the rapid shift to a counteroffensive.[16]

The mounting tension in fortress Kursk continued to grow. Belov wrote in his diary on 13 June:

> Today another two have gone over to the enemy side. That's eleven people already. Most of them are pricks. On 11 June, our neighbours did some battle reconnaissance. They didn't find a thing. We're all sitting in this ravine, it will be a month soon, and there's just silence at the front.[17]

The following day he added, with understatement:

> A big operation is being prepared. Our division is going to attack in three echelons, and our regiment will be in the second. There will be thirty-five batteries working in the division, not including two Katyusha regiments. It's going to be pretty interesting.[18]

# 4

# GIFTS FROM UNCLE SAM

British sailors were angered by the complete lack of gratitude shown by dockyard workers when they delivered supplies to Archangel. Russian indifference resulted in some choice expletives being shouted at the quayside. 'Go to hell, then,' yelled one annoyed sailor, who turned and went below followed by the rest of his disgruntled shipmates.[1] What they did not know was that the dockers were already in hell. The workers were slave labour from Stalin's Gulag and they had nothing to be happy about. The sailors failed to grasp the significance of the guards, whose rifles had fixed bayonets.[2] The British were yet to learn that the Soviet Union did things very, very differently from Britain.

In the Kremlin, Soviet leader Joseph Stalin was far from happy with his gifts from Uncle Sam and the British Bulldog; they were simply not what he wanted. Sat at his desk, he found himself reading a joint communique from President Roosevelt and Prime Minister Churchill that was causing him displeasure. Britain and America in 1943 essentially had three options for victory: bring Germany to its knees by bombing its weapons factories; launch a European second front with an invasion of Sicily and Italy; or a cross-Channel invasion of Nazi-occupied France. The reality was that they could only manage the second with the resources available.

Stalin desperately wanted the third option as that would draw German troops away from the Eastern Front. Looking at his maps, the English Channel looked such an insignificant barrier. At the end of 1942 he had written to Roosevelt:

Permit me also to express confidence that time has not passed in vain and that the promises about opening the second front in Europe, which were given to me by you, Mr President, and Mr Churchill in relation to 1942, will be fulfilled and will anyway be fulfilled in relation to spring 1943 ...[3]

After Churchill and Roosevelt's Casablanca conference in early 1943 Stalin continued to lobby them for a firm commitment to a second front. In a joint reply sent on 12 February the pair stated they were:

Pushing preparations to the limit of our resources for a cross-Channel operation in August ... Here again shipping and assault landing craft will be limiting factors. If the operation is delayed by the weather or other reasons it will be prepared with stronger forces in September. The timing of this attack must of course be dependent upon the condition of German defensive possibilities across the Channel at that time.[4]

Stalin felt that this was too vague and pressed them to commit to the spring or early summer at the latest. Churchill wrote back pointing out the strategic demands on their resources in the Mediterranean, the Far East, the Pacific and the Arctic convoys. Reference to the latter irked Stalin even more. How much time did they need, he scoffed. The slowing down of American and British operations in Tunisia had permitted Hitler to transfer twenty-seven divisions from the West to the Eastern Front. Stalin was thoroughly fed up waiting for them to take the pressure off the Red Army.

The Soviet leader was a wily old fox and knew the one thing that Churchill and Roosevelt feared was not so much the Soviet Union being defeated but making a separate peace with Hitler. If that happened they would never liberate Western Europe in the face of the redeployed might of the battle-hardened Wehrmacht. In light of his victory at Stalingrad neither was a likely outcome, nonetheless he sought to play on their fears by warning of the danger to their common cause if the second front continued to be delayed. On 15 March 1943 he cunningly signalled back:

I recognise these difficulties. Nevertheless, I deem it my duty to warn you in the strongest possible manner, in the interest of our common cause, how dangerous would from the view-point of our common cause further delay in opening a Second Front in France. This is the reason

why the uncertainty of your statements about the contemplated Anglo–
American offensive across the Channel arouses grave anxiety in me
about which I feel I cannot be silent.[5]

In the meantime, Roosevelt and Churchill thrashed out how best to attack
Italy. There would be no shipping available for transporting troops and
equipment to Britain in March and April, while May was also uncertain.
This plus the need to keep supplies flowing to North Africa and preparations for an invasion of Sicily as a stepping stone to the Italian mainland
firmly ruled out any cross-Channel attack at all in 1943. Stalin knew the
Red Army would be on its own in the summer. To further sour relations
with Roosevelt and Churchill, they now closed off the Arctic supply route.

The Battle of the Arctic convoys was a bloody affair with the Luftwaffe
and Kriegsmarine doing everything to stop them getting through. These
convoys were dubbed PQ, with the most infamous being PQ17.[6] Just three
months after the German invasion Britain and America had started shipping
military supplies to their new-found ally. Merchantmen sailed through the
Norwegian and Barents seas to the Arctic ports of Murmansk and Archangel.[7]

'I went to Russia on the third convoy to sail from Scotland,' recalled
news correspondent Walter Kerr of the *New York Herald Tribune*. 'We left
on the night of 13 October [1941], at a time when the German Army was
only sixty-five miles from Moscow and moving so fast we did not know
whether our ships would get to Russia on time.'[8] He and the convoy survived unscathed and he travelled on to Moscow. It became a hazardous
route though and the danger grew as time passed.[9]

Kerr later observed:

During those months of 1942 our ships that sailed to Russia were inadequately armed … they did not have the fire power they needed to ward
off attack, but they also knew how much the supplies were needed by
the Red Army. We began to lose ship after ship.[10]

Russian-born British journalist Alexander Werth managed to persuade
the editor of *The Sunday Times* to let him cover the war in the east from
Moscow. Once funding was approved he caught the first available flight to
Reykjavik and then prepared for the sea journey to Murmansk. Iceland
had been turned into a giant aircraft carrier as part of the war against
Hitler's U-boats. The Icelanders were somewhat bemused that their sleepy
island had become so pivotal to the Allied war machine.

Like Walter Kerr, Werth experienced at first-hand the desperate attempts to get military supplies through to the Soviet Union. He found himself sailing from Iceland on 20 May 1942 with the 10,000-ton cargo vessel *Empire Baffin*, which formed part of the fifty-strong convoy PQ16. The Luftwaffe was soon aware of their departure and a week later more than 100 bombers attacked them south-east of Barents Island. The escort destroyers did everything they could to drive off the attackers.

Werth recalled the terrifying ordeal:

> For 40 long minutes they attacked, usually in twos and threes, usually coming straight out of the sun, some diving low, others dropping their bombs from two hundred feet (60m). From the yellow shark-like bellies one could see the obscene yellow eggs dropping … Then there was another attack. This time they weren't merely dive-bombers, but torpedo carriers as well … Then the Focke-Wulf [fighter-bomber] tried to provoke the destroyers by coming almost within range, and while the destroyers were firing at him, one of the planes which had been quietly hiding in the clouds suddenly came diving down.[11]

The attacks resulted in the loss of four ships and two others heavily damaged. The Luftwaffe struck twice more and just twenty-five ships reached Kola Bay on the evening of 30 May. That night they were attacked again, losing another seven ships. Werth though survived to make his way to Moscow.

Arthur Oakeshott, a correspondent with Reuters, also travelled with one of the Arctic convoys and endured the full fury of the Luftwaffe. He was attacked by more than fifty bombers:

> Shell bursts were soon joined in the Arctic air by long streams of cerise-coloured tracer shells from the Oerlikon guns. Then, as the planes zoomed over the destroyer screen, hell breaks loose … The port guns of the destroyers open up, followed immediately by every gun in the convoy … From then on the battle becomes a whirling maelstrom of shells, bullets, tracers, black, blue, brown and grey smoke-bursts. The zoom of the aircraft, the crashing of bursting shells, adds to the din.[12]

Oakeshott was deeply grateful they had an aircraft carrier for protection. This quickly put its Hurricanes into the air and, having driven off the first wave, intercepted the second group of attackers. 'The carrier seems to shake herself like an outraged angry hen,' he wrote, 'but instead of her chicks hiding in her wings for protection they – the Hurricanes – roar off her deck in pursuit of those who have upset their mother's equanimity – and did they give it to those jerries!'[13]

The subsequent convoy PQ17 was savagely mauled by bombers and U-boats, which together sank twenty-four vessels, with just eleven escaping to reach Archangel. Thanks to poor intelligence the ships had scattered, leaving them to be picked off one by one. The convoy disastrously lost 3,350 vehicles, 430 tanks and 210 aircraft. PQ18 also took a beating, losing thirteen ships.

By early 1943 Hitler was far from happy about how the maritime campaign was going, complaining, 'The tally of our U-boat sinkings has fallen off alarmingly, and there have been serious errors in the conduct of the war in the air.'[14] Hitler was well aware how crucial the battles of the Atlantic and Arctic were to the outcome of the war. Despite his many preoccupations, he still found time to reflect upon the war of the shipping lanes and the role of airpower:

> Apart from submarines, our greatest need is for little ships – powerful corvettes, destroyers and the like – these are the classes that carry on the fight.
>
> The Japanese today possesses the most powerful fleet of battleships in the world, but it is very difficult to use them in action. For them, the greatest danger comes from the air.[15]

During the beginning of 1943, under the cover of perpetual Arctic darkness, Churchill had pushed two supply convoys through to Russia, but with the return of daylight he reluctantly postponed the March convoy. Then, under advice from the Royal Navy, he agreed that supplies by this route would stop until the return of darkness in the autumn. 'This decision was taken with deep regret,' Churchill wrote later, 'because of the tremendous battles on the Russian front which distinguished the campaign of 1943.'[16]

Stalin was livid that Churchill was being difficult. In particular this would delay the delivery of 660 fighter aircraft.[17] Stalin wrote to him on 2 April saying, 'I consider the step as catastrophic. The Pacific and Southern [i.e. Iran] routes can't make up for it.'[18] Four days later Churchill replied, highlighting the achievements of Bomber Command's raids against Germany's cities. He also sought to convince Stalin that the fighters would be sent via the Mediterranean as swiftly as possible.

There was another reason for the halt in the convoys; a diplomatic row had broken out over the inadequacy of Murmansk's air defences, which became the only point of access once Archangel froze. Having run the gauntlet the merchantmen found themselves still under attack even after they had reached their destination. Although 60 per cent of the ships were American the British had responsibility for their protection. Lobbying by London failed to have the desired effect; Stalin did not boost fighter cover over Murmansk and refused to let the RAF help. Besides, Stalin wanted Churchill and Roosevelt to concentrate on opening a second front in Europe.

Stalin was perhaps understandably affronted that they insisted he be grateful for the crumbs from their table. At a meeting with Zhukov and Vasilevsky he had raged, 'Tens, hundreds of thousands of Soviet people are giving their lives in the struggle against fascism, and Churchill is haggling over twenty Hurricanes. And their Hurricanes are no good, our pilots don't like that plane ...'[19]

Stalin found it hard to fathom why the Allies were so persistent about sending pilots and fighters to the Soviet Union. Even General Charles de Gaulle's Free French were trying to get in on the act. In late November 1942 the volunteer Normandy fighter regiment had arrived under Jean Tulasne, having travelled via Africa and Iran.[20] Although declared operational soon after, they had not scored their first victory until the spring of 1943 flying Soviet-built Yak fighters. They were brave but it had been a steep learning curve and casualties were high. The Red Air Force did not really know what to do with the Frenchmen so they were assigned to General Zakharov's 303rd Fighter Aviation Division ready for the summer.

Walter Kerr, who had covered the battles of Moscow and Stalingrad, appreciated there was a good reason for Soviet stubbornness:

> It was not an incident that astonished American and British observers in Moscow, for during all the months of aid to Russia the Russians consistently refused to allow us to operate on Russian soil. Their stand appeared inexplicable at first, but most of us came to the conclusion that it was simply a manifestation of the years of distrust that followed the revolution. The Russians would win their own war in their own way.[21]

Only much later did Khrushchev acknowledge, 'The English helped us tenaciously and at great peril to themselves. They shipped cargo to Murmansk and suffered huge losses. German submarines lurked all along the way. Germany had invaded Norway and moved right next door to Murmansk.'[22]

Stalin cared little that the Americans and British were fighting a desperate convoy war in the Atlantic in order to supply their forces in North Africa and as part of the build-up for the second front. Hitler's submarines were now wreaking havoc on the Allied shipping lanes. During March Admiral Dönitz had more than 100 U-boats at sea and the Allies lost 700,000 tons of shipping that month.

Remarkably, in response to the American shipments to North Africa, Britain and the Soviet Union, German intelligence, known as the Abwehr, established a sizeable spy network in Brazil. Washington used the country as a hub for air ferrying services and as a central location on the convoy routes. Brazil had a population of almost a million Germans, making it a fertile ground for espionage. Although this network suffered a collapse in 1942, the intelligence collected was clearly quite important as the Abwehr attempted to set up two more groups in 1943.[23]

Despite Hitler's best efforts, a lot of equipment was still getting through to the Soviet Union. The Luftwaffe issued a secret intelligence report on 4 April 1943 that assessed around 1.2 million tons of supplies had been delivered via the Arctic route compared to just 500,000 tons via the Persian Gulf and the Far East. It reported, 'Besides raw materials, victuals and mineral oil, it included 1,880 aircraft, 2,350 tanks, 8,300 lorries, 6,400 other vehicles and 2,250 guns.'[24] These inevitably had an impact on the fighting on the Eastern Front

This assessment was surprisingly accurate, according to Alexander Werth. He noted that American deliveries during 1941–42 amounted to 1.2 million tons and British shipments 532,000 tons.[25] Walter Kerr, in 1943, reckoned that in the first year of deliveries Churchill and Roosevelt supplied Stalin with 4,084 tanks, 3,052 planes, 30,031 vehicles and 831,000 tons of miscellaneous goods.[26]

Regardless of all the sacrifice, the Red Army found much of what it received was obsolete. More than half the tanks delivered in 1942 were light types with insufficient armament and armour. The following year the proportion rose to 70 per cent. Even the heavy tanks such as the British Matilda were found wanting and 'as inflammable as a box of matches'.[27]

Armoured vehicles supplied by America, Britain and Canada represented a sizeable chunk of the Red Army's tank forces. By the end of the war some 22,800 armoured vehicles had been provided, of which 1,981 were lost at sea with the Arctic convoys. These deliveries amounted to 16 per cent of Soviet tank acquisitions, 12 per cent of self-propelled guns and all armoured personnel carriers. The first shipment in 1941 totalled

487 British Matilda, Valentine and Tetrach tanks, and 182 American M3A1 light tanks and M3 Lee medium tanks. The following year these shipments had increased to 2,497 from Britain and 3,023 from America.[28] Yet Stalin remained unmoved by such incredible generosity.

Just 300 British Churchill tanks were sent to the Soviet Union with the Arctic convoys. Forty-three were lost at sea and no further examples were sent after 1943. Although Soviet tankers liked the tank's thick armour they did not think much of its puny 6-pounder gun or its speed. The 5th Guards Tank Army deployed to Kursk had just thirty-five Churchills available. The Valentine became the most common type of British tank in service with the Red Army, followed by the Matilda. The Valentine proved popular in Soviet service due to its mobility. However, the Matilda, the Valentine and the Bren gun carrier had narrow tracks that restricted mobility in the winter. They tended to clog with snow and then freeze solid.

Ironically, Red Army soldiers thought that the USA initials stencilled on American-built vehicles stood for *Ubiyat Sukinsyna Adolfa*, meaning 'Kill that son of a whore Adolf'. Although the M3 medium tank was armed with a 75mm gun, this was mounted in the right-hand side of the hull, greatly restricting its traverse. The turret, with a 37mm gun, gave the tank a high profile and Soviet tankers named it the 'Grave for Seven Brothers', or 'the crematorium'. Likewise the Soviets did not like the high silhouette of the M3 light tank either. They also received the M3 Sherman, which again was not greatly liked.

German sources also indicated that the Soviet crews were not happy with the tanks supplied by their allies. Colonel Reinhard Gehlen, who was in charge of intelligence gathering on the Eastern Front, said:

> Our intelligence suggested that about thirty armoured brigades had put in an appearance on the eastern front equipped with British and American tanks. The Russian troops, however, were not very happy with the quality of these tanks, as they were inferior to the Soviet T-34 in every respect, and with their narrow tracks their cross-country performance in Russia was poor; moreover, their engines could not digest the low grade fuels common in the USSR.[29]

Although the Red Army viewed the Lend-Lease vehicles as a blessing and a curse in equal measure, there was no getting away from them. By 1943 around 20 per cent of Stalin's tank brigades had Lend-Lease vehicles, while

10 per cent were completely equipped with them. What was of greatest value to the Red Army were the trucks and lorries, which greatly aided its mobility. Werth noted:

> From my personal observation I can say that, from 1943 on, the Red Army unquestionably appreciated the help from the West – whether in the form of Airacobras, Kittyhawks, Dodges jeeps, spam, army boots, or medicines. The motor vehicles were particularly admired and valued.[30]

Few American- or British-supplied fighters were to see action at Kursk. The Red Air Force units operating on the central part of the front employed almost no Hurricanes, Kittyhawks or Tomahawks as they had failed to live up to expectations. However, at least one unit flew the P-39 Airacobra fighter in a ground attack role. In addition, some of the air armies operated the American Douglas Boston attack bomber.[31]

Aside from Roosevelt and Churchill, Stalin was particularly angry with the US Ambassador Admiral William H. Standley. The latter, along with the American correspondents in Moscow, made it known they felt that the Soviet press, and indeed the Soviet government, was not showing enough gratitude for American and British supplies. Stalin was moved to write to Henry Cassidy of the Associated Press, saying rather tartly, 'As compared with the aid which the Soviet Union is giving the Allies by drawing upon itself the main forces of the German Fascist armies, the aid of the Allies to the Soviet Union has so far been little effective.'[32]

When the letter was published an affronted Standley flew to Washington to clarify exactly what had been sent and how much of it had been successfully delivered. On his return to Moscow in January 1943 he made it his mission to get the Soviets to show some appreciation. No one was forthcoming, not even Foreign Minister Molotov. Two months later at a press conference, Standley dropped a diplomatic bombshell. He issued a statement saying the Russian people had no idea of the help they were getting and this would not encourage Congress to renew aid if it was not appreciated.

Soviet censors were enraged but were authorised by Stalin to issue Standley's statement on 9 March 1943. Stalin appreciated that a public relations war was going on and that for the sake of the bigger picture he needed to give ground. The chief censor, Kozhemiako, was furious as his mother had died of starvation in Leningrad. One of his colleagues cursed, 'We've lost millions of people, and they want us to crawl on our knees because they send us spam. And has the "warmhearted" Congress ever done anything that wasn't in its interests? Don't tell me that Lend-lease is *charity.*[33] No one though was going to defy Stalin and the following day the Soviet press began to report on the generous aid sent by their allies.[34]

Despite the disparaging remarks about spam, like everything else it played its role in Stalin's war effort. 'There were many jokes going around in the army, some of them off-colour, about American Spam,' recalled Khrushchev. 'It tasted good nonetheless. Without Spam we wouldn't have been able to feed our army. We had lost our most fertile lands – the Ukraine and the northern Caucasus.'[35] What he did not mention was that some of the canned pork was also sent to feed the Gulag inmates.[36]

It was very evident to Alexander Werth from his contacts in Moscow that Uncle Sam's gifts were going to have an impact on the impeding fighting at Kursk. He wrote:

On 11 June I recorded a conversation with a Russian correspondent who had just been to Kursk. He said the Russian equipment there was truly stupendous; he had never seen anything like it. What was also going to make a big difference this summer was the enormous number of American trucks; these were going to increase Russian mobility to a fantastic degree. The Russian soldiers were finding them excellent.[37]

# PART TWO

# HITLER INSISTS

# 5

# SHADOW OF STALINGRAD

Just two weeks after the German surrender at Stalingrad Hitler's spin doctor, Joseph Goebbels, found himself in the city of Düsseldorf on a mission. He had a lot on his mind. Goebbels was conducting a trial run for saving the nation and setting out his vision for the future. He was due in Berlin in three days' time to address the country and Düsseldorf presented him with the chance to finetune his speech. When he got back to the capital nothing was to be left to chance.

Following the loss of Stalingrad, at the Nazi Propaganda Ministry in Berlin, Goebbels faced one of the toughest challenges of his life: how did you hide the fact that Hitler had wantonly flushed a quarter of a million men down the toilet? Remarkably, the British had turned their defeat at Dunkirk into a victory, but then they had saved 300,000 men. They had been subsequently humiliated at Singapore but that was a Japanese victory. He summoned his staff and they began to formulate a plan to stage-manage what was an unmitigated disaster for the German armed forces and their allies. German self-confidence could not be left in the doldrums.

So far, the handling of Stalingrad had been a public relations disaster from start to finish. To mark the tenth anniversary of Hitler's rise to power, on 30 January 1943, Göring had made a broadcast ridiculously comparing the German garrison to the 300 Spartans who had died defending Thermopylae. The German Army was not happy that the rotund head of the Luftwaffe was making a 'funeral' speech for their trapped men. Nor did his words do anything to boost the garrison's rock bottom morale.

Later that same day Hitler's speech was delivered by Goebbels. He made but one reference to Stalingrad, warning, 'The heroic struggle of our

soldiers on the Volga should be an exhortation to everyone to do his maximum in the struggle for Germany's freedom and our nation's future ..."[1]
It was a telling admission that all was not well in Russia. Goebbels attempts
at damage limitation had started much earlier. Since mid-December he
had ordered the confiscation of mail from German prisoners of war.

One such intercepted letter was from an anonymous officer known
only as Albert written to his uncle. He had struck a falsely optimistic note:

> You probably know what happened to us; the picture is not rosy, but
> probably we have already passed the critical phase ... they want to gain
> a decisive advantage ... Soon the first half of January will be over, in
> February the situation will still be difficult, but then there will be a turn-
> ing point – and a big success.[2]

It was not made official that the German 6th Army was cut off until
mid-January 1943. Then on 3 February it was announced the Battle of
Stalingrad had come to an end: 'They died so that Germany might live.'[3]
No mention was made of the tens of thousands of prisoners. Inevitably
the news caused alarm across Germany. Within days the German security
service was covertly canvassing public opinion in order to put together an
official assessment. While its findings were not surprising, they also showed
Hitler's decisions were being openly questioned:

> Reports about the termination of the Battle of Stalingrad have shaken the
> entire people once again to its depths. The speeches of 30 January and the
> proclamation of the Führer have taken a backseat in view of this event ...
> ... large segments of the population are debating whether the develop-
> ments at Stalingrad were inevitable and whether the immense sacrifices
> were necessary. Our fellow Germans are specifically concerned with the
> question whether the retreat to Stalingrad was at the time promptly rec-
> ognised. Air reconnaissance should have spotted the concentration of
> Russian armies that were then moving against Stalingrad ...
>     Furthermore, the question is being discussed why the city was not
> evacuated when there was still time.[4]

Goebbels called for copies of the international newspapers. He knew the
Western powers had been gloating throughout the winter of 1942–43.
They had journalists embedded with the Red Army who chronicled in
minute detail the fate of the 6th Army. In addition, the Soviet press agency

Novosti had been swift to issue photographs of bedraggled and half-starved German prisoners going into captivity.

Downtown Stalingrad had been devastated, its multi-storey buildings reduced to shells. In the north the houses were built of clay and straw and when the fighting ended only the brick chimneys remained as a macabre monument. The most lasting and most damaging images were those of the statue of children playing in Stalingrad – this simple sculpture had come to symbolise the German rape of the city and personified what the Red Army was fighting for. In Goebbels' mind Stalingrad represented Germany's stand against Bolshevism. The men of the 6th Army had been heroic crusaders, not conquerors. To stop the Bolsheviks greater sacrifice would be needed.

Also, what Germany needed now was strong leadership from the Nazi inner circle. A unified front was vital, not only to reassure the German people but also Bucharest, Budapest and Rome. At the same time, Goebbels decided to capitalise on his party's rampant anti-Semitism in order to appeal to Germany's baser instincts and the fear of marauding foreign hordes. He was determined not to seek Himmler's help – the two men detested each other. Besides, Goebbels was fed up with Himmler's own propagandists hogging the limelight. Himmler was busy building his own private army with the Waffen-SS, gaining him yet more favour with the Führer.

Goebbels saw captive cinema audiences as a good way of disseminating Nazi propaganda. The movie-going public were always prepared to sit through a newsreel prior to watching the feature they had paid for. In his office Goebbels recalled Leni Riefenstahl's propaganda masterpiece the *Triumph of the Will*.[5] It had hammered home the invincibility of organised Nazi brute force – this message needed to be repeated louder than ever. However, he was jealous of Riefenstahl and had done everything he could to undermine her standing with Hitler and Himmler. Leni was a good-looking woman but she had rebuffed his advances and he never forgave her.

Besides, the public would not sit through a full-length propaganda film on the Eastern Front; there was nothing good to report. Goebbels knew that a propaganda unit had been assigned to the 6th Army, but he doubted that the survivors could offer anything but the unvarnished truth. All those glorious photographs and film taken during the triumphant advance on the Don and the Volga were now useless.[6]

One of Goebbels' special war correspondents had signalled, 'Death has ceased to appall the German soldier on the Russian front; he now regards

it as his inescapable fate.'[7] Goebbels had scoffed at such defeatism; it had
clearly been written by a pre-1933 professional journalist who put integ-
rity before the needs of the Nazi Party. He made a mental note to ensure
older war reporters were given back office jobs out of the way.

Goebbels was an astute operator and understood it was best to tackle
the disaster head-on with a special radio announcement. A noble but
necessary sacrifice had been made at Stalingrad, the public were told
solemnly. The German, Romanian and Croatian national anthems were
then played as troops from all three countries had been involved. In
honour of those lost it was then announced there would three days of
mourning. The cinemas and theatres were shut as this was not a time
for public frivolity. Goebbels knew that despondency and uncertainty
must not be allowed to set in and his printing presses were set to work.
Key amongst his morale-boosting posters were 'The Wheels Must Turn
only for Victory'.[8] Nazi Party members were sent off to paste this on
every available surface.

He then issued a decree on 15 February 1943 to all the regional gov-
ernors and military headquarters calling for complete mobilisation
for victory. To some it seemed a bit late. That day he gave his speech in
Düsseldorf ominously called 'Do You Want Total War?'[9] In his uniform
standing before a crowd, with arms bent at the elbows and fingers splayed,
he warned them that they were facing the risk of a Russian victory thanks
to international Jewry. He promised Germany would retaliate by extermi-
nating the Jews. Goebbels was greeted by ugly rapturous approval.

Deep down though most senior Nazis were very rattled by Stalingrad.
Hitler's Private Secretary, Martin Bormann, began to fear for the safety of
his family. Writing to his wife Gerda, who he called his 'dearest Mummy-
Girl', he warned, 'Should the war take a turn for the worse, either now or
at some later stage, it would be better for you to move to the West, because
you simply must do everything in your power to keep your-our-children
out of any danger.'[10] He then returned to the arms of his mistress.

Goebbels did everything in his power to quickly gloss over Germany's
humiliation at Stalingrad. His actions in doing so headed off Himmler's
aspirations for taking over the Propaganda Ministry. Goebbels felt that his
own pronouncements to the German people were not enough and that
Hitler should speak to the nation; national morale needed invigorating and
the Führer was a master at whipping a crowd into a frenzy. He normally
began a speech calmly, then would slowly build it up to an impassioned
crescendo. Hitler though refused to appear in public because he was in

complete denial and would never admit defeat. Although he was a master orator and rabble-rouser, Hitler was simply too depressed to face crowds of adoring Nazis.

Instead it was a defiant Goebbels who took to the podium at the Berlin Sportpalast to address a finely stage-managed rally on 18 February 1943.[11] Behind him an enormous banner proclaimed 'Total War Makes a Shorter War'. As far as Goebbels was concerned, theatrical flourishes would be far more important than what he actually said.[12] He had ordered that the event be broadcast live by radio into the nation's living rooms. When the cameras began to roll, Goebbels announced only 'Total War' would halt the tide of Bolshevism and was greeted by loud cheering. Afterwards, Goebbels went home to one of his luxury homes to console himself with one of his movie starlets. He considered it a perk of being the head of the German movie industry.

Later that week the Sportpalast newsreel was shown in reopened cinemas across Germany, although many audiences failed to appreciate that the roaring masses were loyal Nazis drafted in especially for the event. Goebbels was rather pleased with himself and his successful manipulation of the public perception of the war. The crowd had worn civilian clothing rather than uniforms to create the illusion that they were just normal everyday German citizens cheering their approval.

'If I had ordered them to jump out of the window they would have done so!' Goebbels later joked dismissively.[13] He convinced himself that his actions had stemmed the tide of pessimism and defeatism and galvanised the national will to continue the war. However, what Hitler really needed rather than Goebbels' fear-mongering Nazi rhetoric was a major battlefield victory before the year was out.

Political infighting and scheming was not helping the Nazi cause. By the spring of 1943 Martin Bormann was impeding Hitler's decision-making process by controlling access to him. No one saw the Führer without going through Bormann. To compound matters, once Hitler was conducting the war from his Wolf's Lair near Rastenburg, this left Bormann a free hand to run German domestic policy as he saw fit. He also attempted to strengthen his position by creating 'The Committee of Three', comprising himself, Field Marshal Keitel and Hans Lammer, Ministerial Councillor and Hitler's chief legal advisor. This was intended to ease the burden on Hitler – or so he claimed.

Goebbels, likewise alarmed at Hitler's refusal to seek a political solution to the war, wanted the Ministerial Council for the Defence of the

Reich to take the lead in such matters. He had lobbied Göring in early March, saying, 'The Führer sometimes wavers in his decisions if the matter is brought to him from different sides. Nor does he always react to people as he should. That's where he needs help.'[14] Goebbels' summation was spot on and Hitler's indecision was to plague his military preparations for the summer of 1943.

Following their catastrophic defeat at Stalingrad, Hitler and his key military advisors Jodl, Keitel and Zeitler sat around discussing what should be done in response. From February 1943, they had cast about trying to find a strategic solution by weighing up all the options. The generals on the ground favoured what they called an 'elastic defence'.[15] This was best exemplified by the successful retreat from the Caucasus and Manstein's remarkable victory in March 1943. Hitler though generally viewed this policy as an excuse by his generals to withdraw.

Field Marshal Kleist in the Caucasus had been grateful that Hitler had seen sense on this occasion:

> When the Russians were only 70 kilometres from Rostov, and my armies were 650 kilometres east of Rostov, Hitler sent me an order that I was not to withdraw under any circumstances. That looked like a sentence of doom. On the next day, however, I received a fresh order – to retreat, and bring away everything with me in the way of equipment … With Manstein's help, we succeeded in withdrawing through the Rostov bottleneck before the Russians could cut us off.[16]

Once back on the Dnieper, Kleist was able to launch a counteroffensive against the Red Army's march westward from Stalingrad and the Don. This resulted in the recapture of Kharkov and stabilised the whole of the southern part of the Eastern Front. It also resulted in a much-needed lull in the fighting that lasted until the summer.

This gave Hitler and his generals time to recover their strength. It also gave him time to ponder his best course of action. Although Manstein had failed to cut his way through to the trapped garrison at Stalingrad, his victory at Kharkov made him flavour of the month again with the Führer. The quandary that faced Hitler was whether to sit tight or attack. Either way the best Hitler could hope for was to wear down the Red Army sufficiently that Stalin would have to accept a stalemate. Hitler knew that time was not on his side, as the growing Allied victories in North Africa meant that it would not be very long before they opened a second front in France.

Since the end of 1942 Mussolini had been lobbying Hitler to 'Stop all offensive operations in Russia. Hold the line with fewer men and assign troops to North Africa.'[17] Hitler had little desire to do this as it was Mussolini's troops who had proved his Achilles heel in the Balkans and on the Eastern Front. Likewise, Italian forces had not been able to stand up to the British in North Africa, which had obliged Hitler to step in.

Zeitzler, Kluge and Manstein all wanted Hitler to put an insurance policy in place. This was to be in the form of a static defence line anchored on the Dnieper. Started early enough it could provide in-depth defence secured on a series of stoplines either side of the river. This proposal was anathema to Hitler because he hated giving up ground and felt that his generals would retreat to it at the earliest opportunity. This attitude first manifest itself in the winter of 1941–42 when General Guderian wanted to withdraw his frostbitten 2nd Panzer Army to the relative shelter of prepared positions. Hitler's response was to sack him. Also, in reply to Zeitzler's idea, Hitler stated that all fortification materials were required for the Atlantic Wall on the French coast. Hitler did not relent until the summer of 1943 with the construction of the Hagen Line.

All of Hitler's generals had been deeply shocked by the loss of the 6th Army at Stalingrad, none more so than General Zeitzler. He had repeatedly pleaded with Hitler to let them withdraw, and he even went on hunger strike, all to no avail. Zeitzler had watched in dismay as Manstein's relief column failed to cut its way through to the beleaguered garrison. Its commander, General Paulus, lacking authorisation from Hitler, refused to move. Zeitzler took the failure to avoid the capitulation of the Stalingrad pocket as a personal failure, although responsibility rested firmly with Hitler. It is quite likely that a rift developed between the two men, with Zeitzler secretly despising his Führer. If this is true then it goes some way to explaining Zeitzler's actions over the next few months.

Hitler undoubtedly underestimated Zeitzler, as did Albert Speer, Hitler's armaments minister, who recalled:

A straight forward, insensitive person who made his reports in a loud voice. He was not the type of military man given to independent thinking and no doubt represented the kind of Chief of Staff that Hitler wanted: a reliable 'assistant' who, as Hitler was fond of saying, 'doesn't go off and brood on my orders, but energetically sees to carrying them out'.[18]

Hitler became ever more withdrawn after Stalingrad. He was clearly shaken and Zeitzler took advantage of this opportunity. Guderian noted Hitler had become more solitary and shunned the company of his generals:

> His meals, which, until the Stalingrad disaster, had provided him with brief periods of rest in company with the men of OKW [Oberkommando der Wehrmacht – armed forces high command], were thereafter brought to him separately. Only very rarely would he invite one or two guests to eat with him. He would hastily swallow his dish of vegetables or of farinaceous food. He drank with it either cold water or malt beer.[19]

Hitler's decision-making was greatly impaired by his worsening health and deteriorating state of mind. His angry outbursts with his staff and general lethargy were a result of nervous stomach pains and insomnia. The cramps were greatly aggravated by his vegetarian diet and lack of exercise. Hitler's anxiety also manifest itself with him scratching at his neck and ears until he drew blood. In addition, he chewed his finger-nails. His personal physician, Dr Morell, kept him going with a cocktail of dubious drugs.

Walking his German shepherd dog Blondi for ten minutes before breakfast did little to help Hitler's condition. Before Stalingrad he had always made it a point of standing during his daily conferences. Now his legs and back were painful and he had to sit at the table, which made it difficult for his generals, who were used to leaning over the maps.

Wholly unfairly, Hitler held his generals responsible for Stalingrad and the worsening situation on the Lower Don. To calm his nerves he took solace in the company of adjutants Otto Günsche and Heinz Linge, his female secretaries plus Morrel and Martin Bormann. Linge had the dubious honour of administering the opium prescribed by Hitler's doctor. While Hitler was at a low ebb the ineffectual Göring took the opportunity to worm his way back into the Führer's favour.

Although Hitler was ill after Stalingrad he managed to rouse himself enough to try and shore up his alliance with Italy. At the end of February he despatched his Foreign Minister, Ribbentrop, to Rome with a sixty-page letter for Mussolini. In it he outlined his plans for a new offensive against Stalin. This, however, was not what Mussolini wanted to hear. While Hitler was obsessed with Russia, Mussolini was obsessed with

North Africa and wanted the Axis to concentrate their war effort in the Mediterranean and Tunisia.[20]

Zeitzler resolved to make it his mission to avenge Stalingrad, stabilise the Eastern Front and deliver such a blow to the Red Army that the balance would tilt back in favour of Nazi Germany. He looked at the situation maps of the front-line and began to formulate a plan. German resources were limited, he appreciated that, so he scaled his proposed operation accordingly. All that mattered was that they gave some payback and that the morale of the German armed forces was boosted.

Zeitzler had every confidence in Manstein's abilities to fend off the Red Army to the south of Kharkov in southern Ukraine. Despite Manstein's failure to reach Stalingrad his actions had been exemplary since. Besides, everyone knew that Manstein's thwarted relief effort, Operation Winter Storm, had been a desperate gamble because he had inadequate forces for the job.

What Hitler and his generals could not foresee was Stalin's long-term strategic objectives. If Britain and America were incapable of assaulting France for another year would Stalin bide his time and coordinate his efforts with them? Soviet confidence had been boosted thanks to Stalingrad, but had subsequently experienced a setback at Kharkov. It was highly improbable that Stalin would acquiesce to Hitler's continued occupation of Mother Russia while he waited for the second front.

If Stalin persisted in applying pressure on the southern part of the Eastern Front, did he have his eye on the Balkans? If that was so the Western Allies would face some tough choices over invading France or Italy. Looking at his maps, Hitler's attention was continually drawn to the vital coal mining and industrial region of the Donetz and the granaries of the Ukraine. If Stalin sought to recover these it would eventually put him on the road to Romania's oilfields and the Balkans.

Manstein's advice seemed to offer the best of both worlds. He told Hitler that they had insufficient troops to hold the whole of the Eastern Front. Inevitably if they remained on the defensive stretched across such a huge area the Red Army would eventually break through again. Therefore, using superior generalship and their better forces and equipment they should conduct a mobile defence or 'elastic defence'.

Unfortunately, Hitler took this to mean that attack was the best form of defence, which is what Zeitzler was also advocating. What Manstein really meant was a flexible mobile deployment that could conduct tactical counterattacks to send the Red Army packing. Manstein told Hitler:

There were two possibilities for the conduct of operations in 1943, after the period of mud had passed.

The first would be to prevent the Russians attacking by a German offensive ... The other way – and the better one – would be to await the Russian offensive ... then – with all our strength – make a counter-attack ... with the aim of rolling up their whole front in the south.[21]

In February 1943 Manstein's Army Group South sent Hitler a plan advocating the second option. If the Red Army launched a pincer attack on the Donets area with a supporting offensive around Kharkov, Army Group South could then withdraw west toward the Lower Dnieper ready to strike back. Once reinforced it could trap the Soviets against the Sea of Azov. Such a plan was unacceptable to Hitler, who could not countenance giving ground to the enemy. Instead, Zeitzler was advocating pinching off the Soviet salient at Kursk, which would gain him territory, not lose it.

Rivalry between Jodl and Zeitzler played a part in swaying Hitler's eventual decision. Zeitzler reasoned that their enemy's forces were too weak and communications too poor to permit the Soviets to take the initiative. Jodl, in his role as Hitler's Chief of Staff, pointed out that with an Allied victory looming in North Africa they needed to send men and equipment to Italy and the Balkans as a matter of urgency. Now, he argued, was not the time for a major commitment on the Eastern Front. Zeitzler, who had no influence over operations in the West, felt that Jodl was meddling and urged that the Eastern Front should be given priority.

# 6

# CITADEL TOO LATE

At the beginning of April, Zeitzler ordered General von Mellenthin, Chief of Staff of the 48th Panzer Corps, to Lötzen in East Prussia. This command was one of Army Group South's principal armoured formations, which had fought well south of Kharkov at the start of the year. He sounded out Mellenthin regarding the proposed Kursk offensive. Zeitzler was pleased to find him fully supportive, though Mellenthin cautioned against any excessive delay.

On leaving picturesque Lötzen, Mellenthin recalled his military history. He was reminded of the decisive German victory at Tannenberg fought in 1914 around the Masurian lakes. Although he was Silesian, he understood Tannenberg was burned into the psyche of the Prussians, indeed all Germans. It was their Trafalgar or Waterloo and had expunged a much earlier defeat at the hands of the Lithuanians and Poles.[1] The latter had halted the first *Drang nach Osten* or 'Drive to the East'. So bitter was the memory that the first thing the Germans did when they entered the city of Kraków in 1939 was to tear down the Polish monument to the battle.[2]

Mellenthin knew they needed another Tannenberg, but could such a victory be achieved at Kursk? In 1914 the Imperial Russian Army had become divided and trapped, then defeated piecemeal.[3] The Red Army was certainly not the same as the Tsar's old military. Nonetheless, he noted a certain weakness: 'in two important respects the Russians have not changed. They are still addicted to mass attacks, and they still show an extraordinary indifference to wireless security.'[4] Both cost them dearly.

Zeitzler wanted to strike in the middle of April but such a deadline was impossible; early May was the best he could hope for. Clearly Zeitzler intended to get the Army Group commanders on board, but while Kluge in charge of Army Group Centre was also supportive, Manstein wanted to retreat. What Zeitzler did not know was that there was a mole in the midst of the German High Command and that they ensured that Stalin was warned of Zeitzler's intentions on 1 April 1943.[5]

Every time Zeitzler asked for situation reports from the German armies around the Kursk salient it went through General Erich Fellgiebel's offices.[6] He was head of communications for both OKW and OKH (Oberkommando des Heeres – Army High Command). Along with his deputy, Lieutenant General Fritz Thiele, he was an ardent anti-Nazi. To some they were patriots trying to undermine Hitler, to others they were dangerous traitors intent on Germany's defeat. Every step Zeitzler took to formulate Operation Citadel was relayed by Fellgiebel to the 'Lucy' spy ring in Lucerne and on to Moscow.[7]

News of Mellenthin being called to Lötzen was particularly interesting; it signalled something important was afoot. Word was that his corps had been doing sterling work with the heavy Tiger tank. Hitler had high hopes for his new tanks, assault guns and self-propelled guns that German industry was currently churning out. Fellgiebel would have known if Zeitzler had requested Mellenthin bring a briefing from General Hoth on the combat readiness of the 4th Panzer Army ready for the forthcoming campaigning season.

Zeitzler clearly sowed a seed with Hitler, who discussed the matter with Jodl and Keitel at some length. After Stalingrad Hitler needed to impress upon his Italian, Hungarian and Romanian Axis allies that all was well with their cause. This was a bitter pill to swallow as it had been the collapse of their armies that resulted in the loss of Stalingrad. Despite viewing the Italians and Romanians as little more than cowards, he was going to have to welcome them with open arms once more.

Keitel, Jodl and Zeitzler were ordered to conduct a public relations campaign that involved a certain level of subterfuge. Jodl was instructed to prepare a map of the Eastern Front on a scale of 1:1,000,000 that was wholly unrepresentative, as were the respective strengths of each side. It made the Kursk salient look insignificant and Operation Citadel a safe bet for success. Hitler's generals were told they would inform their allies about 'alleged positions' rather than worry them about actual ones. During the first two weeks of April Hitler hosted Mussolini, Antonescu and Horthy in the ostentatious surroundings of the Klessheim bishop's palace near Salzburg.

To distract his guests Hitler regaled them with how Manstein had smashed the Red Army before Kharkov, killing or capturing more than 80,000 enemy troops the previous month. This did not balance the books with the losses incurred at Stalingrad and it conveniently ignored the massive Soviet build-up in the Kursk salient and behind it. Thanks to reinforcements sent by Stalin, the Red Army still threatened the whole region from Kharkov to Belgorod and Kursk. Such information was but a trifle.

Mussolini and Antonescu left completely reassured. Regardless of the loss of his soldiers, Horthy was not even interested in the Eastern Front, but rather wanted to complain about the presence of German troops on Hungarian soil. When Tiso, the President of the puppet state of Slovakia, arrived, he was simply given lunch and no briefing. This was despite Slovakia having troops fighting and dying in the Soviet Union. Hitler's other piece of unpalatable humble pie was to award General Gariboldi, who had commanded the Italian forces at Stalingrad, the Knight's Cross. It was all a shameless charade to keep the Axis allies together, because whatever their shortcomings Hitler was stuck with them.

Ironically, Mussolini had promised himself that he would stand up to Hitler. He wanted immediate peace with Russia and the withdrawal of his armies from abroad to protect Italy from the encroaching British and Americans. Goebbels was amused by the Italian dictator's transformation, recalling, 'When he got out of the train on his arrival the Führer thought he looked like a broken old man; when he left again he was in high fettle, ready for anything.'[8] Mussolini remained wed to the Axis alliance.

Mussolini was not well and his condition was aggravated by the very imminent demise of his forces trapped in Tunisia. The previous summer he had been suffering from stomach pains, brought on by the Axis defeat at El Alamein, which had variously been diagnosed as amoebic dysentery or an ulcer. On the train journey to Salzburg, Mussolini's stomach problems flared up again. He was further stressed by the Hungarian Prime Minister, who had earlier been in Rome urging that the smaller Axis powers should make a separate peace with Stalin. Although Hitler offered the services of his own doctor, Mussolini declined and a day was lost because the Italian dictator was too ill to attend the meetings.[9]

Major Otto Günsche, Hitler's adjutant, got the distinct but mistaken impression that Operation Citadel was the Führer's idea rather than Zeitzler's. Once a week Zeitzler travelled from Lötzen with

General Adolf Heusinger, Chief of the Operations Department of Army High Command, for their Obersalzberg briefing. In early April Hitler announced to them and his other assembled officers:

> The situation on the Eastern Front permits no large scale multi-directional offensive. We need to pull a few important pieces out of the Russian Front in order to gain the initiative again. We must finally be able to talk of success again. The sops I threw at the Allies at Klessheim will not keep them sweet forever.[10]

He bent over the map spread out on the conference table and put on his spectacles. Then, jabbing at the chart, he added, 'Here, at Kursk, we have the opportunity of giving the Russians a blow and threating Moscow again.'[11] Hitler motioned to Günsche and held open his hand. His adjutant passed him a green pencil, which he used to draw two arrows on the map; one from Orel and the other from Belgorod meeting behind Kursk. Thus, publicly Operation Citadel was born.

Hitler looked up full of enthusiasm and said:

> Zeitzler, in my opinion, we should launch the main offensive here, at the centre of the Kursk salient that leads out of the areas of Belgorod and Orel. I am hoping for a great success. Work the plan out! Send your best staff officers out to have a look straight away. They need to examine the area properly.[12]

Zeitzler's proposal seemed to gain no traction with the others according to Guderian, who recalled: 'In view of the heavy blow suffered so recently at Stalingrad and of the consequent defeat of the whole southern flank of the German front in the East, large-scale offensive operations seemed scarcely possible at this time.'[13]

Nonetheless, on 15 April 1943 Hitler issued a Top Secret signal for commanding officers only. Fatefully it read:

> As soon as weather conditions permit, I have decided to launch the Citadel offensive, the first offensive operation this year …
>      The aim of this offensive is a concentrated thrust carried out decisively and rapidly by the forces of one main attack force from the area around Belgorod and another from the area to the south of Orel to surround forces in the Kursk area by a concentric offensive and destroy them …

For purposes of secrecy, only those persons whose involvement is absolutely necessary should be informed of the plans of this operation.[14]

Despite this, Zeitzler did not give up and continued to push Hitler.[15] At the beginning of May 1943 another conference involving Zeitzler, Guderian, Kluge, Manstein, Model (commander of Kluge's 9th Army) and armaments minister Albert Speer, took place in Munich. Unhelpfully for Hitler, opinion was completely divided and no consensus could be reached. Guderian, implacably opposed to the whole enterprise, arrived spoiling for a fight.

For two heated days they debated the merits of Operation Citadel. Hitler had opened proceedings by droning on for forty-five minutes about the situation on the Eastern Front, but still showed every sign of being uncommitted. Not only did he run through Zeitzler's plan but also Model's opposition. The latter had intelligence showing Stalin was busily fortifying the Kursk salient and had withdrawn the bulk of his armour. This could only mean that the Red Army was anticipating a pincer attack. The generals were then surprised when Hitler did not adopt his usual tactic of dismissing Model for being a defeatist.

Publicly at least only Kluge supported Zeitzler's proposals. Model's view was that they would have to have a rethink or abandon Citadel altogether in light of his latest intelligence. Model though was only an army commander, so did not really have a casting vote. Manstein also felt that they had left it too late, if they had struck in April then they might have succeeded. Looking at the gathered faces he said, 'Now its success was doubtful.' His commitment to the plan seemed ambiguous when he said to carry it out he would need two extra infantry divisions. This was not the time to be discussing reinforcements and Hitler told him so.

Guderian was very disappointed by Manstein's performance at the meeting, observing, 'Manstein, as often when face to face with Hitler, was not at his best.'[16] Guderian made his position perfectly clear when he declared that the attack was pointless. Manstein railed against Hitler's facilitation:

Hitler decided – against the advice of the two army group commanders – to postpone 'Citadel' till June, by which time he hoped, our armoured divisions would be stronger still after being fitted out with new tanks. He stuck to his decision even after it had been pointed out to him that the unfavourable developments in Tunisia could mean that if 'Citadel' were put off any longer, there would be a danger of its coinciding with an enemy landing on the continent.[17]

Guderian felt he and Speer 'were the only men present at the session who were prepared bluntly to oppose Zeitzler's plan'.[18] General Hans Jeschonnek, the Luftwaffe's Chief of Staff, who was also present said that postponement offered the air force no advantages either. In his planning appraisal Jeschonnek had warned, 'Red Army Air Force units had recently gained extraordinary strength, and their flight personnel were now better trained, had a high morale, and were ready for a large-scale offensive.'[19]

The constant delays were driving Colonel Gehlen to distraction. When Citadel slipped to June this completely derailed Operation Silver Lining. Although Hitler was adamantly opposed to encouraging Russian nationalism, Gehlen had persuaded Zeitzler of the merits of conducting a major propaganda operation at the same time as Citadel.[20] Given the green light he had trained 1,500 Red Army officers and propaganda workers held at Dabendorf prison camp south of Berlin. They were to be formed into special reception teams who were to welcome deserters at the front. Leaflets were also printed promising Soviet soldiers they would be well treated if they surrendered and that they could join the 'Russian Liberation Army'.

On 3 May the code word Silver Lining was issued to the Luftwaffe. Citadel had initially been scheduled for 6 May 1943 and that night, before they could be stopped, Luftwaffe bombers dropped 18 million leaflets. The net result was just thousands rather than the tens of thousands of deserters that had been hoped for. Gehlen despaired, saying the whole thing 'went off half cock'.[21] The only benefit of this wasted mission was that it confused the Red Army when the leaflet drop was not followed by a German offensive.[22]

The operation almost had the reverse effect by alienating Soviet soldiers even more. While Silver Lining was the designation for German propaganda operations, to his alarm Gehlen discovered that it meant something entirely different to the Luftwaffe. 'There was a last moment panic when we learned that Silver Lining was a long existing Luftwaffe code word for commencing poison gas warfare, but this caused no real problems.'[23] In the meantime the leaflets had to be reprinted and the operation rescheduled to support Citadel in June.

Gehlen, along with Colonel Martin and Captain von Grote from OKW's military propaganda section, struggled with Hitler's intransigence over giving the war a more political approach rather than just relying on military force. Reichsminister Alfred Rosenberg, in charge of the Ministry for Occupied Eastern Territories, while sympathetic had dragged his heels over issuing the Smolensk Committee proclamation. In the meantime, Himmler's SS units were terrorising the population.

On 10 May 1943 General Wolfgang Thomale stood at the back of the dignitaries gathered around the conference table. Thanks to his post as Chief of Staff to Heinz Guderian he was attending yet another interminable meeting about tank production and Operation Citadel with his boss.[24] The others present included the Führer, Field Marshal Keitel, Guderian and Albert Speer's principal assistant, Karl Saur of the Armaments Ministry. Guderian was not happy with Saur, who had opposed moving the tank factories to safer locations out of the reach of the Allied bombers. Saur argued that the Allies were concentrating on the Luftwaffe's aircraft plants and had no intention of targeting the tank production centres. Guderian was unconvinced and felt even as just an insurance measure they should be moved as soon as possible.

Thomale marvelled at Heinz's persistence in opposing Citadel to Hitler's face. They had been discussing the vexed issue of the new Panther tank, when Guderian leant forward and grabbed Hitler's hand. For a moment the Führer was taken aback by such familiarity from a once disgraced general. Guderian said he needed to speak frankly about plans for the summer on the Eastern Front and Hitler acquiesced. Guderian explained he felt they should sit tight for the rest of the year. He reasoned that for the expenditure of a great deal of resources they would gain little and that necessary defensive preparations in France would be harmed.

Keitel, suddenly responding on Hitler's behalf, said, 'We must attack for political reasons.'[25] Guderian was of the opinion that this was a feeble excuse and retorted, 'It's a matter of profound indifference to the world whether we hold Kursk or not. I repeat my question: "Why do we want to attack in the East at all this year?"'[26] However, Hitler, Jodl and Keitel were well aware that their Axis allies, Italy, Hungary and Romania, were beginning to waver in their commitment to the war.

Thomale was eager to hear the Führer's reply and leaned forward. Hitler looked uneasy and it was evident that he was still dithering over the whole enterprise. His unexpectedly honest reply did not engender any great confidence. Looking at Guderian he said, 'You're quite right. Whenever I think of this attack my stomach turns over.'[27] There was a moment's stunned silence while everyone digested the implications of this. 'In that case your reaction to the problem is the correct one,' replied Guderian soothingly. Then, to emphasise his position, he retorted, 'Leave it alone!'[28]

Thomale was Guderian's 'confidant'[29] and knew that his boss was concerned about the influence Zeitzler seemed to have over Hitler and his
'yes' men, Generals Jodl and Keitel. Guderian was well aware that Zeitzler
was constantly advising the Führer that they must not sit idle while Stalin's
Red Army capitalised on their victory at Stalingrad. Guderian felt that was
all very well, but his first priority was to rebuild Hitler's exhausted Panzer
forces, not watch them being foolishly squandered.

Keitel, Saur and Thomale all remained quiet. Flustered, Hitler said he
had not yet made up his mind. The following day Guderian and Thomale
travelled by train to Lötzen, where his staff were temporarily housed.
On 13 May Guderian saw Speer to discuss production issues and in the
afternoon had yet another conference with Hitler. Notably Citadel was
not mentioned again. Guderian had once more pushed things too far with
the Führer.

In trying to get support for his Kursk operation Zeitzler may have discussed the matter with Field Marshal Erwin Rommel, who had been recalled
from North Africa. Just nine days after the German surrender in Tunisia,
Rommel wrote to his wife, Lucie, on 15 May: 'Dined with Zeitzler (Halder's
successor) this evening and had a very pleasant conversation. Our views
coincide in everything.' Later, whilst at Hitler's HQ in Rastenburg, Rommel
cryptically noted, 'I'm confidently hoping that we'll pull it off.'[30]

At the end of the month Zeitzler sought to get Hitler to commit to
Citadel with an attack on 10 June or at the end of June at the latest. Jodl
urged caution following Zeitzler's suggestion that a counterattack might
be better than an attack. 'We must be careful, my Führer,' said Jodl, 'not to
saddle ourselves with another lost battle.'[31]

Hitler was angry and well aware that the initiative was slipping away
from him:

> Listen to me, Jodl, I can't simply wait for weeks until Herr Stalin is
> obliging enough to attack. I must seize the initiative from him as quickly
> as possible. The situation is going to change overnight. No one can tell
> me that this coalition of the Western powers and Russia is going to last
> indefinitely – it will last only until problems start to arise. One day it will
> collapse of its own weight, and the more relentlessly we hammer at the
> Russians, the sooner that day will come.[32]

While Hitler hoped that the Allied coalition against him would collapse,
he was concerned that the Axis faced the same prospect. The reverses

Germany had suffered at Stalingrad and in Tunis, plus mounting U-boat losses in the Atlantic, were not a good advert for the merits of the Axis alliance. He knew he had to do something to stop the rot, but just could not decide what. The reality was he had simply run out of options.

In mid-June, before Citadel was launched, Hitler transferred his HQ from the Obersalzberg back to the Wolfschanze in East Prussia. Although it was officially a neutral country, Hitler needed to court Turkey as it was supplying him non-ferrous metals. He knew that Citadel was a good way of impressing the Turkish government. Late that month a delegation of senior Turkish generals and general staff officers were invited to tour the Panzer divisions massing in the Kharkov–Belgorod area.

Field Marshal von Manstein personally hosted the visitors and pulled out all the stops to impress them. A display of German firepower was laid on that included Tiger tanks and Stuka dive-bombers being put through their paces. Two waves of Stukas pounded targets into oblivion on the open steppe.[33] The exercises culminated in a massive explosion that caught the gathered staff officers by surprise, causing them to spin around to see a huge cloud of dust and smoke rising hundreds of feet into the air.

As usual, a German propaganda camera crew were on hand to capture the proceedings on film. The newsreel subsequently reported the Turkish delegation was witness to a 'full-scale battleground exercise' and that 'the Turkish officers were able to convince themselves of the state of readiness and the attacking power of the troops'.[34] They then visited Hitler at Rastenburg the very day after his offensive commenced. It was a public relations opportunity he could not afford to miss.[35]

In the meantime, the debate rolled on and so did the wavering over a start date. Hitler called his army group and army commanders to Rastenburg in mid-June. Then, much to Zeitzler's relief, Hitler agreed to launch the attack in early July. It was as if they had been worn down, as his field marshals did not object despite all the previous concerns. Behind the scenes though some generals remained far from happy.

Afterwards, General Adolf Heusinger, in charge of the army's planning operations, motioned to Jodl and said, 'Something must be done to stop this headlong progress toward disaster.' Jodl shrugged and replied fatalistically, 'I agree entirely – we're simply hastening to meet our doom, but the man who is leading us is our destiny, and one does not escape one's destiny.'[36]

After leaving Rastenburg the generals gathered at Army High Command Headquarters in the Mauerwald. Meeting in Heusinger's office, the conversation turned to North Africa. He complained about the division between the Army High Command with responsibility for the Eastern Front and the Armed Forces High Command with responsibility for everything else. This had greatly hampered combined operations in the Mediterranean. Heusinger pointed out that Hitler's refusal to take Gibraltar and Malta had condemned their forces in North Africa. 'We should have saved part of Rommel's armies,' he said, 'but instead we tried to hold out in a hopeless situation, and none of them were able to get out.'[37]

On this gloomy note the conversation turned to Kursk. Looking around at the others, von Kluge asked if they were now not too late, after all 10 June had come and gone like so many deadlines, to launch Citadel. 'I am afraid so,' replied Heusinger. 'The risk seems to be much greater now. It would be better to prepare a counterattack, but the field marshals didn't raise any serious objections this evening.' Heusinger sighed, adding, 'You must encourage your generals to show some initiative before it's too late.'[38] It was too late though, the dice had been cast and Zeitzler had finally got his way.

Zeitzler though must have known he was gambling with Nazi Germany's very future. He had originally envisaged Citadel as a limited decisive surprise attack for the spring, but the high command now saw it as an all-out frontal assault that would be an uncompromising trial of strength with the rejuvenated Red Army.

It was with a certain hypocritical irony that Hitler told Martin Bormann one evening in mid-June:

> It is quite extraordinary how many men there are who are incapable of facing reality and who, when face to face with danger, cannot calmly make plans to meet it. Such people are, for the most part, cowards, and fear of the unknown is ineradicably engrained in them.[39]

It was as if he was describing himself.

# 7

# HITLER'S ARMOURED FIST

Relentless Nazi propaganda played a part in convincing Hitler that Operation Citadel was a good idea. In one ear the Führer had Zeitzler urging him to punish the Red Army for Stalingrad, in the other he had Reichsführer-SS Heinrich Himmler persuading him that his Waffen-SS were the ones to do it.[1] Himmler was feeling particularly vindicated. His Waffen-SS had performed extremely well in recent months and covered themselves and him in glory. This had validated expanding his motorised infantry formations into Panzergrenadier divisions equipped with tanks. He was fed up with the pompous Reichsmarschall Hermann Göring swanning around telling everyone how marvellous his Luftwaffe was. Himmler felt he should be Hitler's designated successor, not a man who dressed as if he were starring in a comic opera. His pearl-grey uniform and ostentatious rings were a source of amusement to many.

Regular German radio broadcasts were abruptly interrupted by a fanfare from the Horst Wessel song on 14 March 1943,[2] to be followed by a triumphant announcement that the Waffen-SS had recaptured the Ukrainian city of Kharkov. The five-day battle over the Soviet Union's fourth largest city was the climax of a two-month campaign by the Wehrmacht to halt the advancing Red Army following Stalingrad. By early February Soviet tanks were thrusting toward the Dnieper, Kharkov was threatened, as were the German forces hurriedly retreating from the Caucasus through the Rostov gap. Himmler was delighted his SS Panzer Corps had saved the day.

The fact that his commander, SS-General Paul Hausser, had initially withdrawn from the city against the explicit orders of Hitler was neither here nor there. No one wanted the facts to get in the way of a good story; least of all Nazi propaganda minister Joseph Goebbels, whose broadcasters were extoling the virtues of Himmler's soldiers. Hausser's actions had enabled the army's weak Kharkov garrison to escape and put his SS Panzer Corps in a position from which Manstein could launch a highly successful counterattack.

Himmler took every opportunity to tell Hitler, and anyone else who would listen, that his highly motivated Nazi soldiers were far better fighters than the regular army's recruits. Just imagine, he said, what the Waffen-SS could achieve if they were permitted to field an independent army that did not have to answer to the Wehrmacht. Hitler, while weighting up his options for Kursk, seemed to be seduced by the prowess of these tough SS divisions.

After Goebbels saw Hitler, the propaganda minister observed, 'He was exceptionally happy about the way the SS *Leibstandarte* was led by "Sepp" Dietrich. This man personally performed real deeds of heroism and had proved himself a great strategist in conducting his operations.'[3] Hitler, recalling the performance of his Axis allies at Stalingrad, declared, 'The SS Panzer Corps is worth 20 Italian divisions.'[4]

In the back of his mind Hitler continued to blame the army for the defeat at Stalingrad. Field Marshal Paulus had shamed Germany by taking the coward's way out and surrendering. Hitler ungratefully felt that Manstein and Hoth had failed him by not cutting their way through to the besieged garrison. Göring had also let him down; his grandiose promises of being able to keep the garrison resupplied from the air proved spectacularly hollow. Hitler looked at Himmler and his highly able generals as clearly men who got things done and who could be trusted.

Looking at intelligence maps of the southern edge of the Kursk salient, Hitler asked himself, could Hausser's SS Panzer Corps cut its way through to Kursk? Tiresome questions about the number and quality of their tanks mattered little. However, it would take more than a handful of SS divisions to pierce fortress Kursk.

Guderian was vexed that Himmler's Waffen-SS was duplicating the army's efforts. He saw Himmler early in the year to try and get him to standardise his armoured units with those of the army's. More importantly, he wanted Himmler to stop raising new units, but he would not agree. The Waffen-SS was riding high in the popularity stakes with Hitler after its performance at Kharkov. As far as Guderian was concerned, the Waffen-SS and elements of the Luftwaffe's ground forces were an unwelcome drain on vital manpower. He took a cynical view of Hitler's motives for indulging Himmler:

> Hitler's idea was to make himself independent of the Army, whose leaders he never trusted, by forming this private army in which he believed that he could place implicit confidence; it would thus be a Praetorian guard that would be ready for anything, should the Army ever refuse to follow him on account of its Prussian-German traditions.[5]

The emergence of Himmler's Panzergrenadier divisions was not just a political vanity project; there were sound strategic reasons for upgrading them from the early motorised units. The expansion of German strength in 1943 was clearly accelerated after Rommel's defeat at El Alamein in November 1942, the Allied landings in French North Africa that same month and by the destruction of the German army trapped at Stalingrad in early 1943. *Liebstandarte Adolf Hitler*, *Das Reich* and *Totenkopf* were transformed into Panzergrenadier units for the spring 1943 counteroffensive in the Soviet Union, each with an integral tank battalion. This increase in combat power had been authorised in early 1942 but was not implemented until the second half of the year. Notably, the 5th SS *Wiking* division was also allocated a tank battalion but instead of being withdrawn to France to re-equip it stayed in the line.

As early as June 1941, *Liebstandarte* expanded to a full motorised infantry division and took part in the invasion of the Soviet Union as part of Army Group South and was involved in the fighting at Kiev and Rostov. The division was sent to France for refit in 1942 and upgraded. Sent back to the Eastern Front in 1943 under SS-Brigadeführer Theodor Wisch, it fought at Kharkov. The SS-VT-Division *Reich* was also sent to France in March 1942, with the exception of a small Kampfgruppe, where it was upgraded to become SS-Panzergrenadier Division *Das Reich*. It was sent back to the Eastern Front in January 1943, where under the leadership of SS-Obergruppenführer George Keppler it also took part in the capture and recapture of Kharkov.[6]

The 5th SS Panzergrenadier Division *Wiking* was the first and best of the foreign units raised by the Waffen-SS. *Wiking* first took part in the invasion of the Soviet Union as a motorised division. The following year it fought in the Caucasus and was redesignated a Panzergrenadier division. In the spring of 1943 the 5th SS was involved in the counteroffensive between the Don and Dnieper. The least well known was the 3rd SS *Totenkopf*, initially raised from concentration camp guards.

To take Kursk Hitler massed two armoured fists with fifteen armoured divisions and eighteen infantry divisions. To the north Field Marshal von Kluge's Army Group Centre would commit General Model's 9th Army. This comprised three Panzer corps and two infantry corps with a total of five Panzer, one Panzergrenadier and eight infantry divisions. Model had about 335,000 troops and 900 Panzers.

In the south Manstein's Army Group South would commit Hoth's 4th Panzer Army and General Kempf's command, known as Army Detachment Kempf. Between them they had three Panzer and two army corps with about five Panzer, four Panzergrenadier and ten infantry divisions. The most powerful armoured commands were Hausser's SS Panzer Corps with the three SS Panzergrenadier divisions and Knobelsdorff's 48th Panzer Corps, which included the *Grossdeutschland* Panzergrenadier division. These forces totalled 350,000 men with some 1,270 Panzers and 245 assault guns.

On paper these were impressive forces; however, on closer inspection this was far from true as a large element of the Panzers were obsolete. Almost 630 tanks were the inadequate Panzer III, these consisted of 432 armed with a 50mm gun, 155 with the short support 75mm gun and 41 flame-thrower tanks. The last two types were not suitable for tank-to-tank combat. This meant that the army's Panzer and Panzergrenadier divisions, as well as the SS Panzergrenadier divisions, were equipped with large quantities of these ineffective tanks. For example, 4th Panzer Army's 11th Panzer as well as the 2nd SS and 3rd SS Panzergrenadier each had about fifty Panzer IIIs. Similarly 9th Army's 2nd and 4th Panzer Divisions each had forty. All the other armoured units had between a dozen and twenty.

Hitler mustered about 2,600 armoured vehicles but this included the Panzer IIIs plus 200 obsolete light tanks and more than 530 turretless assault guns. The latter were really defensive rather than offensive weapons as they lacked rotating turrets, which greatly restricted their field of fire. To complicate matters, they were considered self-propelled guns so came under the command of the artillery and not the Panzerwaffe. By the summer of 1943 there were twenty-eight independent assault gun or Sturmgeschütz (StuG) detachments, four divisional StuG detachments, two remote control companies and twelve StuG platoons with the weak Luftwaffe field divisions.

When Guderian was appointed inspector general of armoured troops in early 1943 he was given a wide remit to resuscitate and revitalise every aspect of all the armoured units. Answering directly to Hitler, he was responsible for recruiting, training organising and equipping the Panzer divisions, both Army and Waffen-SS. Working with Armaments Minister Albert Speer, he sought to centralise weapons production. This put an end to the private industries the SS had created in the face of the army's intransigence over supplying modern equipment.

Guderian soon found himself with a power struggle on his hands that resulted in him having no say over the infantry divisions' assault guns. In his view this greatly impeded improving the infantry's anti-tank capabilities. He observed with some rancor, 'The results of this decision were far-reaching: the assault artillery remained an independent weapon; the anti-tank battalions continued to be equipped with ineffective, tractor-drawn guns, and the infantry divisions remained without adequate anti-tank defence.'[7]

Production of the Panzer III came to a stop in February 1943 in favour of the StuG III assault gun, although the support variant of the tank continued to be built until August. Guderian wrote:

> The construction of the Panzer III was now entirely discontinued, the industrial capacity thus freed being given over to the building of assault guns. The production figure for assault guns was to reach 220 per month by June 1943, of which 24 were to be armed with light field howitzers. This gun, with its low muzzle velocity and its very high trajectory, was undoubtedly well suited to the requirements of the infantry, but its production resulted in a fresh weakening of our defensive power against hostile tanks.[8]

Delivery of the first production series of the howitzer-armed StuH42 did not commence until March 1943, with the highest monthly output being reached in September 1944 with 199 vehicles. These were armed with the StuH42 L/28 105mm gun fitted with a muzzle brake, similar to the leFH18(M), to allow it to fire more powerful ammunition, giving it greater range. When the Battle of Kursk started the German Army Groups Centre and South had sixty-eight StuH42.

Likewise, Guderian was not pleased that Panzer IV production was weakened by the need to build yet more assault guns. In April 1943 he gained agreement that Panzer IV production would continue and be expanded during 1943–44 until mass production of the Panther could be assured. Hitler though was not perturbed by the inadequacy of his existing Panzers; Guderian was overseeing his zoo of weird and wonderfully named armoured fighting vehicles that were armed with high-powered anti-tank guns. It was these that would slice through the Soviet defences, creating a breach for the rest of his forces to flood through.

To support the ground attack Göring's Luftwaffe was ordered to gather every aircraft it could spare. Hoth's Panzers were allocated Luftflotte (Air Fleet) 4 under the operational command of General Hans Seidemann, while Model got Major General Paul Deichmann with Luftflotte 6. To reinforce both these air fleets additional units were redeployed from France, Germany and Norway. Flying tactical air support at Kursk meant an immediate end to the limited strategic air attacks that were being conducted against Stalin's weapons factories.

Deichmann knew that Citadel was an all or nothing operation for the air force. Hitler had made it clear he was prepared to sacrifice the Luftwaffe if necessary. Deichmann attended the last Führer conference, noting with some alarm:

> Two days before the German offensive began, Hitler addressed the commanding generals of the participating armies and corps near his headquarters in East Prussia. He spoke about the latent threat, and declared that if the Russians launched a counterattack he would throw into action his last available aircraft to block it.[9]

A total of seventeen Luftwaffe air wings were deployed near Kursk. The main airfields were clustered around Orel to the north and Belgorod and Kharkov to the south. One of the key Luftwaffe headquarters was at Mikoyanovka, south of Belgorod. These were backed by more than 200 bombers based at Kirovograd, Smolensk, Stalino and Zaporozhe. To create an aerial fist Hitler massed 1,200 bombers, 600 fighters, 100 ground-attack and 150 reconnaissance aircraft.

Elsewhere on the Eastern Front, the other Luftwaffe commands were stripped bare and greatly weakened. In northern Russia Luftflotte 1 was left with just one unit each of bombers, fighter-bombers and light bombers. In the Arctic, where the Luftwaffe was still busy attacking Allied convoys, Luftflotte 5 was left with a bomber group, fighter group and elements of a Stuka group. In the Black Sea area the reduced 1st Air Corps was left relying on the Romanian air force for help.

Nor was all well in the Luftwaffe's hierarchy. General Jeschonnek, Chief of the Air Staff, was not a happy man; his deep depression was mounting daily. Caught in the middle, his position with Hitler and Göring had become completely intolerable. After Stalingrad the Reichsmarschall was shunned by Hitler, so Göring set about creating a separate air staff under Colonel Ulrich Diesing to deliberately sidestep Jeschonnek. In the absence of Göring it was always the unfortunate Jeschonnek who was berated by a furious Hitler for the Luftwaffe's latest failures. The Chief of the Air Staff felt his key task was operational matters so he never troubled himself much with air defence. However, every time Allied bombers successfully attacked the weapons factories he was now Hitler's first port of call. Jeschonnek found the strain increasingly unbearable at a time when he should have been helping to oversee preparations for Citadel.

Air Marshal Erhard Milch, who was Guderian's equivalent with the air force, likewise had a very troubled relationship with the Reichsmarschall. He felt Göring ought to step down, especially after the debacle of Stalingrad. Milch also felt the Luftwaffe should concentrate its resources on the defence of the Reich to fend off the Allies' mounting bomber offensive. However, Göring preferred to pretend that there was not a war going on. To this end he devoted himself to his leisure pursuits, hunting and amassing a vast illegally acquired art collection.

Milch, who had overseen the herculean but futile Luftwaffe airlift to Stalingrad, let it be known he was implacably opposed to a summer offensive. He also wanted Zeitzler and Göring replaced. He dined alone with Hitler on 5 March 1943 and argued that Germany should remain on the defensive until 1944 and that the armed force's leadership should be overhauled. Milch pointed out that transport was simply insufficient to keep the troops resupplied over the enormous distances on the Eastern Front. The front line should be shortened. Hitler was not receptive, saying, 'You cannot persuade me.'[10]

Milch recommended that Hitler stop his daily staff meetings and appoint Manstein as a new chief of the general staff. It was evident that Milch wanted Hitler to sidestep Keitel, Jodl and Zeitzler. 'Give him control of all fronts, not only one area,' advised Milch. 'All under your command. You remain supreme commander while he acts as your assistant.'[11] Milch then suggested getting rid of Göring by giving him a combat command on the Eastern Front. 'Otherwise he'll be off shopping in Paris again.'[12] Hitler could not bring himself to part with Göring, even though he had referred to him disparagingly as 'this fat, well-fed pig!'[13]

After the meal their discussions went on until 03.15 and Milch feared he might have overstepped the mark as Hitler kept jotting dots on his note-pad. He tried to make amends by apologising to the Führer for speaking his mind. 'You have contradicted me twenty-four times,' said Hitler with-out malice. 'I thank you for telling me this. No one else has given me such a clear picture.'[14] At such an early hour in the morning Milch struggled to tell if Hitler was being genuine or not.

While Milch fought in Berlin to get approval to devote one month's worth of fighter production to the Reich's defence, Göring holidayed in the Obersalzberg. Milch kept sending Göring reports, which were ignored. The pair eventually came together at Rominten, Göring's hunting lodge in East Prussia. The Reichsmarschall had finally summoned his Luftflotte commanders to discuss Operation Citadel. A row broke out over aircrew morale, with Göring raging at Milch, 'You don't imagine that I actually read the rags you send me!'[15] Milch pointed out that his inspection trips as Inspector General were pointless if the Reichsmarschall took no heed of his assessments. Göring agreed and Milch returned to Berlin hating his boss more than ever.

The SS-Kriegsberichter of Colonel Günther d'Alquen's war cor-respondent unit were on hand to record the build-up of the Waffen-SS divisions. The cameramen were soon busy photographing and filming the massing SS Panzergrenadier divisions of Hausser's 2nd SS Panzer Corps. Just as Himmler had instructed, special attention was lavished on the mighty Tigers of the 2nd SS *Das Reich*.

One such cameraman had been loitering with two Panzergrenadiers who had just finished digging a foxhole for their machine gun. The land-scape, although open, undulated in the distance where small hills rose either side of dry river gullies. He turned to look behind him where there were a number of thatched farmhouses. In front of the buildings and rum-bling toward the foxhole was a 56-ton Tiger tank belonging to *Das Reich*. The machine-gunner glanced over his shoulder, alerted by the noise and slightly alarmed at the proximity of the tank.

Before it drew level with them the cameraman stood and took a three-quarter shot of the beast. The tank commander had better things to be thinking of than the snap happy photographer. Instead, with just his head poking out of the hatch, he stared off at the horizon. Long after the photographer's death this image would become famous. While the Tiger looked incredibly formidable, *Das Reich* had just fourteen of them available serving with the Panzer regiment's 8th Company. Later, the

SS-Kriegsberichter also snapped a Panzer IV stopped on a dirt road while three cows wandered aimlessly in front of it. When battle started he made sure he rode with the armoured columns photographing *Das Reich's* assault guns and its captured T-34 tanks going into action.

The cameraman assigned to *Totenkopf* was also kept busy photographing the division's obsolescent Panzer IIIs and assault guns. The latter were usually covered in Panzergrenadiers hitching a ride, so made for a good photo. In one village he stood at the roadside and caught a column of four Panzer IIIs, their tough-looking crews ready for action. The tanks were painted a two-tone camouflage of sand and brown, then for good measure to break up their outline, further foliage from nearby bushes or tress had been added. What the SS-Kriegsberichter probably did not know was that the crews were not terribly happy going into battle with the tank's inadequate 50mm gun. Compared to Soviet weapons it was a spud gun.

The 24th Panzer Corps under General Nehring, consisting of the 5th SS Panzergrenadier Division *Wiking* and 17th Panzer Division, was held as Manstein's reserve. Early one morning the reporter assigned to the *Wiking* photographed about a dozen Panzer IIIs, the bulk of which were parked on the reverse side of a slope for cover. By the nearest tank four parka-clad crewmen had gathered around their portable stove to keep warm. The commander sat happily puffing on a cigar. Somewhere amongst the crews was Kurt Eggers, one-time editor of *The Black Corps* newspaper, now himself a Panzer commander.

The Luftwaffe sought to ensure it got its fair share of the limelight. Famous German pilot Colonel Hans-Ulrich Rudel stood in the sunshine posing for the camera. Behind him was a clear blue sky, in front a wooden trestle table. On this was a scale model of a Soviet T-34 tank. Jabbing his right hand downward, his fingertips tapped on the engine grille of the model just behind the turret. The photographer clicked his camera, capturing Rudel's demonstration for prosperity. 'Gentlemen,' said Rudel, 'that is how you destroy the T-34.'[16]

Rudel gained his reputation as a daring Junkers Stuka dive-bomber pilot. He did not smoke and was a teetotaller, eschewing the hedonistic mess lifestyle of his more rowdy comrades. Rudel preferred sport when not flying. His exploits on the Eastern Front were legendary and included destroying a battleship. He had headed up an experimental anti-tank Stuka unit, seeing combat in the Kuban.[17] For that operation he had gained the Oak Leaves to his Knight's Cross.

He laughed when his pupils asked him if it was true that he had personally sunk seventy enemy landing craft in the Kuban. Turning back to his
lesson, he pointed out that tank exhaust smoke made an ideal aiming point
at the back of the hull. Rudel recommended that pilots drop as low as 15m
when making their attack run, the Stuka's slow speed would ensure sufficient time to target the tank. The new crews of the Luftwaffe's 'Cannon
Birds', or tank busters, were today learning the best way to stop an enemy
tank was by tearing out its engine using 37mm cannon fire. He also taught
them that shooting off the tracks or road wheels to immobilise an enemy
tank was another good outcome. This would leave them vulnerable to
other aircraft circling overhead armed with bombs.

Rudel had a disarming smile that turned into a broad grin, but the
truth was that his career had got off to a rocky start. Problems with colleagues and superior officers had resulted in him sitting out a number of
the Luftwaffe's early campaigns. Rudel had few worries over missing out
on Hitler's coming summer offensive – they needed him.

At the same time, Captain Bruno Meyer was familiarising himself
with the new Henschel tank buster aircraft carrying 20mm cannons,
supplemented by a 30mm cannon.[18] Tests with the latter fitted beneath
the aircraft's fuselage at Rechlin showed it could punch through 8cm of
armour plate.[19] Meyer had been summoned to Germany to conduct further gun trials. He liked what he saw, an aircraft with real punch though
it was no faster than the Stuka. Meyer watched the armourers at work.
The 30mm cannon round, including the shell casing, was the length of
a man's forearm. Pumping those into an enemy tank would have the
desired effect.

Meyer was instructed to create the 4th Anti-Tank Group comprising four squadrons each with sixteen aircraft.[20] It was to be assigned to
General Seidemann's 8th Air Corps in time for Operation Citadel. The
twin-engine Henschel Hs 129 ground attack aircraft handled really well
and Meyer could not wait to try it in combat with its new armament.
The flying tank busters were to play an important supporting role. What
he had yet to learn was that the Henschel did not like operating from
forward airfields.

Not everyone though was pleased with the Luftwaffe's expanding
ground support role. 'The Luftwaffe High Command viewed with mixed
feelings,' observed General Deichmann, 'the gradual move from providing
indirect air support to the Army to providing an increasing proportion of
direct support missions.'[21] This was the artillery's role, not the Luftwaffe's.

Ironically, on the eve of the battle for Kursk Stalin was taken to see an exhibition of captured Luftwaffe equipment in Moscow. This included bombers, dive-bombers and fighters. Notably, he was photographed hands clasped behind his back examining the feared Junkers Ju 87, better known as the Stuka. This weapon had terrorised the Red Army in 1941 and helped bring it to the brink of defeat. His propagandists were soon at work and to help dispel the myth of the Luftwaffe's invincibility the exhibition was opened to the public. It was not long before well-dressed Muscovites were wandering around the aircraft and school children were clambering all over the exhibits.

# 8

# GUDERIAN'S ZOO

The Panzertruppen crew stood to attention and saluted as the general approached. They had tidied their heavy Panzer the best they could but this time of year it was filthy. Nonetheless, it was running, which was the main thing. He returned their salute and the vehicle commander could not help but give a wry smile. It was not every day that you got to give a general a driving lesson with a 56-ton tank. He was adamant though that he wanted 'a go'.

General Mellenthin, as Chief of Staff of 48th Panzer Corps, felt his job should have some perks. It was March 1943 and 'Marshal Winter' had turned to 'Marshal Mud' as the ice and snow of the Russian winter began to melt. This brought all combat operations to a halt because very little could cope with the appalling mud. Life had a routine air to it as he leafed through his papers at the Corps HQ outside Kharkov.

Four armoured divisions had been pulled out of the line and placed under 48th Panzer Corps. They were given time to refit and, just as importantly, conduct training and live firing exercises. Mellenthin had issued orders to the divisional commanders that they were to commence troop and platoon level exercise working up to divisional level. Once this had been done he decided to abuse his position and have a little fun. He later confessed:

> I personally set out to make myself proficient in handling the Tiger tank; I learned to drive this massive vehicle and fire its 88mm gun. With this powerful gun and very strong armour the Tiger was the most successful

and effective tank in the world until the end of the war; it had already shown what it could do in the counterattack at Kharkov.[1]

Mellenthin though had an ulterior motive for closely familiarising himself with the Henschel-built Tiger, as he knew that the senior commanders were taking a close interest in its performance. A VIP visit was scheduled for the end of the month. General Guderian arrived wanting to be briefed and Mellenthin recalled:

Guderian particularly wanted to discuss the experiences of the Tiger battalion of the 'Grossdeutschland' Division in the recent offensive, and Count Strachwitz, the very dashing commander of their Panzer regiment, was able to give him many interesting details regarding the performance and limitations of the new tank. As a result of his visit Guderian ordered a speed up in the production of Tigers and Panthers.[2]

Guderian was very interested to hear how on one occasion Strachwitz, concealed in a village, had lain in wait for a column of eighty unsuspecting Soviet tanks. Within a space of minutes thirty-six of them had been torn apart before the rest turned and fled. Strachwitz had claimed the first kill by decapitating the lead tank. The 100mm armour of Strachwitz's Tigers suffered little more than a few dents and scratches. Afterwards his men were photographed examining the superficial damage.[3] Bernd Freytag von Loringhoven, who served with him, remarked, 'This large Silesian landowner was also a dedicated soldier, possessed of flair and intuition ... Strachwitz did not know the meaning of fear.'[4]

In stark contrast, the debut of the Tiger in late 1942 in the Leningrad area had been a complete shambles. Speer remembered:

The Russians calmly let the tanks roll past an anti-tank gun position, then fired direct hits at the first and last Tiger. The remaining four thereupon could move neither forward nor backward, nor could they take evasive action to the side because of the swamps, and soon they were also finished off. Hitler silently passed over the debacle; he never referred to it again.[5]

The loss of these Tigers was Hitler's own fault. 'His staff remonstrated that the terrain he had chosen,' adds Speer, 'made tactical deployment of the tanks impossible because of the marshy subsurface on both sides of the road.'[6] Hitler, though, was not one to listen to advice at the best of times.

Crucially, Tiger tanks were in short supply; Army Group Centre was supported by a single unit. The Heavy Panzer Battalion 505 was created in early 1943 and by May had twenty Tigers supported by twenty-five Panzer IIIs. At the end of April it was assigned to Army Group Centre and shipped to the Eastern Front. Between 8 and 10 June it received eleven more Tigers. Therefore at the start of Operation Citadel the battalion had thirty-one Tigers, plus its supporting Panzer IIIs, and four days into the fighting on 9 July was joined by the 3rd Company, boosting total strength to forty-five. Army Group Centre was also allocated the 656th Panzerjäger Regiment, with the two battalions of Ferdinands likewise armed with 88mm guns.

Army Group South had a total of 102 Tigers deployed with the 2nd SS, 3rd and 48th Panzer Corps. Heavy Panzer Battalion 503 had been earmarked to join Rommel in North Africa but instead found itself in southern Russia during the Don campaign and the retreat from Stalingrad. It had anticipated receiving the Porsche-designed Tiger, but with the cancellation of this programme the unit was equipped with twenty Henschel Tigers and twenty-five Panzer IIIs in late 1942. By April of the following year it had forty-five Tigers on its strength. The battalion was able to muster forty-two operational Tigers in time for the Kursk offensive, but these were divided up between three Panzer divisions. These included 13th Company 1st SS Panzer Regiment, 8th Company 2nd SS Panzer Regiment and 9th Company 3rd SS Panzer Regiment, which had twelve each, serving with the 1st, 2nd and 3rd SS Panzergrenadier Divisions respectively.

*Grossdeutschland* received the Tiger before many other units, forming a heavy Panzer battalion from the summer of 1943. In fact, as early as January 1943 the *Grossdeutschland* Panzer Regiment had formed a heavy tank company that consisted of nine Tiger Is and ten Panzer IIIs. These were shipped to the Eastern Front the following month, arriving at Poltava for the offensive to retake Kharkov. By the time of Citadel the unit had been officially dubbed the 9th Company and was equipped with about a dozen Tigers.

In late April 1943 Guderian was visiting Paris and Rouen inspecting armoured units on occupation duties when he was summoned to Munich by Hitler. Arriving on 2 May, he spent the next few days in discussions with the Führer, Zeitzler, Manstein, Kluge, Model and

Speer regarding the desirability of a summer offensive on the Eastern Front. Guderian thought that this had been abandoned. To his dismay, Zeitzler seemed to think the Tiger and Panther were now ready to deliver a decisive blow:

> I pointed out that the Panthers, on whose performance the Chief of the Army General Staff was relying so heavily, were still suffering from many teething problems inherent in all new equipment and it seemed unlikely that these could all be put right in time for launching the attack. Speer supported these arguments of mine from the standpoint of arms production.[7]

Guderian greatly respected Albert Speer, Hitler's armaments minister. They enjoyed each other's company and its clear the general and former architect were friends. Guderian described Speer as 'a good comrade', adding, 'I always found working with this sensible, natural man both easy and pleasant. Speer's ideas and decisions were the product of a healthy intellect …'[8] They worked together 'without friction'[9] and tried to assist one another as much as possible, something that could not be said for most of the squabbling Nazi hierarchy.

Speer and his factory directors were not involved in the design of the Panther and the Tiger tank; their job was to build them. Nonetheless, he was fully aware of 'Hitler's bias for super-heaviness'[10] when it came to his Panzers. Speer noted, 'Hitler insisted that more would be gained by increasing the range of the guns and the weight of the armour.'[11] Hitler argued that tanks were like warships, they would outshoot smaller faster vessels, forcing them to retreat. By his logic, a faster tank would have to avoid a heavier tank, but he conveniently ignored pack tactics.

Speer was well aware of the results of the Führer's meddling in the design of Guderian's new Panzers:

> We decided to develop a new thirty-ton tank whose very name, Panther, was to signify greater agility. Though light in weight, its motor was to be the same as the Tiger's, which meant it could develop superior speed. But in the course of a year Hitler once again insisted on clapping so much armour on it, as well as larger guns, that it ultimately reached forty-eight tons, the original weight of the Tiger.[12]

Guderian and Speer tried to prevail on Hitler the importance of spare parts for the front-line units. However, to increase provision of adequate spares would have cut new tank production by some 20 per cent and Hitler would have none of it. Speer despaired that Hitler ignored the fact that it was easier, quicker and cheaper to maintain existing tanks: 'General Guderian, the Inspector General of Tank Ordnance, frequently pointed out to me that if we could repair our tanks quickly, thanks to sufficient spare parts, we could have more available for battle, at a fraction of the cost, than producing new ones.'[13]

The issue of getting the Panther ready in time not only caused Guderian a headache, it also played a part in messing up Zeitzler's plans. In late May he had badgered Hitler to commit to the attack by the end of June at the very latest. He was alarmed by the intelligence that showed the Red Army was continuing to strengthen its position at Kursk. 'The enemy is bringing up fresh troops, and I don't want to wait until they've brought up their new tanks and assault guns as well,' said Zeitzler.[14]

'You mustn't say such things Zeitzler,' warned Hitler. 'Our Panther tanks are far superior to any of the Russian tanks, and two battalions of Panthers will give us a powerful impetus to out attack … what I need is a totally decisive military victory, and as soon as possible, but the odds must be heavily in our favour.'[15]

Zeitzler though was fed up waiting for conditions to be just right, he had been advocating Citadel since April yet there seemed unending excuses for delaying it – not least the wretched Panther. Zeitzler pointed the finger at Guderian and Speer by pressing Hitler to get a commitment that the Panther would be ready by 10 June at the latest. 'Otherwise,' said Zeitzler, 'let us begin the attack without them, or else use them in a counterattack, but only after the Russians have launched their offensive.'[16]

It was not only the Panther causing trouble. Dr Ferdinand Porsche had not been very happy that his rivals at Henschel had beaten his design for a heavy Tiger tank. It had been argued his design was much too complicated for a production tank but what did they know; he was forward thinking, they were not. His designers had sought to marry an 88mm flak gun to his prototype chassis, he had recommended modern air-cooled engines and electric transmission. This would have been ideal for service in North Africa. Production had been instigated but it was halted in the summer of 1942 and only five were ever built. These were sent to be used for driver training.

Hitler had been disappointed that the Tiger could not take the latest version of the 88mm anti-tank gun because the designers could not make the turret big enough. This would result in the Tiger II but that would not be ready until early 1944. As an interim it was decided to produce an assault version using the gun. In light of the wasted Porsche design, Hitler instructed the company to look at using the chassis for just such a task, but it was to be a rushed job from start to finish. On 6 February 1943 Hitler had ordered ninety Ferdinands to be built as quickly as possible. Those that had been built and were kicking about the factory floor were fitted with a large box superstructure to mount the 88mm gun.

Now Lieutenant Colonel Baron Ernst von Jungenfeld stood with his two battalion commanders, Major Steinwachs and Major Noak. None of them were very pleased. The battle-proven Sturmgeschütz III assault gun was a good piece of kit but this new hunting tank was something else; the thing was almost 10 tons heavier than the Tiger tank. Noak and Steinwachs knew what it was – it was an abomination. It was an unloved bastard of a vehicle based on the rejected Porsche design for the Tiger tank.

When the crews had first climbed in they immediately noticed that there was no hull machine gun. The two majors wanted to know what their men should do if they became stuck and surrounded by enemy infantry? Should they surrender? The vehicle commanders and drivers hated it. No side vision ports were provided for the driver, who could only see directly ahead via a slightly raised view port. To make matters worse, the commander could only assist the driver if his head was poking out the hatch in the roof, as no raised cupola had been fitted with vision blocks. On top of this it was 10kmph slower than Hitler's medium tanks, meaning it could not keep up with the Panzers.

Dubbed the Ferdinand after its designer, fewer than 100 had been issued to the two battalions. Major Karl-Heinz Noak remonstrated with Jugenfeld; how on earth was this unwieldy beast supposed to make much impact in Hitler's forthcoming summer offensive? Jungenfeld shrugged and pointed out that the Ferdinand's 88mm gun was a version that was more powerful than that installed in the Tiger. Therefore their gunners had better get as proficient with the weapon as quickly as possible.

Jugenfeld tried to put a brave face on things but his regiment's third battalion was in no position to help the Noak and Steinwachs men. It was equipped with the clumsy-looking Brummbär consisting of a turretless Panzer IV armed with a 150mm assault howitzer. This gun was designed for bunker busting and to support infantry. Just like the Ferdinand, it lacked a machine gun to protect it from enemy infantry. All in all, his regiment was a lame duck. His only hope was that the units he fought alongside would be able to protect them while they went about their allotted tasks.

Conversion to the Panther caused some of the Panzer divisions a real problem. For General Walter von Huenersdorff it greatly weakened his 6th Panzer Division, which had fought so valiantly to reach Stalingrad. He had arrived to take command in February 1943 only to find two months later that he had lost one of his tank battalions. The 1st Battalion, stripped of its tanks and equipment, was sent back to Germany to train on the Panther. This left him with the regimental headquarters and a single battalion equipped mainly with the Panzer IV.

Luckily for Huenersdorff and his men the front opposite them remained quiet. Nonetheless, he was not happy at the prospect of starting the summer campaigning season with a depleted division. When Huenersdorrf took stock he found he had fewer than ninety tanks, of which more than a third were the inadequately armed Panzer III.

General Walter Krüger, commanding the 2nd SS Panzergrenadier Division, had exactly the same problem. At the beginning of May one of his tank battalions was shipped to Mailly-le-Camp, France, to convert to the Panther. It would not be combat ready until late August, which was way too late for Citadel. All *Das Reich* would have to give it some real punch were a dozen Tigers. It was not until late July that the 1st, 3rd and 5th SS divisions were supplied with a small number of Panthers. Like many Panzer division commanders, Huenersdorff and Krüger were left asking where were the Panthers and why were they taking so long to get into service.

Waiting for Guderian's zoo to be got ready infuriated Manstein:

> As a result of the delays in the delivery of our own new tanks, the Army Group was not ultimately able to move off on 'Citadel' until the beginning of July, by which time the essential advantage of a 'forehand' blow was lost. The whole idea had been to attack before the enemy had replenished his forces and got over the reverses of the winter.[17]

Albert Speer was of the view that all the new armoured fighting vehicles, but especially the Ferdinand, swayed the Führer's decision-making when it came to committing to Citadel:

> The delivery of new weapons encouraged Hitler to make preparations for an offensive in spite of the winter's losses of materiel … It kept being postponed because Hitler counted heavily on the effectiveness of the new tanks. Above all he was excepting wonders from a new type of [Ferdinand] tank with electric drive construction by Professor Porsche.[18]

Hitler seemed to have an inflated opinion of the Ferdinand's capabilities, saying, 'The monster will be the pile driver with which we shall smash the Russian positions. No T-34 will stop it.'[19] Clearly he was oblivious to the Ferdinand's shortcomings and may have been unaware of just how few of them there were. 'The Ferdinand, a self-propelling, over heavy gun, had just been introduced in great numbers for use on the Eastern Front,' claimed Otto Günsche, Hitler's adjutant.[20]

Hitler was not just staking Citadel's success on the Ferdinand, Panther and Tiger; he also had making their debut the Brummbär, Hornisse and the Hummel, which were essentially self-propelled guns. Only the Hornisse (or Hornet) though carried an anti-tank weapon and was armed with the same 88mm gun as the Ferdinand.

Hitler could muster, not including the Tiger, about 390 Panthers, Ferdinands and Hornisse in a tank-to-tank role, which essentially represented two Panzer divisions. On paper this looked a formidably powerful strike force. However, all three had their drawbacks: both the Panther and Ferdinand were mechanically unreliable and had not been combat tested. The Hornisse had an open fighting compartment, the sides of which were inadequately armoured to take on enemy tanks.

Despite Hitler's excessively high hopes for them, Guderian's zoo held no horrors for the Red Army. 'Their new tanks were very menacing indeed,' acknowledged Khrushchev, 'but our troops learned quickly how to deal with them.'[21] Soviet soldiers were given extensive training on how to cope with the Panzers and the rifle divisions got to train using T-34 tanks acting as the enemy. They also got to practise using heavy percussion grenades and Molotov cocktails. These were sometimes combined, using two grenades and a Molotov bound together using telephone wire.

Even though the Ferdinand and Panther had not yet been committed to combat, the Soviets seemed to have very good intelligence on them. Mansur Abdulin was quite confident:

We knew all the technical characteristics of Tigers, Panthers, Ferdinands and other enemy tanks and self-propelled guns … We veterans explained to the greenhorns the particular weaknesses of the Tigers, Ferdinands, Panthers, and so on. You should always act in pairs. The enemy tank must ride over you, over your trench, then one soldier fires at the accompanying infantrymen, while the other throws the bottle or grenade.[22]

Stalin had a very good idea of the problems Guderian was suffering with Panther tank production thanks to the 'Lucy' spy ring and the wealth of classified intelligence it was providing. On 15 April 1943 Radó had transmitted to Moscow Hitler's order of battle for Citadel. Just two days later he helpfully listed the creation of new Panzer and infantry units. Then, on 28 June, Radó provided a summary of Panther production, meaning Stalin knew that Hitler had three or four battalions' worth of his new tank. This intelligence may have included technical specifications.[23]

The German General Staff and the Abwehr intelligence organisation had come to the conclusion that someone high up was aiding Stalin. Colonel Gehlen noted:

> Canaris and I repeatedly observed quite independently of one another that the enemy was receiving rapid and detailed information on incidents and top-level decision making on the German side. Admiral Canaris came to my headquarters at Anderburg one day and told me in the course of a lengthy conversation whom he suspected to be the traitor, though I believe that he knew more than he was prepared to tell me.[24]

However, both were looking in the completely wrong direction; they convinced themselves wrongly that the traitor was Hitler's private secretary, Martin Bormann.[25]

In Switzerland the 'Lucy' spy ring's days were numbered. By June 1943 Foote was aware that he was being watched by the local police. Three months earlier the Abwehr had placed Radó and most of his co-conspirators under surveillance. He had not helped matters by having an affair with one of his female wireless operators, who was half his age. The girl concerned was also seeing an Abwehr agent. Foote had wanted to reduce the rate of his transmissions but Moscow refused. Germany was now putting diplomatic pressure on the Swiss to arrest the ring and it was becoming increasingly difficult for the authorities to turn a blind eye. In terms of Kursk though, their work was more than done.

It is also possible that intelligence on Guderian's zoo was passed to Stalin by his Bletchley Park spy, John Cairncross. His decrypts allegedly encouraged the Soviets to develop more powerful shells in response to German armament reports.[26] It is likely that Bletchley was well aware of Hitler's constant demands for updates on the Panther and Ferdinand. Certainly Churchill was alerted to what he called 'the new "Tiger" tanks'.[27] In light of the Tiger I appearing in mid-1942, it was hardly new by the summer of 1943 so he must have been referring to the Ferdinand.[28]

Even in Germany the preparation of these new weapons for Operation Citadel seemed to be common knowledge. Jewish academic Victor Klemperer, living in the city of Dresden, jotted down in his diary in early July, 'We are now producing whole series of "Tiger" tanks; and all of it, arms and men, is going east on a massive scale, a train every fifteen minutes! Our offensive is sure to start in the next few weeks ...'[29] Armed with such information Stalin already had a low-tech solution to Guderian's zoo. 'Because the Germans had much better quality equipment and super-tanks like the Tiger,' said Captain Jerry Roberts, 'the Russians needed greater quantities of armoured vehicles in order to compete.'[30]

# 9

# A FLAWED PLAN

In London, British war commentator Major General Sir Charles Gwynn astutely wrote about Hitler's Russian conundrum after Stalingrad:

> What can the Germans do to retrieve the situation? A merely defensive attitude would almost certainly mean the acceptance of the inevitability of further disasters. Yet they have already learnt that premature and inadequate counter-strokes only adds to their losses ... I feel sure that the Germans would wish to postpone counter-offensive operations to the spring ...[1]

German intelligence and counterintelligence were well aware that Stalin knew all about Hitler's troubled plans. Colonel Gehlen recalled:

> On 28 April an untried agent reported that the Russians expected their enemy would soon mount a major offensive in the area between Kharkov and Kursk. From these and similar Abwehr reports there was no doubt that the Soviet high command had learned of our intentions and were taking necessary counter-measures.[2]

Gehlen grew increasingly petulant, saying, 'I had taken every opportunity ... to warn the German command against this major offensive.'[3]

Despite the friction between Churchill and Roosevelt on the one hand and Stalin on the other over the delivery of weapon supplies and intelligence sharing, the prognosis for the rejuvenated Red Army was good.

The British Joint Intelligence Committee doubted Hitler's chances of victory over Stalin in 1943. It assessed 'the prospect of a German defeat of Russia has receded to vanishing point'.[4] By April 1943 it was also of the view that Hitler had now passed the point where he could hope to reach a peace settlement with Stalin. Churchill was in agreement and wrote, 'The Russians, both on land and in the air, had now the upper hand, and the Germans can have had few hopes of ultimate victory.'[5]

Thanks to the decoders at Bletchley Park, Churchill was forewarned that a battle was looming at Kursk. Not only had Bletchley cracked Enigma used by the German armed forces but also the Lorenz system used by the German High Command. He resolved to inform Stalin but as always was at pains to conceal the true source of the information. Captain Jerry Roberts, working at Bletchley, explained:

> We were able to warn the Russians that the Germans were planning this – how the attack was going to be launched, and the fact that it was going to be a pincer movement. We were able to warn them what army groups were going to be used. And most important, what tank units were going to be used.
>
> Now I can remember myself, strangely enough, breaking messages about Kursk. You know, the name sticks in your mind. We had to wrap it all up and say it was from spies, that we had wonderful teams of spies, and other sources of information.[6]

It has been speculated that Bletchley intelligence was passed through Rudolf Roessler and the 'Lucy' spy network in Lucerne, but there is no evidence to support this. The warning was simply sent via diplomatic channels on 30 April to Moscow. Stalin did not altogether trust Churchill and it is doubtful he took much heed of Britain's efforts. After all, these simply confirmed what he already knew. Although Soviet military intelligence was aware of Bletchley Park, which they called 'Krurort', they were unaware of the exact nature or indeed the scale of the work being conducted there.

Stalin was convinced that British help came with an agenda. In 1941 he had largely ignored Churchill's warning about the impending German invasion. His main concern was that if the Germans had broken the Soviet cipher system then the British had as well. Ironically, Stalin had a spy right in the heart of Bletchley, Captain John Cairncross, who was passing large quantities of decrypts to the Soviet Embassy in London.[7]

He worked at Bletchley from 1942 until the summer of 1943, when he transferred to MI6.

Cairncross, by his own admission, passed intelligence about Kursk to his controller, Anatoli Gorsky. Stalin did not really need Churchill's official or Cairncross's unofficial help, as his own military intelligence was already well aware of Hitler's build up around the Kursk salient. Ironically, the intelligence provided by Cairncross helped convince Stalin that the 'Lucy' ring was part of a deliberate German deception operation because some of their information matched. It seems Stalin and his intelligence services could not accept or appreciate that Bletchley Park and his Swiss spies were drawing on the very same sources within the German High Command.

Churchill and Roosevelt, who had enough on their hands planning the Mediterranean campaign and the war in the Far East and Pacific, found Stalin's ingratitude perplexing. On 10 June Stalin wrote to the American President with an air of petulance, saying, '… you and Churchill have decided to postpone the Anglo-American invasion of Western Europe till the spring of 1944. Now again we've got to go on fighting almost single handed.'[8] He then tried bullying Churchill by warning, 'The preservation of our confidence in the Allies is being subjected to severe stress.'[9]

This was the final straw for Churchill, who on 27 June pointed out that England had fought alone until June 1941. Then bizarrely and contrary to Bletchley Park intelligence, he said, 'You may not even be heavily attacked by the Germans this summer. This would vindicate decisively what you once called the "military correctness" of our Mediterranean strategy.'[10] Quite what Stalin made of this is anyone's guess.

The Soviet salient at Kursk presented problems for Hitler and Stalin. For Hitler it was a tempting target to slice off. At the same time, the German bulges to the north and south were tempting targets for Stalin. For Manstein the German defence stretching south from Kharkov to the Sea of Azov was the fulcrum for holding the Donetz Basin. Rather than attacking Kursk, Hitler would have been better to have flattened out the bulges and straightened the Eastern Front. Manstein was acutely aware of the danger in the Kharkov region:

> The bulge in the German front, which ran down the Donetz and Mius from a point below Kharkov, embracing the valuable coalmining and industrial region south of that city, was just begging to be sliced off. Should the enemy succeeded in breaking through around Kharkov or

even the Middle Donetz, he could still achieve his aim of the previous winter and destroy the German southern wing on the Black Sea.[11]

Churchill and Roosevelt understood only too well the dilemma facing Hitler. Major General Gwynn, writing for the benefit of the British public, was spot on with his assessment:

> It is too early yet to speculate on whether the disasters the Germans have suffered will compel them to attempt a drastic general withdrawal in order to shorten their communications and to establish a straighter front. Such a course was contemplated last year, but it was realised that it would be too desperate an undertaking to carry out in the mid-winter. This year it would probably be even more difficult, but the alternative of holding on at all costs might be even more disastrous if the momentum of the Russian offensive is maintained.[12]

Ironically, Stalin dithered just as much as Hitler over what to do about the Kursk salient. Kharkov to the south was seen as the key to the region, to date there had been three battles fought for the city and each time the Red Army had been soundly defeated.[13] He could not decide whether to let the Germans attack and wear themselves out or to strike first. The differing advice offered by his generals did not help matters.

Zhukov, having lifted the German siege of Leningrad, was available to help elsewhere in early 1943. In mid-March he was summoned to the Kremlin to see Stalin to discuss events just to the south at Kharkov. 'I arrived in Moscow late in the evening,' Zhukov recalled. 'I was extremely tired as we had had to travel by jeep along extremely rough roads.'[14]

He endured an interminable meeting with Stalin and the Politburo about defence industries that went on until 3 a.m. He then met with Stalin and members of the Military Council and that went on for another two hours. Dinner soon became breakfast. An exhausted Zhukov then departed for the south:

> About seven o'clock I was already at the Central Airport and was flying to the headquarters of the Voronezh Front. It was necessary to analyse the situation which had developed there and render help on the spot. As soon as I had taken my seat on the plane, I fell into a deep sleep and was only awakened by the bump during the landing at the airfield.[15]

Once Manstein was held at Belgorod, Zhukov and General Vatutin, the new commander of the Voronezh Front, spent until early April touring units and assessing the situation. Zhukov was particularly concerned about the 52nd Guards Rifle Division dug in to the north of Belgorod. To the left and right of them were the 375th and the 67th Guards Divisions. These units formed part of Chistyakov's 21st Army, which had been rechristened the 6th Guards Army. Zhukov assessed that the weight of any enemy attack would fall on the 52nd Division and resolved to reinforce them with artillery.

In the Kremlin Stalin leafed through the reports coming from Sándor Radó, who was known as 'Dora' to Soviet military intelligence. It was clear that Hitler was planning something big for Kursk. Stalin, publicly at least, despised spies and disparaged their information. He saw their actions as purely politically motivated or based on financial gain; they could not be trusted. Nonetheless, what 'Dora' was saying was corroborated by intelligence from Soviet partisans behind German lines and by Red Air Force reconnaissance flights.

Zhukov and Vatutin's intelligence also indicated that Hitler would renew his efforts:

> Evidently the enemy, collecting maximum of his forces, including up to 13–15 tank divisions, supported by a large amount of aviation, will deliver a strike by his Orel-Kromy groupings to envelop Kursk from the south-east ... One must expect that this year the enemy will count on tank divisions and aviation for the offensive, since his infantry is considerably weaker for carrying out offensive actions than last year.[16]

Zhukov advised that the Red Army should not go over to the offensive, reasoning, 'It would be better if we wore down the enemy on our defences, knocked out his tanks, and then, introducing fresh reserves, by going over to the general offensive finally finish off his main forces.'[17]

A day or two later Vasilevsky arrived at the Voronezh Front HQ and he and Zhukov were in agreement over the proposed approach. By mid-April Vatutin and Khrushchev had good intelligence on the dispositions of Manstein's Army Group South. It assessed that the Voronezh Front was confronted by nine infantry and three Panzer divisions in the first line, with a further six infantry and three Panzer divisions in the second. Another three Panzer divisions were expected in the area. Vatutin concluded:

The enemy is not yet ready to launch a big offensive. The offensive is not expected to begin earlier than 20 April but most likely in early May.

However, individual attacks may be expected at any time. Therefore, we demand that our forces be in a constant state of full combat readiness.[18]

Rokossovsky's Central Front had a slightly different view of the situation. His Chief of Staff, General Malinin, signalled a situation report to Moscow suggesting that they take pre-emptive action, warned that an enemy offensive was expected in the second half of May and called for reinforcements for both the Central and Voronezh Fronts. However, Rokossovsky also wrote to Stalin recommending the defence option.

By late April Vatutin had convinced himself that they needed to act and began to lobby Moscow. He was rightly concerned about their window of opportunity. He first began to press Vasilevsky and then Stalin in May and June, urging them to begin their summer offensive otherwise they might lose the benefit of the weather. Stalin began to waver with their sit tight strategy and it took the combined efforts of Zhukov, Vasilevsky and Antonov to dissuade him from attacking first. Despite all their preparations, Rokossovsky and Vatutin's long wait continued until the first week in July.

Hitler's procrastination with Citadel did not help Stalin make his mind up. The German offensive looked imminent on 10 May, 20 May and again on 2 June and the fronts stood to, only to be stood down shortly after each time. This waiting game greatly fuelled Stalin's temper, which was vented on aircraft designer Alexander Yakovlev and the Aircraft Production Commissar Pyotr Dement'ev after faults with the Yak fighter had been reported to him.

Before the meeting Stalin had sat examining a piece of torn wing covering that had come from a damaged Yak-9 fighter. He was extremely displeased by the explanatory letter that had come with it signed by a number of front-line pilots. They were making serious allegations against the People's Commissariat of the Aviation Industry. The latter had blamed a series of crashes at the factory on pilot error, but there had also been complaints from the fighter regiments deployed to Kursk. The pilots said the cause of the crashes was the fabric on the aircraft's wings being ripped off while in flight.

'I have never seen Stalin in such a rage,' said Yakovlev.[19] Stalin knew that the aviation industry had been cutting corners and killing his pilots. According to his source, there had been at least ten cases and they now had several hundred defective fighter aircraft. Stalin asked them were they aware of the problem and Yakovlev tried to explain by blaming someone else:

> This was caused by the poor quality of nitro dyes delivered by one of the Ural chemical enterprises where hastily tested substitutes were employed. The paint was not durable and was quickly affected by atmospheric conditions. It would crack, and the fabric gluing of the wing would come loose from the plywood.[20]

Stalin was furious and demanded to know why they had not done anything about it. Yakovlev responded that the problem had not been discovered until after the aircraft had been delivered to the front-line, where they were left 'under open skies, exposed to rain, sun and other atmospheric elements'.[21] This seemed spurious in light of several hundred having already been delivered. Stalin not only accused them of trying to wreck his preparations at Kursk but also of being 'Hitlerites'.

Yakovlev was left shivering and Dement'ev went scarlet. In a panic they promised to fix the planes within two weeks. Teams were sent to the fighter factory and the paint and varnish plant to investigate. Stalin later learned that the crashes were not caused by the paint or glue, but the lack of priming on the plywood wing before the fabric was glued on. This had been done to speed up production.

Despite these production problems, by May 1943 the Red Air Force was three times the size it had been a year before. Like the ground forces, the various elements of the air force were beneficiaries of Lend-Lease planes. These were shipped by the Arctic convoys to Murmansk or shipped to the Persian Gulf and Abadan or Basra for collection by Soviet ferry pilots. They were also flown over the South Atlantic ferry route to Abadan or over the Alaskan–Siberian ferry route, with Soviet pilots collecting the aircraft from Fairbanks. The Arctic route proved the most costly; convoy PQ16 carried 200 aircraft but lost seventy-seven; PQ17 suffered even greater losses: of its shipment of almost 300 aircraft, it only delivered eighty-seven.

While Hitler's ground preparations were under way the Red Air Force ensured the Wehrmacht got no peace. On 3 May bombers attacked the rail junction at Minsk; the next night they set about Orsha, followed by Gomel and Bryansk. The Luftwaffe was also attacked between 6–8 May when bombers, fighters and ground attack aircraft struck seventeen airfields. This pressure was kept up when twenty-eight Luftwaffe bomber bases in the Orel–Bryansk and Kharkov–Belgorod areas were attacked between 8 and 10 June.

The fighters of the Red Air Force also fought to ward off Luftwaffe bomber raids that included the fighter plants at Gorky and Saratov, the aero engine factory at Rybinsk and the rubber plant at Yaroslavl. After the raids on the Kursk rail junction in early June, the Luftwaffe hit the Yelets marshalling yards, vital for suppling the Kursk salient, on 13 June.

In the second week of May Stalin received a reassuring report that stated, 'The 16th Air Army has intensified aerial reconnaissance and is keeping the enemy under vigilant observation. Air formations and army units are alerted to repulse enemy air attacks and possible enemy offensive action.'[22]

At the same time General Mellenthin despaired that Hitler would not listen to the growing warnings that the Kursk salient was turning into a giant trap. He recalled even in the early May conference:

> Model produced air photographs which showed that the Russians were constructing very strong positions at the shoulders of the salient and had withdrawn their mobile forces from an area west of Kursk. This showed that they were aware of the impending attack and were making adequate preparations to deal with it.[23]

Early in April two Ju 88 bombers, kitted out for photographic reconnaissance work, flying at 17,000ft photographed around 12,000sq. km of the Kursk salient. This was the largest area ever taken in a single sweep.[24] Marked 'Russian positions north-east of Belgorod: Top Secret', these showed dense trench networks and artillery positions. Luftwaffe photo reconnaissance also revealed the presence of dug-in Red Army tanks.[25] Hitler dismissed the intelligence, saying, 'That won't save them either this time.'[26]

Field Marshal von Kleist, commanding an army group in southern Ukraine, felt that the withdrawal of the Red Army's tanks made Citadel a pointless venture. He argued:

> If it had been launched six weeks earlier it might have been a great success – though we no longer had the resources to make it decisive. But in the interval the Russians got wind of the preparations. They laid deep minefields across their front, while withdrawing their main forces farther to the rear, so that comparatively few were left in the bag than our high command had hoped to enclose.[27]

Zeitzler's plan had always been flawed but the delay was fatal. Throughout April, German intelligence was fully informed about what was going on in the Kursk salient. 'My own branch reported in compelling detail on Soviet defensive preparations,' recalled Colonel Gehlen in charge of Eastern Front intelligence gathering.[28] His sources indicated that infantry and tank units had been deployed to the area opposite the starting point for the Germans' southern attack. In addition, this intelligence showed 'that every day tanks, engines and tank guns were leaving the factories at Kazan and Gorky, bound for the sector of the front between Kupyansk, Kursk and Orel' in the area of the northern attack.[29]

Gehlen fretted about the constant delays. 'With each week that passed,' he wrote, 'our prospects of success lessened; whereas initially the War Department and my own branch had been confident of victory at Kursk, by late June we were certain of defeat.'[30]

Finally, on 1 July, the Führer summoned his generals to Rastenburg and ended the terrible waiting game. He told them Operation Citadel would commence in four days' time. Gehlen had convinced himself that Citadel was doomed to failure and warned that it would be met by 'powerful' counteroffensives. On 4 July he wrote, 'I consider the operation that has been planned a particularly grave error, for which we shall suffer later on.'[31] His opinions mattered little as strategic decisions were being taken well above his pay grade.

While the British codebreakers at Bletchley Park were fully aware of the arguments over German preparedness for Citadel, German efforts to cover their intentions were half-hearted at best. In an effort to confuse Stalin and his generals over the timing of Hitler's attack, Manstein was sent to Bucharest. There he decorated Romanian dictator Antonescu before flying back to the Kursk front.[32]

Manstein, having fought with the Romanians in the Crimea, greatly respected Antonescu and was full of praise for his loyalty to Hitler's cause. Kleist, in contrast, despaired of him and his antiquated armed forces. Antonescu was still busy reconstituting his shattered army and those units remaining at the front were largely kept out of harm's way. Since its mauling at Stalingrad the Romanian Army was capable of little more than security duties. Zhukov and his fellow generals were well aware of this state of affairs. Although Antonescu supported the continuation of the war against Stalin, he wanted peace with the West.

It is possible that Hitler and Manstein hoped Stalin would be distracted into thinking the large German and Romanian garrison in the Kuban bridgehead, which maintained a toehold in the Caucasus, was planning something. Hitler wanted to bide his time before striking once more toward Stalin's vital oilfields. Certainly if nothing else the bridgehead was thwarting the Red Army's desire to liberate the Crimea, which was occupied by yet more German and Romanian troops. The Luftwaffe committed considerable resources to protecting and supplying the garrisons. Nonetheless, by early July the Red Air Force had wrestled control of the skies over the Kuban from the Luftwaffe.

Manstein made his presence in the Romanian capital very public by paying his respects to Romania's Tomb of the Unknown Soldier in Carol Park. Despite this it is doubtful that Soviet spies in Bucharest were fooled by his very brief visit or that many people took much notice.[33]

In the mean time, General von Knobelsdorff had called his divisional commanders together, including 'Papa' Hörnlein, for a briefing. His 48th Panzer Corps was to be deployed on the left-hand flank of the southern assault at Kursk. Hausser's SS Panzer Corps would be in the centre and Breith's 3rd Panzer Corps on the right with his tanks to the east of Belgorod. Knobelsdorff's command left to right consisted of Westhoven's 3rd Panzer, Hörnlein's *Grossdeutschland* and Mickl's 11th Panzer.

They were not happy. In the good old days of the Blitzkrieg you simply went around enemy defences, leaving the infantry to mop up. Here there was nothing to go around, meaning they would have to bludgeon their way through. Knobelsdorff and his men were going to have to take Gertsovka and Butova before reaching the first Soviet defence line anchored on the fortified village of Cherkasskoye. Afterwards, getting over the Pena River would not be easy and *Grossdeutschland*, once through the first line, would have to get past Syrtsevo to get to the town of Verkhopenye.

Mickl was instructed to attack Cherkasskoye from the east with Combat Group *Count Schimmelmann* using flamethrower tanks. Hörnlein's boys would have to tackle it head on. Hausser would have the same problem reaching Prokhorovka and the Psel. Nonetheless, there was cause for at least some optimism. Manstein, unlike Model to the north, had massed his 700 Panzers into an armoured fist that on the face of it stood a good chance of punching through.

# PART THREE

# LET BATTLE COMMENCE

# 10

# STALIN SHOWS HIS HAND

In late June Major General Kosykh found himself assigned to the head-quarters of Pukhov's 13th Army, acting as liaison for Rudenko's 16th Air Army. Kosykh had been briefed to expect the full weight of Model's Panzers in Pukhov's defensive zone. As such he was given priority in requesting air support and allocating air strikes to help defend 13th Army's positions. Pukhov was delighted by the presence of Rudenko's deputy; not only had he been granted extra artillery but also first call on an entire air army. The generals and their aides gathered around maps of the defences to calculate how close they could drop bombs without imperilling their own troops, or wiping out the minefields.

Pukhov called his front-line divisional commanders Generals Barinov, Janjgava and Yenshin and told them what to expect. The first two officers were holding the line from Podolyan, through Butyke, Alexandrovka and Pervyye Ponyri. Nothing was to get through, the Germans would be met by a maelstrom of bombs and shells. If any of them survived and reached the wire they would be mown down by Soviet machine guns.

The Luftwaffe operated from airfields about 20km from the front line, but on the eve of Citadel some fighter squadrons flew into advanced air-strips just 5km from the front. The Red Air Force, partly out of respect for the Luftwaffe's skill at hitting forward airfields, operated its tactical airstrips much further back. Soviet fighters were placed up to 40km away, ground attack aircraft 70km and bombers up to 130km.

Both the Soviet 16th and 2nd Air Armies were commanded by men who had fought at Stalingrad. General Rudenko kept command of the

16th, with General Krasovski replacing Smirnov in command of the 2nd, after handing over the 17th Air Army on the South-Western Front to General Sudets. They were backed by Goryunov's 5th Air Army, which had been reconstituted after its move from the North Caucasus. Combined with the flanking 17th Air Army, up to 3,000 Soviet aircraft were ready to meet Hitler's offensive.

Stalin's Red Air Force held a numerical superiority, with twice as many fighters as the Luftwaffe and many times the number of ground attack aircraft. This was largely due to Zhukov's insistence that their fighter strength be substantially increased to meet Citadel. Only Stalin's day bomber force was inferior to the Luftwaffe, with about half the number available. Overall coordination of air operations, as at Stalingrad, was the responsibility of Air Marshal Novikov, aided by his deputy General Vorozheikin and his newly appointed Chief of Staff, General Khudyakov, subordinate to Zhukov as Stalin's deputy supreme commander. The deputy air army commanders were posted to the ground armies' HQs and a network of secondary command and control centres was established inside the salient.

While waiting for Citadel, Soviet engineers built or renovated 154 airfields. They also constructed fifty dummy airfields that were so effective that the Luftwaffe attacked them repeatedly on 29 June. The Red Air Force kept itself in a state of readiness. For example, on the Voronezh Front the 2nd Air Army kept thirty-six fighters and ground attack aircraft on a permanent thirty-minute standby. These aircraft could only be tasked under the direct authorisation of the army's commander, General Krasovski.

It was not long before Soviet patrols caught German soldiers, who confirmed an attack was imminent. Zhukov recalled:

> Somewhere between two and three in the morning Pukhov rang Rokossovsky to tell him that a captured sapper of the 6th Infantry Division had informed him that German troops were ready to begin an attack. This was to happen at approximately 3 a.m. on 5 July.[1]

On the night of 4 July and on into the early hours there was no rest for the Luftwaffe. Citadel was scheduled to start at 03.30 on 5 July and the Luftwaffe was to put 1,700 aircraft into the air to bomb and strafe Soviet defences. To the north Model was to be supported by the 1st Air Division with 730 aircraft based around Orel under Major General Paul Deichmann. He was responsible for the 6th Air Fleet's combat operations. To the south under General Hans Seidemann, 1,100 bombers, ground attack and fighter aircraft drawn from the 4th Air Fleet were to fly from airfields around Kharkov and Belgorod.

Meanwhile, the Luftwaffe's radio eavesdroppers had picked up heightened chatter from the Red Air Force in and around the Kursk salient. There was a sudden surge in communication amongst the Soviet air regiments that indicated something was going to happen. The operators peered at their screens being fed information from the Freya radar units in the region.[2] They revised their initial count up from 100, 200, 300, to finally more than 400 aircraft coming in their direction. This was not a normal raid; an entire Soviet air army was on its way. In a panic one of the men picked up the field telephone and frantically called Mikoyanovka, which was the location of the 8th Air Corps' HQ 27km south of Belgorod.

The Luftwaffe's bases were scenes of organised chaos as row upon row of aircraft stood at cockpit readiness. The plan was that the slower bombers would take off first and circle around while they waited for their fighter escorts to get airborne. However, the Red Air Force had other ideas. Its intelligence showed that Seidemann's 8th Air Corps, with its extensive experience of flying close air support, had redeployed from the Crimea to the Kharkov–Belgorod sector. This confirmed that Hitler was planning to attack imminently.

After taking the call from the Freya stations, the duty officer at Mikoyanovka hastened to find Seidemann and the Luftwaffe's Chief of Staff, General Hans Jeschonnek, who just happened to be visiting. On hearing the news both men looked ashen-faced. Their heavily laden bombers were about to take off but if they did they would run straight into enemy fighters. If they did not they would be smashed on the ground or as they lumbered skyward. Operating from Mikoyanovka were not only bombers but also their valuable tank-busting aircraft.

The five main airfields around Belgorod and Kharkov were now packed with aircraft. A signal immediately went out for the bombers to stand down. Men then ran out across the airfields with thumbs up for the fighter squadrons to go first. Pilots buckled up and the Messerschmitts began taxiing through the ranks of waiting bombers to reach the runways.

The Soviets were clearly up to something. Earlier, Deichmann's command post near Orel airfield reported that Soviet artillery and rockets had started pounding Model's 9th Army in the darkness. They were not hitting much but something had spooked them. News filtering into Model and Manstein's headquarters suggested some sort of spoiling attack, or worse, the Red Army was going to go on the offensive first.

Zhukov noted:

On 4 July I was at Central Front Headquarters. In a telephone conversation over a high security line with Marshal Vasilevsky, who was
at Vatutin's headquarters, I learned about the outcome of an engagement with advanced enemy detachments near Belgorod. I was also told
that information received earlier that day from a captured soldier of
the [German] 168th Infantry Division – to the effect that the enemy
offensive would be launched at dawn on 5 July – had been confirmed
and that, in accordance with the plan of Supreme Headquarters, the
Voronezh Front was ready to open fire with its artillery and air units
preliminary to the counter-attack.[3]

The prisoner's division, belonging to General Breith's 3rd Panzer Corps,
was deployed north of Belgorod and to the south of Shopino. On its left
was the 3rd SS Panzergrenadier Division. In response to this intelligence
orders had been issued to Rudenko's and Krasovski's HQs, who in turn
signalled their air corps commanders – the attack mission was a go.

The Red Air Force was prepared to take on this daring first strike
because of its new-found confidence. During the early part of the year it
had fought to gain dominance over the Kuban region to the east of the
Crimea. Throughout April and May, at a time when the Luftwaffe should
have been resting and re-equipping ready for Citadel, it had been required
to fly up to 400 sorties every twenty-four hours over the Kuban.

Due to Hitler's insistence on holding the Kuban, the Luftwaffe was
forced to sacrifice precious resources needlessly. During the third week
of April, Soviet pilots claimed almost 190 German aircraft; this would
increase to nearly 370. Such was its mauling that the Luftwaffe was obliged
to half its sortie rate and Hitler's hold on the Kuban was greatly weakened.

On 28 June, courtesy of the 'Lucy' spy network, Stalin had received the
Luftwaffe's complete order of battle for Citadel.[4] This meant the Red Air
Force knew exactly what it was up against. John Cairncross, spying for the
Soviets at Bletchley Park, claimed he played a role in Stalin's surprise air
attack at Kursk. He said that the German language intelligence 'I supplied
was genuine, giving full details of German units and locations, thus enabling
the Russians to pinpoint their targets and take the enemy by surprise'.[5]

Krasovski and Sudets were not only targeting the airfields at
Mikoyanovka, Pomerki, and Soloniki outside Belgorod and Osnova
and Rogan outside Kharkov, but also the airfields at Barvenkovo and
Kramatorskaya. Aerial reconnaissance had shown that some of these were
hosting up to 150 aircraft each. It was too good an opportunity to miss.[6]

It is unclear why they did not first attack the Luftwaffe's Freya and Würburg radars, which had deployed to the Belgorod and Kharkov areas in the spring of 1943. These were capable of detecting large formations of aircraft out to 150km or single aircraft at 90km. The Red Air Force was well aware of them, but instead chose to ignore them at its peril.

At Mikoyanovka, Seidemann and Jeschonnek watched anxiously as Soviet aircraft formations droned overhead toward the Luftwaffe's network of airfields. Had they been quick enough reversing the take-off orders or was Stalin about to devastate Hitler's air support before Operation Citadel had even started? If the Red Air Force succeeded with its audacious surprise attack then Citadel would be stillborn. To make matters worse, the forward airfields were overflowing with munitions. Seidemann's forces had enough stored ammunition for ten missions, while Deichmann had bombs for fifteen days of major operations.

Also at Mikoyanovka was Captain Bruno Meyer, who was unsuccessfully trying to get some sleep. During the night he had overseen his ground crew and armourers preparing his squadrons for battle. Later in the morning his anti-tank group was to provide support for the advancing Panzers and to fend off Soviet tank counterattacks. His squadron leaders, Major Matuschek, First Lieutenants Oswald and Dornemann and Lieutenant Orth, had been well briefed and they all knew their role.[7] Principally they were to break up Soviet armoured formations at the first opportunity. Understandably there was a keen sense of rivalry with Hans-Ulrich Rudel's tank-busting unit.

Meyer was anticipating his new tank busters would come as a nasty surprise to the Soviet tankers. The Red Army was familiar with his Henschel Hs 129 aircraft but they were normally used to drop fragmentation bombs and make low-level strafing runs using their machine guns. Even the addition of 20mm cannon had posed little threat to the T-34 tanks' armour plating, the new 30mm cannon though was a different matter.

He had been alerted to a problem at the sprawling Mikoyanovka air base by the mad scramble as the fighters took to the skies. After all their training it now seemed as if the Red Air Force was going to destroy his unit before it even got off the ground. His headquarters field telephone began to ring as his squadron leaders called to find out what was happening.

Tense moments passed until it was confirmed that the 3rd and 52nd Fighter Groups were safely airborne. It was now a case of waiting to see if the Luftwaffe's superior tactics and skill could prevail. The Soviet attacking force included 285 fighters and 132 ground attack aircraft from the 2nd and 17th Air Armies.[8] All of a sudden their pilots were caught out as they assumed they would pounce on an unsuspecting Luftwaffe. Instead they found themselves under attack by angry swarms of Messerschmitts that, having climbed, darted out of the haze of the early dawn.

Across Belgorod and Kharkov the air-raid sirens began to wail. It was so early in the morning that few could be bothered to move out of bed – night raids were nothing new. In Kharkov some of the remaining long-suffering residents and the German garrison headed for the shelters. A few of the elderly went to the Assumption and Annunciation cathedrals hoping for divine protection – the old ways still survived in the Soviet Union. Although both cathedrals had long been closed by the Soviet authorities, the Germans had recently reopened Annunciation for services.

Kharkov's enormous Dzerzhinsky Square, now renamed 'Leibstandarte SS Square', was deserted except for German military police doing the rounds. The garrison commander suspected the Red Air Force might be going for the railyards or the old aircraft and tank factories. The latter was being used by the SS, who were re-employing captured Soviet T-34 tanks that they had taken as their own.[9]

The Soviet formations tried to press on toward their targets and as they did so their ranks were thinned by German fighters and flak. Over the air corridor between Belgorod and Kharkov it turned into a turkey shoot. Soviet tactics were simply not flexible enough to fight an air battle and bomb ground targets at the same time. The Soviet Lavochkin and Yakovlev fighters were outclassed, although the newer version of Lavochkin had a much improved climb rate. Those bombers that did reach the Kharkov sector scattered their bombs over a wide area, achieving little damage.

Senior Lieutenant Simutenkov, piloting an Il-2 Sturmovik, had a narrow escape with the flak:

> As we approached our target I could see the anti-aircraft fire ripping through the sky. I held my course and could just make out some enemy aircraft taking off. This was a shock as we were convinced that we would achieve surprise and record a major success, but before I had a chance to make my attack my aircraft was hit in the fuselage and then the right wing … I feared that the engine would burst into flames but it did not but it stuttered and lost power. I instinctively swung the aircraft south and within seconds was making a forced landing somewhere within our lines.[10]

The sky filled with swirling vapour trails as aero engines were pushed to their limit. Desperate dogfights took place as aircraft scattered in all directions. It became a case of every man for himself. Wingmen tried to stay together but were often separated in the confusion. Those bombers and ground attack aircraft still with their bombs were separated from their squadrons and picked off.

General Hermann Plocher reported:

> The air battle, which broke out at relatively low altitude, could be observed from the ground, which was also facilitated by the lack of clouds. The German defenders demonstrated a doubtless superiority over the attackers. Such large-scale air engagements were rare for the Eastern Front, and the neighbouring terrain was soon covered with debris ... Jeschonnek, who was at the forward command post of the 8th Air Corps, personally saw the defeat of the Soviets.[11]

General Seidemann could not believe his good luck. Not long before his bomber units had been threatened with obliteration. He was deeply thankful that the god of war had favoured him:

> It was a rare spectacle. Everywhere planes were burning and crashing. In no time at all some 120 Soviet aircraft were downed. Our own losses were so small as to represent total victory, for the consequence was complete German air control in the 8th Corps sector.[12]

Jeschonnek was equally thankful their fighters had saved the day; the Führer would have been furious if the Luftwaffe had been caught napping. He could just imagine how the conversation would have gone if he had to personally report to Hitler the loss of an irreplaceable air corps on the very brink of Citadel. Jeschonnek hoped that the rest of the operation went as well.

The stunned Red Air Force had no choice but abandon the mission and its remaining aircraft, many of them damaged, turned and headed for home. The Messerschmitts gave chase and the German flak batteries kept firing.

Hungarian Miklós Keyneres, flying a German Bf 109, found himself in the thick of it dodging the flak and in hot pursuit of a fleeing Il-2. The Soviet pilot swinging out of formation hoped to escape by dropping down to tree level. Keyneres clung to his tail:

On my right hand side, three Germans are pursuing too. One of the
Germans dives on it, but fails to bring it down ... I aim ahead of the
engine but hold my fire for another moment ... Then I squeeze both
firing buttons. I pull up in an instant to avoid colliding ... I get on its
left side again and from above and behind I shoot at the cockpit ...
From a close distance I open up with the cannon. The machine shud-
ders and hits the ground with its right wing tip. It slides along a creek,
violently burning.'[13]

The surrounding countryside became littered with the broken remains of
Soviet aircraft. Those crews lucky enough to survive being brought down
were swiftly rounded up and taken prisoner. The aircraft that got back had
to be patched up, refuelled and rearmed, and all that took precious time.
Likewise the shaken pilots had to be debriefed and prepared for their next
combat sorties.

Zhukov was angry that the pre-emptive air strikes had been completely
botched: 'The air force made an insignificant, and to be quite honest, ineffective contribution; raids on enemy aerodromes at dawn did not fulfil
their purpose in any way at all as the German Command had its aircraft in
the air by that time to assist its ground troops.'[14]

All the Red Air Force achieved was to delay the Luftwaffe very slightly.
Crucially the loss of so many aircraft from Rudenko and Krasovski's air
armies meant the Red Air Force was unable to challenge the Luftwaffe
over the Kursk salient during the opening stages of Operation Citadel.
It was a major setback for the Red Air Force sending so many fighters on
this abortive pre-emptive strike.

The result was that Soviet aircraft were not in a position to contest
Luftwaffe supremacy on the southern flank of the Kursk salient and in the
north their response to Luftwaffe attacks were often completely ineffectual. Certainly in the northern sector Soviet fighters only began to react
to Citadel in the late afternoon and German Fw 190s had brought down
110 Soviet aircraft by nightfall.

It was round one to Hitler. The Red Air Force attacks had done nothing to really impede or stop the Luftwaffe and at about 04.30 their aircraft
began to attack Soviet defences.[15]

Joseph Stalin, on the advice of his generals, decided to fortify the Soviet-held Kursk salient in the summer of 1943 and let Hitler's forces exhaust themselves before striking back. (Via author)

Marshal Georgi Zhukov was instrumental in persuading Stalin to turn Kursk into an enormous tank trap and planning the Red Army's powerful counter-offensives. (Novosti)

General Konstantin Rokossovsky was charged with holding the northern shoulder of the salient against General Model's offensive. (Przekrój)

General Nikolai Vatutin commanded the southern shoulder, defending it against Field Marshal von Manstein. (Russia State Military Archive/RGVA)

Conditions in the Kursk region were grim but the steady build-up of Red Army units reassured the surviving population they would not be left to the Germans again. (RGKAFD)

Soviet tank production was ramped up in 1943 to an average of 2,000 a month; this was in part thanks to Yevgeny Paton's welding technique. (Via author)

Winston Churchill, despite being an ardent anti-Bolshevik, resolved to help Stalin with the provision of weapons and vital intelligence. (Yousuf Karsh, Library and Archives, Canada)

**ARMS FOR RUSSIA** . . . A great convoy of British ships escorted by Soviet fighter planes sails into Murmansk harbour with vital supplies for the Red Army.

'Arms for Russia' became Churchill's mantra but Stalin was not grateful, which greatly strained Soviet relations with Britain and America at a crucial point in the war. (Frederick Donald Blake – The National Archives, UK)

The Arctic convoys helped sustain the Red Army through 1942 and into early 1943 while relocated Soviet weapons factories got up and running. (Via author)

Admiral William H. Standley, US Ambassador to the Soviet Union, centre, caused an almighty row on the eve of Kursk by publicly denouncing Stalin's ingratitude for Lend-Lease. (Associated Press/*Ithaca Journal*)

In the summer of 1943 Adolf Hitler, seen here with Heinrich Himmler to his left, faced a dilemma over whether to attack the Red Army or sit tight. (Via author)

After his catastrophic defeat at Stalingrad, Hitler moved swiftly to reassure his Axis allies, especially Benito Mussolini, that he would prevail with Operation Citadel. (Via author)

The daring recapture of Kharkov in March 1943 by Himmler's tough Waffen-SS suggested that a much larger victory could be achieved. (Via author)

German aerial reconnaissance in the spring of 1943 warned that an enormous build-up by the Red Army was taking place in and around the Kursk salient. (Via author)

Codebreaker Captain Jerry Roberts and his colleagues at Bletchley Park knew exactly what Hitler intended. (Mei Roberts)

Captain John Cairncross was Stalin's spy in Bletchley Park. Known as 'Liszt' by his handlers, he smuggled out secrets in his trousers. Stalin also had a network of spies in Switzerland feeding him intelligence. (Via author)

After Stalingrad Hermann Göring, head of the Luftwaffe, fell from grace with Hitler. In denial that the war was going against Germany, he ignored his Chief of Staff General Jeschonnek and his Air Inspector General Marshal Milch, hampering preparations for Operation Citadel. (Via author)

To give Hitler's armoured fist at Kursk much-needed punch a number of powerful tanks such as the Tiger I were deployed, but there were not enough of them. (Via author)

Hitler had high hopes for his brand new Panther tank but Heinz Guderian called it his problem child. Production glitches caused a critical delay to Citadel's start date. (Via author)

Hitler's 'pile driver' – the Ferdinand made use of an abandoned Porsche Tiger tank design. (Via author)

A large proportion of Hitler's armoured fist mainly comprised the obsolete Panzer III armed with an inadequate gun. (via Author)

On the eve of the Battle of Kursk the Red Air Force attempted to smash the Luftwaffe on the ground using dive bombers such as this Il-2. (Via author)

Stalin's surprise air attack pre-empting Citadel ended in dismal failure thanks to the Germans' early warning radar. (Scott Pick)

The Soviets lost 120 aircraft with a similar number damaged before Citadel even started. (Scott Pick)

A German soldier picks through the debris of a Soviet plane. The Red Air Force's mauling ensured the Luftwaffe briefly enjoyed air superiority. (Scott Pick)

German Panzer IIIs moving up for the attack; they soon found themselves pounded by the Red Army's very in-depth defences and then swamped by Soviet T-34 tanks. (Via author)

Soviet troops hated German spotter planes, such as this Focke-Wulf Fw 189, as they were harbingers of death and made them a priority target. (Via author)

Ferdinand moving up for the attack at Ponyri – there were simply too few of them and they were cut off. (Via author)

Knocked out T-34 – Red Army tankers had to get alarmingly close to the Panzers to neutralise their longer range guns. (Via author)

On the northern shoulder of the salient the Red Army soon dealt with the cumbersome Ferdinand, which could not defend itself against enemy infantry. (Via author)

The deployment of Guderian's zoo failed to produce the desired results. In particular, the Panther proved a complete shambles despite knocking out numerous enemy tanks. (Via author)

Abandoned T-34s. Ponyri and Prokhorovka became massive tank graveyards for both sides. Stalin though was left in possession of the battlefield and Hitler's tank forces had exhausted themselves. (Via author)

Red Army sightseers scramble over a destroyed Panther – it meant the Soviets enjoyed an intelligence windfall with Hitler's brand new Panzer. (Via author)

A British-supplied Churchill tank. A few of these took part in the battle, as did some American tanks, notably during the liberation of the Orel salient. (Via author)

The shattered remains of German Panzers, including a Ferdinand, in the Orel salient. (Via author)

A Soviet tank column rumbles past by a knocked out Panzer. The Red Army's victory at Kursk ensured Hitler was never able to regain the strategic initiative. (Via author)

Members of the 5th SS waiting to go into action in the Belgorod salient. The Waffen-SS slowed the Red Army but could not save the day, nor prevent the liberation of Belgorod and Kharkov. (Via author)

Kharkov was liberated once more and for good this time. (Scott Pick)

Panther tank destroyed outside Kharkov, a symbol of Hitler's bitter harvest in the summer of 1943. (Via author)

# 11

# PONYRI OR BUST

At Ponyri General Pukhov and his Corps and divisional officers had toured the ground, making sure their defences were as comprehensive as they could be. Like all commanders he would have liked more resources but as his positions were backed by the added weight of the 4th Artillery Corps he could hardly grumble.

His defences at Ponyri were anchored on Maloarkhangelsk to the east and Muravl to the west. The whole front was held by six rifle divisions with a tank division in reserve. From Muravl ran the villages of Gnilets, Podolyan, Butyrke, Alexandrovka and Pervyye Ponyri. These were defended by the 132nd, 15th and 81st Rifle Divisions. The first was drawn from the 28th Rifle Corps belonging to Galanin and the other two came from Pukhov's 29th Rifle Corps. If the enemy broke through Podolyan and then penetrated the defences at Bobrik and Soborovka they would be able to reach Olkhovatka, which was just 60km from Kursk.

Pukhov appreciated that should the Germans pierce his first echelon then he would have to hold them at Olkhovatka and Ponyri at all costs. He had sent Colonel Rukosuyev's 3rd Anti-Tank Artillery Brigade to set up their guns at Olkhovatka. To the east General Yenshin's 307th Rifle Division had burrowed into the dark soil at Ponyri. They were not alone for they were bolstered by the firepower of the 5th Artillery Division, the 13th Anti-Tank Artillery Brigade plus the 11th and 22nd Mortar Brigades. Yenshin was confident that should the Nazis get to his lines his lads would drop such a deluge on them that they would be halted in their tracks.

At 02.20 on 5 July 1943 Rokossovsky gave the order for his artillery and Katyusha rocket launchers to open fire on Model's gathering forces. This unleashed what Zhukov called 'a "symphony" from hell'. Also at Rokossovsky's HQ was Malinin, his Chief of Staff, Boikov, the operations chief, and Colonel Nadysev, the front's artillery Chief of Staff. The latter's boss, General Kazakov, was with the 4th Artillery Corps supporting Pukhov.

All of a sudden they could feel and hear the tremendous roar of the opening bombardment. The gathered officers looked at each other, knowing that, for better or worse, the Battle of Kursk had finally commenced. Zhukov was fully aware of the horrors they were was hurling at the Germans:

> The distance between our headquarters and the enemy troops was no more than 20 kilometres as the crow flies ... Taken unawares, the enemy officers and men probably pressed themselves to the ground or threw themselves into the first convenient hole, ditch or trench, any crack to protect themselves somehow or other from the frightful explosions of the bombs, shells and mines ...[1]

Although Rokossovsky had reason to believe Model was going to attack within forty minutes, he initially hesitated and consulted Zhukov, who told him not to waste time. Nonetheless, Zhukov immediately telephoned Stalin in Moscow to let him know what they had decided. 'I got the impression that he was tense,' Zhukov recalled. 'In fact, all of us, despite our long-prepared defences in depth, despite our powerful striking potential, were in a state of high excitement. It was night, but none of us felt like sleeping.'[2]

Nikolai Belov was snoozing in his trench near Maloarkhangelsk when he was woken by the rolling thunder of the guns. He could feel it in the pit of his stomach as hundreds of artillery and rocket batteries launched hot metal in the direction of the Germans. The most intense fire was coming from his left, some 15km distant, as much of the Central Front's firepower was concentrated behind Ponyri. The early morning gloom was like some enormous firework display with the rockets streaking up and away toward their targets.

Belov and his comrades knew that this vast expenditure of ammunition must herald the battle they had waited so long for. He almost pitied the Germans on the receiving end of this rain from hell. The shockwave would suck the air from their lungs and burst their eardrums. The almost instantaneous explosion would wrench men from their trenches and hurl them skyward with the eviscerating shrapnel. It was best not to look at what came back down as it had ceased to be human. The twisted and naked remains were a test even for the strongest stomach.

Stalin was clearly very anxious because ten minutes later he called Zhukov back to find out how things were going. Zhukov explained that German artillery had attempted some counterbattery fire but it had been swiftly silenced. Stalin said he would ring again later.

Model's artillery was caught out and there was damage to his observation and control systems, but the Soviets were largely firing blind. They were uncertain where Model's troop concentration and jump-off points were. German radio traffic could not be entirely trusted because the Germans used it as a way of spreading misleading intelligence. Although Rokossovsky and Zhukov did have good information on Model's order of battle it did not mean they knew exactly where each division was located. Not only were Rokossovsky's guns firing at broad areas to the east and west of the Oka River rather than at specific locations, he had been premature in giving the order. Most German soldiers were still dozing in their dugouts, foxholes and trenches, while the Panzers were concealed under cover.

Later Zhukov deeply regretted the decision to open fire so soon. He felt that if they had waited half an hour German losses in men and tanks would have been far greater. Instead they wasted ammunition and lit up their own positions. Ironically, the Red Air Force helped save Model's men by delaying his start, because the Luftwaffe were busy dealing with Soviet pilots over Kharkov. This meant even if Model had been planning to attack at 03.00–03.30 the Luftwaffe could not make the deadline. Like the abortive air attack, Soviet artillery counter-preparations did little to disrupt Operation Citadel other than to delay it. The second round of the battle seemed to have gone Hitler's way.

While the Soviet barrage rolled forward Pukhov's troops braced themselves – the men of the 15th Rifle Division looking out across the Oka valley knew that they were going to be in for a rough time. Model commenced his own attack about two hours later. Zhukov recalled:

Between 0430 and 0500 the enemy's planes took to the air, and simultaneously artillery fire opened up against the positions of the Central Front, especially the 13th Army sector. A few minutes later the enemy began his offensive, with three tank divisions and five infantry divisions in his first line of attack. These forces struck the 13th Army and the adjoining flanks of the 48th and 70th Armies.[3]

Model and his corps commanders had thoroughly assessed the aerial photos of Soviet defences and the intelligence gained from prisoners. It was self-evident from the Red Army's preparations that the key defences on the road to Kursk lay at Olkhovatka and Ponyri. In particular the hills between Soborovka to the north and Olkhovatka to the south were strongly fortified. Model set his sights on taking the low ridge centred on the latter village and Hill 274. This showed a lack of flair because he was going to have to barge his way through the strongest part of Rokossovsky's defences.

The Luftwaffe, now fully recovered from its Belgorod and Kharkov distractions, ensured Model had the support he needed. Stuka dive-bombers repeatedly hit enemy artillery positions, with pilots flying up to six missions that day. The heavier bombers sought revenge for their earlier inconvenience by attacking the Red Air Force's crowded airfields around Kursk. The mission rate was extremely high. The Soviets counted up to 1,000 German sorties against the northern part of the salient by 11.00 hours.

North of Alexandrovka, Model unleashed one of Hitler's new secret weapons – the Ferdinand. Like the Tiger and Panther, the Ferdinand looked a formidable monster and its propaganda value was not wasted. A camera crew was despatched to photograph the Ferdinands of Panzerjäger Regiment 656 as they lumbered their way to the front. The new crews in their mixture of *feldmütze* sidecaps and *einheitsfeldmütze* field caps and mishmash of uniforms looked confident as they rode on their mighty machines. Their commander, Lieutenant Colonel Jungenfeld, had done everything he could to boost their morale, principally by extolling the virtues of the powerful 88mm Pak43 L/71 gun. This could outshoot the version on the Tiger tank.

A Ferdinand detachment moved forward supporting Kluge's 292nd Infantry Division. They drove straight through the positions of Barinov's 81st Rifle Division to reach Alexandrovka, only to find themselves on their own. On Kluge's left flank by the late afternoon the 86th Infantry Division had reached Ponyri to take on Yenshin's 307th Division. Kluge's division then managed to capture the northern part of the village and the railway embankment.

Further to the east the German 78th and 216th Infantry Divisions launched attacks towards the heavily defended road junction at

Maloarkhangelsk held by at least three dug-in rifle divisions. They were also supported by a detachment of Ferdinands, but were repulsed by a determined counterattack by the Soviet 129th Armoured Brigade.

In the centre, at 06.20 General Grossmann's 6th Infantry Division moved to secure the Oka valley supported by two companies of Tigers from the Heavy Panzer Battalion 505. The Tigers ploughed through the Soviet defences, turning the flank of the 676th Rifle Regiment. By lunchtime they were in Butyrki, threatening Barinov's left flank.

In fact, of his six Panzer divisions Model only committed General von Kessel's 20th Panzer. Despite getting off to a slow start, by 09.00 his tanks had forced their way through Pukhov's defences between Gnilets and Bobrik, which formed the junction with Galanin's 70th Army. The Panzers broke through the 321st Rifle Regiment and took Bobrik. This exposed the flank of Janjgava's 15th Rifle Division.

Like Stalin, Hitler was desperate to know how Citadel was progressing and Zeitzler had the Führer's adjutants constantly calling him for situation reports. These interruptions were far from helpful but to be expected. Finally, at about 12.30 Zeitzler went to brief Hitler in person. Before he had even unpacked his briefing materials Hitler was demanding, 'Zeitzler, how is it going at Kursk?'[4] The truth was he did not really know as the fighting was bitter and confused. One thing was clear, the Red Army was barely giving any ground and that was something Hitler would not want to hear.

Trying to distract the Führer, he explained that the Luftwaffe had scored an early success over Kharkov. Hitler was not interested as he had already heard this through Luftwaffe channels. He wanted to know how ground operations were going. 'The element of surprise was clearly not there,' explained Zeitzler diplomatically. Hitler, displaying his unwavering confidence in his new weapons, ranted, 'The Ferdinand! The Ferdinand must immediately be thrown at the front! We have to break through, whatever the cost!'[5]

Zeitzler was not sure what the Ferdinand could achieve that the Tiger could not. Besides, the Ferdinands had been committed.

In Pukhov's forward command centre the field telephones were ringing furiously and the radios crackled continuously as garbled reports came in from his commanders. There was a constant stream of situation reports and requests for help. He needed to get a clear picture of the situation in order to report to Zhukov and Rokossovsky exactly how the battle was developing. During the course of the day Model had launched five attempts to break through his defences. Despite some penetrations, on the whole Pukhov's positions held up well.

'It was not until the very end of the day,' wrote Zhukov, 'that the enemy drove a wedge into our defences to a depth of from three to six kilometres in the Olkhovatka area.'[6] Model's gains though had been at the cost of at least 100 armoured fighting vehicles. Zhukov singled out the 15th, 81st and 307th Divisions for praise as well as the 3rd Anti-Tank Artillery Brigade. A battery from the latter unit died to a man but not before knocking out nineteen Panzers. Zhukov noted with pride 'they did not allow the enemy to get through'.[7]

To the north-east of Maloarkhangelsk the Germans failed to make any substantial gains against units of the 15th Rifle Corps. In particular, Colonel Gudz's 8th Rifle Division and General Mishchenko's 149th Rifle Division firmly held their ground. Improbably, it was estimated that Pukhov's artillery alone had accounted for 15,000 German troops and 110 Panzers.

Zhukov and Rokossovsky were also very pleased with Galanin's 70th Army on the far left. His 132nd Rifle Division deployed to the west of Gnilets was attacked by three German infantry divisions but had given up very little ground. This army, said Zhukov, 'made up of frontier guards from the Far East, the Transbaikal area and Central Asia, fought valiantly'.[8]

In contrast he was not happy with the sluggish performance of the Red Air Force, which was slow to recover from its mauling over Kharkov. Although Rudenko had more than 1,000 serviceable aircraft, he had managed only about half the sortie rate of the Luftwaffe before noon on 5 July. That evening Stalin called the Central Front HQ wanting to know, 'Have we gained command of the air?' Rokossovsky was very diplomatic in his response, saying, 'Fierce air battles are going on with alternating success.'[9]

Eyeing their maps, Zhukov and Rokossovsky could see that the most immediate threat was to Olkhovatka, because it was here that Model's Panzers were applying the most pressure. Pukhov's 29th Rifle Corps, which had borne much of the fighting, desperately needed help. It was decided to bring up not only the two armoured corps of Rodin's 2nd Tank Army, but also the 19th Tank Corps ready to conduct counterattacks the following day. The latter unit was sent to the west of Olkhovatka while Rodin's 16th Tank Corps was deployed to the north-east. Rodin was also instructed to send his 3rd Tank Corps to the south of Ponyri. The 18th Guards Rifle Corps was sent to help reinforce Maloarkhangelsk, while the 17th Guards Rifle Corps was tasked with reinforcing the main defensive zone.

The Communist Party political instructors did everything they could to boost the morale of the troops. That night meetings were held with the men of the 6th Guards Rifle Division that came under 17th Corps. At a rally for the 8th Company, 25th Guards Regiment, all the Communist Party members and candidate members pledged that they would not let the enemy pass.

Early on 6 July the 100 tanks of the 16th Tank Corps counterattacked, only to be repulsed by General Lubbe's fresh 2nd Panzer Division. They brought with them Tiger tanks and the German armour was able to capture Soborovka. At this stage Scheller's 9th Panzer Division joined the other armoured units fighting between Soborovka and Pervyye Ponyri. In the air groups of up to 100 planes relentlessly bombed Soviet positions.

Model had committed around 1,000 armoured vehicles by midday. These were funnelled into the Soviet 'Pakfronts' that consisted of clusters of dug-in T-34 tanks, anti-tank guns and anti-tank rifles. Any Panzer disabled by mines was soon under attack by Soviet infantry armed with grenades and Molotovs. While the petrol bombs could not damage the armour, thrown on to the engine deck the entire tank was soon engulfed in flames. If the crew tried to escape the inferno they were gunned down as they emerged.

While both sides relentlessly shelled and bombed each other, the Panzers nonetheless kept regrouping and renewing their attacks. The 17th Guards Rifle Corps fought heroically to hold the line. Most notably Major Konovalenko and his 203rd Guards Rifle Regiment, from the 70th Guards Division, beat off about sixteen attacks. That day the German 292nd Infantry Division was joined by the 86th and 78th Infantry to renew the assault on Ponyri. The entire village had been fortified with the railway station, the school, water tower and tractor station all turned into impregnable strongpoints. The Germans struggled to make any progress against the well dug-in garrison.

This was not just a tank battle; when the German infantry and Panzergrenadiers closed with the Soviet riflemen both sides resorted to their 'pocket artillery'. In the case of the Germans this was the stick grenade, while the Soviets used their F1 'pineapples'. Throwing such weapons took practice and had to be timed just right or they were thrown back. One rifleman said, 'It is nerve-racking to lower the safety switch and wait those two seconds.' Then he added with some satisfaction, 'Grenades explode like shrapnel over the heads of enemy troops.'[10] Once the infantry were face to face they resorted to 'entrenching shovels, shooting them point-blank with machine guns, pistols, and even with flare guns'.[11]

That night soldiers on both sides tried to sleep despite the intermittent gunfire, the sound of tanks 'cooking off' and the cries of the wounded. The Soviet tank crews did not get any rest as they were ordered to dig in all their tanks. Although relatively few in number, the longer range 88mm guns on the Tigers and Ferdinands had reaped a deadly harvest amongst the newly arrived exposed T-34 tanks. Crews were told to only leave their turrets visible. To reinforce the battered front line Rokossovsky also ordered the 60th Army to give up a division and 65th Army to redeploy two tank regiments.

Digging in a tank manually without the help of a bulldozer was no easy task. Creating a scrape that was deep enough, wide enough and with a high enough earth embankment was a back-breaking job. Ideally the latter needed to be almost level with the gun barrel. The sweat-drenched, dirt-caked crews understood their lives depended on making a good job so few complained for very long. It was better to get on with it and consider it a competition with the rest of the platoon.

Being hull-down, while making the front of the tanks safer, posed a problem for the crews. A tank is designed to be cross-country mobile, not static. If the Panzers got past them they would swing round behind and shoot at the tanks' thinner rear armour. This meant the crews either had to leave the engine running or the driver had to hold his hand over the starter button ready for a quick getaway. By reversing quickly they could keep the thicker frontal and side armour facing the enemy. The crews though had to keep their wits about them or they could be rear-ended if they backed into a friendly tank. In trained hands the T-34 was a very agile vehicle – in untrained hands it could become a blundering monster, especially when reversing blind.

Starting a tank was not a straightforward procedure – the driver had to carry out a number of steps to prime the engine. Regardless of what was going on around him, the driver had to concentrate on the job in hand. In the case of the T-34 he had to switch on the battery master switch, select a fuel tank and make sure the gears were in neutral. The oil pump switch had then to be pressed to prime the engine lubrication system. Failure to do so meant starting the engine dry, which could cause damage. It was best to do all this before the firing commenced.

On pressing the starter button and depressing the foot throttle the engine should start immediately. Engaging the foot clutch and throttle pedal moves the tank forward or back and using the steering levers causes the vehicle to turn. The latter was vital when weaving amongst enemy tanks. Each gear change required going into neutral, which meant without sufficient revs the tank could come to a halt between first and second gear. Backing out of an earth entrenchment only required reverse, until such time as the commander decided to spin the tank around. In action all this had to happen while the main gun and machine guns were firing and the commander was yelling orders down his throat mike to the crew.

Model was determined to capture Ponyri and decided to renew his assault using elements of General Scheller's 9th and Schleiben's 18th Panzer Divisions on 7 July. Up to 200 German tanks spread out to the north-west of the village, but Yenshin's much reinforced 307th Rifle Division withstood their determined attack. As the Panzers approached Yenshin's defences they were swamped by field gun, howitzer, mortar and Katyusha rocket fire from the 5th Artillery Division. Those that were not hit ran into dug-in anti-tank guns and T-34s. They were also set upon by Soviet ground attack aircraft, which claimed at least sixty Panzers.

Zhukov recalled with evident pride, 'The din of fierce fighting on the ground and in the air continued unabated all day long around Ponyri. The enemy hurled more and more tank units into battle, but he did not manage to break through the defences here either.'[12]

Model gained little more than a foothold in the northern part of the village. The ground before Ponyri was left dotted with German corpses and wrecked tanks, and the survivors withdrew to regroup. Model reverted to shelling the village with his 105mm and 150mm field guns.

There was no hiding Operation Citadel from Hitler's Axis allies once it was under way. In Bucharest Romanian writer Mihail Sebastian was baffled by Hitler's logic. On 7 July he sat down and astutely wrote in his diary:

> For two days a great tank battle has been raging in the Kursk sector ...
> I cannot gauge either the scale or significance of the battle. The official communiqué claims that when the Russians responded to a local offensive with powerful counter-attacks, the German commander threw large reserves into the struggle ...
>
> Is this the beginning of a wider German offensive? That's hard to believe, with the spectre of a landing at their rear. Or is it just a limited action, designed to reduce the 'Kursk salient' or to probe the Russian forces ... In any event, it is this summer's first real episode of war.[13]

The following day Model instructed his Panzers to redouble their attempts to break through at Olkhovatka. In a bid to help end the deadlock, Seidemann's 8th Air Corps was ordered to send 30 per cent of its

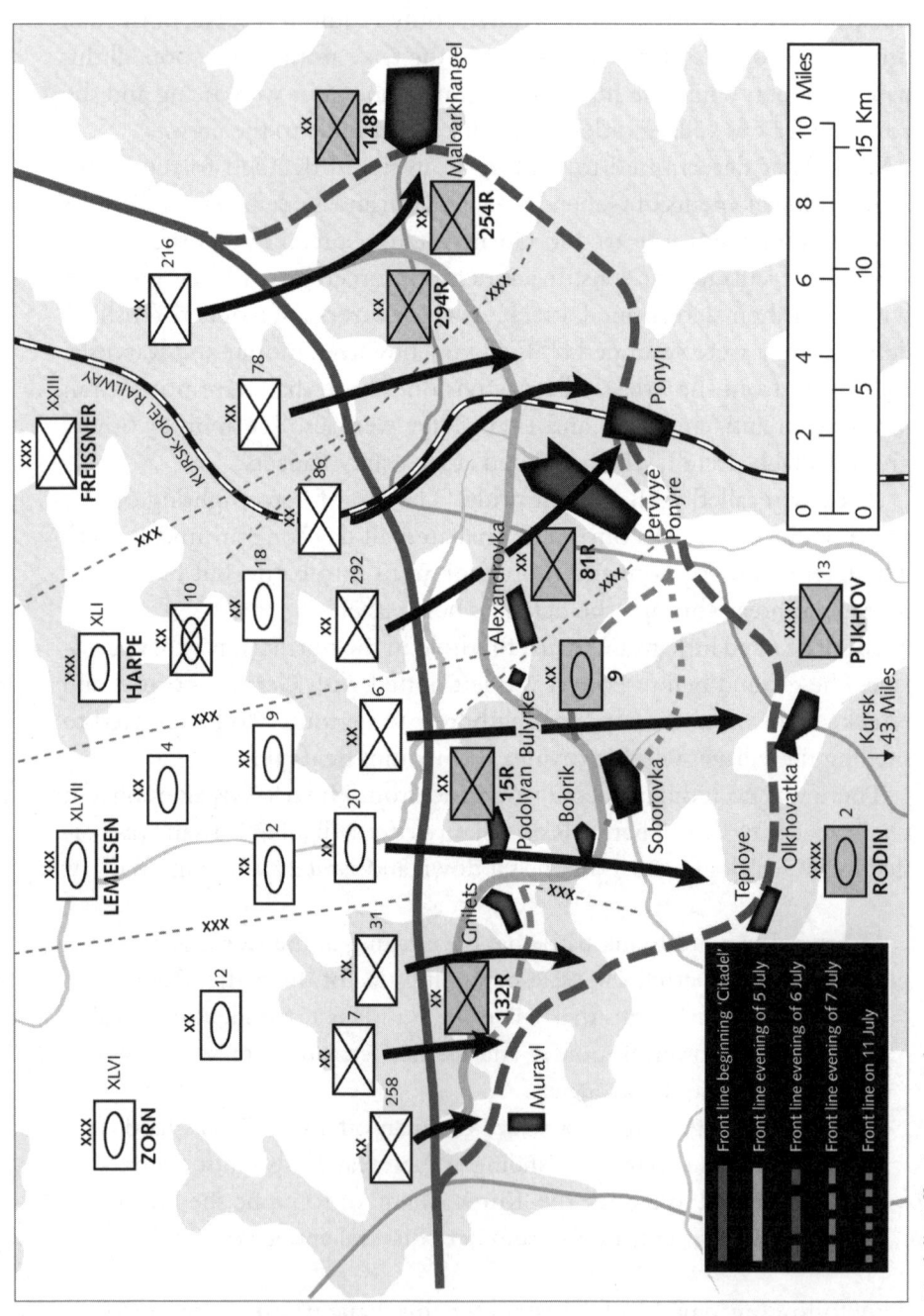

Model's Offensive, 5–11 July 1943.

bombers and 40 per cent of its fighters to help in the Orel sector. Massing 300 Panzers, which were preceded by artillery and rocket fire as well as dive-bombers, Model hit the positions before Colonel Rukosuyev's brigade. The force was simply overwhelming and it quickly overran the Soviets' forward positions.

Desperately Rukosuyev signalled:

The enemy has captured Kashara, Kutyrka, Pogoreltsovy, and Samodurovka. He is bringing up 200 tanks and motorised infantry in the direction of Tyoploye [Teploye] and preparing for another attack … The 1st and 7th batteries have fought bravely and died, but they did not retreat an inch. We have destroyed 40 tanks. The 1st Anti-Tank Rifle Battalion has sustained 70 per cent casualties. I have prepared the 2nd and 3rd batteries and the 2nd Anti-Tank Rifle Battalion to repulse the enemy. I have communication with them. We shall fight. We shall hold fast or die.[14]

The attack saw the 9th and 18th Panzer Divisions trying to crack Olkhovatka, while to the west the 2nd and 20th Panzer pushed on Samodurovka–Teploye–Moltychi with Saucken's 4th Panzer Division in reserve. Model ended up with four Panzer divisions supported by the 6th Infantry Division crammed into a front stretching from Samodurovka to Pervyye Ponyri. Although they eventually took Teploye, they failed at Olkhovatka because the defences on Hill 274 were just too strong.

Despite the continued intensity of the fighting, Stalin was eager to launch his Orel counteroffensive. He rang Zhukov in the early hours of 9 July and upon learning how Model's forces were being bled dry he asked if the time was right to strike. Zhukov responded:

I said that the enemy no longer had the strength to break through our defences on the Central Front and, unless we wanted to give him time to organise the defensive positions we were forcing him into, we should promptly go over to the offensive with all the forces of the Bryansk Front and the left wing of the Western Front. Without these the Central Front would be unable to carry out the planned counter-offensive.[15]

They agreed that the counteroffensive against the Germans Orel bulge would start on 12 July.

The German 508th Grenadier Regiment, supported by half a dozen Ferdinands, was ordered to assault Hill 253.3 at Ponyri on the 9th. To avoid the attentions of the Red Air Force's dive-bombers the Ferdinands drove along the tree-lined railway embankment in order to get as close to the village as possible before attacking. A German photographer ran ahead up the line and turned to photograph two of the monsters sheltering under the trees.

It was hoped that thanks to their heavy armour the Germans would be able to roll on through the Soviet defences. Although the hill was taken, once out in the open one of the Ferdinands quickly ran over a mine and caught fire. Soviet gunners then rained shellfire down on the others. Zhukov was aware that Model was running out of options, especially once it was apparent his remaining armoured reserve was moving south-east in the direction of Ponyri.

Model's setbacks at Ponyri and Olkhovatka forced him to pause operations on the 10th while he got his reserves into place ready to attack again. Armour backed by 31st Infantry Division was tasked with helping clear Ponyri on 11 July.[16] Time was now running out for Model. In the course of four days' bloodletting he had managed to drive a wedge about 12km deep and 10km wide into Pukhov's defences between Olkhovatka and Ponyri. However, it had been extremely hard-won ground. The Soviets claimed to have inflicted 42,000 casualties and destroyed 800 tanks.

# 12

# PROKHOROVKA BLOODBATH

Khrushchev claims that he and Vatutin were tipped off about the start of Hitler's southern attack the night before:

> We got a call from the 6th Army. The commander told us that a German soldier had defected from a frontline SS division and that he had important information: 'He says the Germans are going to attack tomorrow morning at three o'clock.' We ordered that the prisoner be brought to us immediately. Vatutin and I interrogated him.

It transpired that the man was an unwilling recruit from French Alsace serving with one of the SS Panzergrenadier divisions and readily answered their questions. Khrushchev was suspicious that the soldier seemed so well informed. He said:

> Naturally I didn't actually see the orders for the offensive but the troops can sense what's about to happen. And it's more than just intuition. First, we have been issued with dry rations for three days. Second the tanks have been moved all the way to the front lines. Third, an order has been given to stack ammunition right next to the heavy artillery and field pieces so not to lose time loading once the artillery opens fire.

'But what makes you so sure the attack will start at three o'clock in the morning?' asked Khrushchev.

'Well, figure it out yourself. At this time of year dawn begins to break at about that hour, and that's when the German command likes to open an attack,' replied the soldier.[1]

Following the interrogation a call was made to Moscow to seek permission to commence a pre-emptive bombardment.

Zhukov observed:

At 16.10 on 4 July the enemy's advanced detachments began offensive operations. The aim of these operations was apparently reconnaissance. On 5 July, following artillery and air bombardment, the enemy launched an offensive from the Streletski–Tomarovka–Zybino–Trefilovka area, with no less than 450 tanks.[2]

General Hoth knew he had his work cut out. Even if he got through the deep Soviet defences Katukov's tanks were blocking the way to Oboyan. Likewise, the presence of Rotmistrov's tanks posed a major threat to his left flank. When Rotmistrov was committed to the battle he would inevitably come via Prokhorovka. Examining his maps, Hoth appreciated that once through the enemy's defences he would have to swing north-east to defeat Rotmistrov. After that was achieved he could swing westward toward Oboyan with a view to linking up with Model at Kursk.

Therefore Hausser's three SS Panzergrenadier divisions were given the role of slicing their way through to Prokhorovka. In their path lay the 52nd Guards Rifle Division and the 375th Rifle Division from Chistyakov's 23rd Guards Rifle Corps. To the right of 4th Panzer Army, Kempf's Army Detachment was supposed to hook Breith's 3rd Panzer Corps to the north-west past Belgorod to catch Rotmistrov in the left flank.

Vatutin though moved first to pre-empt Hoth's attack. At 02.30 Chistyakov and Shumilov gunners opened up and pounded German positions to their south. An hour later Hoth's artillery replied, then at 04.00 4th Panzer Army's two westerly Panzer corps rolled forward between Gertsovka and Belgorod with 700 Panzers and assault guns. Luftwaffe dive-bombers and anti-tank aircraft set about the Red Army's surveyed artillery and tank positions. The ground shook and great clouds of dust filled the air.

Hörnlein's *Grossdeutschland* Panzergrenadier division formed the centre of Knobelsdorff's 48th Panzer Corps. His officers and men were relieved to be going back into combat after all the monotonous training. They had spent time examining their tactical maps showing their lines of attack and objectives. They had every faith in their abilities as they were the army's elite. Their immediate goal was the small town of Cherkasskoye held by the Soviet 67th Guards Rifle Division.

Nonetheless, Major General Mellenthin was far from happy about the ground they would have to fight their way across:

> The terrain, over which the advance was to take place was a far-flung plain, broken by numerous valleys, small copses, irregularly laid out vil-lages, and some rivers and brooks; of these the Pena ran with a swift current between steep banks. The ground rose slightly to the north, thus favouring the defender. Roads consisted of tracks through the sand and became impassable for all motor transport during the rain. Large corn-fields covered the landscape and made visibility difficult.[3]

Strachwitz's Tigers and Lauchert's Panthers formed the armoured spearhead supported by the older Panzer IIIs and IVs. Magold led his assault guns into action with his head poking from the commander's cupola. Although dangerous it made it easier to control the battle and he did not like to close up his vehicle until the last moment. Then he would have to rely on the vision blocks in the cupola and the periscope. Meanwhile, Frantz's self-propelled guns followed the Panzergrenadiers ready to provide artillery fire support when and where it was needed. On Hörnlein's left Westhoven's 3rd Panzer, supported by Schaefer with the 332nd infantry, attacked to the west of Gertsovka with the goal of reaching the Pena River.

To the west the Soviet front line of General Chistyakov's 6th Guards Army was shelled and subjected to dive-bomber attack. On the receiving end of things were Colonel Nekrasov's 52nd Guards Rifle Division and Colonel Baksov's neighbouring 67th Guards Rifle Division. They then braced themselves to face Hausser and Knobelsdorff's Panzer corps and began to fire back with their field guns, mortars and rocket launchers. The 5th Guards Mortar Regiment supporting Baksov dropped two salvos on to the advancing Panzers, claiming eleven tanks.

Initially the *Grossdeutschland* and 11th Panzer's frontal attacks on Cherkasskoye did not get off to a good start. To the left of the town the new Panthers ran into an uncleared Soviet minefield and had to be retrieved by sappers whilst under artillery fire. To the right, although 11th Panzer broke through the crust of the Soviet defences, they could not reach their objec-tive, which was the bridge over the Psel River.

Nonetheless, by 09.15 the Germans had barged through the first line of defences and reached the outskirts of Cherkasskoye.

Despite his best efforts Nekrasov's resistance was overwhelmed by Hausser's Panzers, led by the Tigers, and they captured half a dozen fortified villages held by Nekrasov's division. In quick succession they overran Berezov, Gremuchi, Bykovo, Kozma-Demyanovka and Voznesenski. Soviet riflemen were left reeling and dazed, others tried to escape to their second line of defences.

Will Fey was with a Tiger company gathered to the west of Tomarovka. As the heavy tanks rumbled forward, 'Enemy infantry ran through the cornfields, trying to avoid us and to reach the village in the next valley'.[4] The tank's turret and bow machine guns opened up and cut them down. To their right they spotted a Soviet lorry trying to escape through some woods until tracer fire caused 'it to burst into flames'.[5] Then he and his crew soon found themselves engaging a force of at least forty counterattacking tanks. All the Tigers fired together, including Fey's:

> We counted the torches of the enemy tanks that would never fire on German soldiers. After one hour, twelve T-34s were in flames.
>
> The other thirty curved wildly back and forth, firing as rapidly as their barrels would deliver. They aimed well, but our armour was very strong. We no longer twitched when a steely finger knocked on our walls. We wiped the flakes of interior paint from our faces, loaded again, aimed, fired.[6]

This success inevitably exposed Baksov's defences, particularly around Cherkasskoye. Thanks to support from 11th Panzer attacking the eastern approaches to the town, by late afternoon Hörnlein's men had broken in.

German attacks involved up to 100 Panzers each time and by nightfall they had pierced the positions of the 67th Guards Rifle Division. Baksov had no option but to withdraw to Krasny Pochinok.

During the fighting his 196th Guards Rifle Regiment became encircled, but its continued resistance helped cover the retreat of the rest of the division. That night the regiment was ordered to break out. Junior Lieutenant Aleko and a platoon of fifteen submachine-gunners were ordered to act as rearguard and for several hours they bravely held at bay repeated attacks by the Germans.

To the west, despite fierce resistance by the 71st Guards Rifle Division, Westhoven's Panzers reached the Pena by nightfall. To the east of Belgorod

Shumilov's 7th Guards Army found itself under attack by Breith's Panzer corps and Raus corps. They were stopped from getting to Korocha.

That day Will Fey was in combat for six long gruelling hours: 'Our Tiger half-company, with the help of medium and light support forces, knocked out, on the record, twenty-three American tanks and T-34s of a large superior force, and drove back the rest.'[7]

By the end of 5 July German troops were stunned by the weight of fire the Soviets were able to bring to bear despite the best efforts of their own artillery and the Luftwaffe. 'I fought in many countries but I never saw anything like the Russian artillery,' remarked Grenadier 1st Class E. Wulf from the German 332nd Infantry Division.[8]

However, Knobelsdorff and Hausser's men had driven a wedge up to 10km deep in two sectors. In support of these advances the Luftwaffe had flown more than 2,000 sorties. Vatutin suffered heavy casualties and lost sixty tanks and seventy-eight aircraft. It was clear to him that Chistyakov was under the most pressure and that night he ordered Katukov's 1st Tank Army plus the 2nd and 5th Guards Tank Corps to reinforce the 6th Guards Army's second line of defences.

Vatutin was all for counterattacking in the morning, but Katukov warned him that their tanks were being knocked out at long range by the Panthers and Tigers. It would be foolish to venture out into the open when the Panzers' strength was far from spent. As they had done on the Central Front, the tank crews were ordered to dig in, so as to present the smallest possible target, and fight from these static positions.

On 6 July the 1st SS and 2nd SS with 120 tanks fought their way to the north-west up the Belgorod–Oboyan road. Around Yakovlevo *Liebstandarte* encountered forty-two tanks of the Soviet 1st Armoured Guards Tank Brigade. At 1,000m they engaged each other and after sixty minutes twelve T-34s had been destroyed. Rolf Erhardt, serving with the 1st SS, did not get off to a good start. 'My experience as a Panzer driver in the few days since 5 July consisted of a gigantic bang,' he said, 'when I ran over a mine on 6 July, and a few meaningless missions.'[9]

By 11.00 the Soviet 155th Guards Rifle Regiment had been forced out of the way and *Das Reich* had taken Luchki to the east of Yakovlevo. This cut a sizeable hole in the defences between Chistyakov and Kryuchenkin and put Hausser firmly amidst the Soviet second defence line. The slowness of Breith's forces exposed Hausser's flank to Soviet infantry counterattacks. This was a setback for Manstein because it meant a third of his armour was being used as flank guards rather than as the cutting edge.

Things did not go well for the powerful 48th Panzer Corps either, as Mellentin wrote:

On the second day of the attack we met our first setback, and in spite of every effort the troops were unable to penetrate the Russian line. *Grossdeutschland*, assembling in dense formation and with the swamp in its immediate front, was heavily shelled by Russian artillery. The engineers were unable to make suitable crossings, and many tanks fell victim to the Red Air Force ...[10]

According to Zhukov's intelligence, Hoth's 4th Panzer Army had lost tens of thousands of men, as well as 200 tanks and 100 combat aircraft, by the close of 6 July. Although Hausser had penetrated some of the second line of Soviet defences, Knobelsdorff had been halted in front of them.

When Vatutin spoke with Stalin that night he explained that Chistyakov had fought off twelve attacks that day and that the total tally of Panzers amounted to 332. It was rather optimistically claimed that Shumilov's troops had killed some 10,000 Germans. At 23.00 Pavel Rotmistrov was ordered to route march his tanks 190 miles to get them to Prokhorovka by the 9th. Rotmistrov, with his small round glasses and moustache, had the look of a teacher rather than a tank general. Nonetheless, his academic appearance belied a steely determination.

The next day, 7 July, Hoth renewed his attacks with the bulk of his Panzers striking Chistyakov's and Katukov's forces in the Oboyan–Prokhorovka area. At 04.00 the 48th Panzer Corps threw 400 tanks at Katukov's 31st Tank Corps and 3rd Mechanised Corps. Pressure was exerted on Soviet positions between Syrtsevo and Yakovlevo. Dubrova, between the two, was quickly captured. Breith also launched 200 tanks against Shumilov in the Korocha area. The plan was to widen the breach on the flanks and deepen it toward Prokhorovka. 'On 7 July ... we at last achieved some success,' said Mellentin. '*Grossdeutschland* was able to break through ... and the Russians withdrew ... The fleeing masses were caught by German artillery fire and suffered heavy casualties.'[11]

At Rastenburg Hitler drove Zeitzler to distraction with his constant demands for updates. In particular he wanted to know how the Waffen-SS was doing. In the end the suspense got the better of Hitler and he ordered Major Günsche to fly down to Belgorod to find out first-hand. It was not a trip that Günsche particularly looked forward to as the Red Air Force was increasingly aggressive. Fighter escort or not, the thought of running into Soviet fighters was a worrying prospect.

Finally safely touching down to the north of the city, he located the headquarters 1st SS. All around him was evidence of a fierce tank engagement. Günsche claimed divisional commander Sepp Dietrich did not welcome his intrusion, nor did he welcome Hitler's questions. He made no attempt to sugar-coat the situation for the benefit of the Führer.

Dietrich was reportedly bitter:

Over there are ten kilometres of what I was supposed to be able to take, but at what price! Of the more than 150 tanks I started out with, not even twenty are still battleworthy. The infantry has sustained heavy losses. The neighbouring division has fared no better. Who knows how deeply manned the Russian's lines are? It is easy to talk when you are in East Prussia, but here it looks different.[12]

When Günsche asked the burning question, Dietrich snapped back, 'We are not going to break through.'[13] A dejected Günsche flew back to Hitler. He was worried about delivering his briefing because he was all too familiar with Hitler's terrible rages. Instead he found the Führer almost resigned to the situation. 'Forget it,' said Hitler, 'I know … Even Dietrich has been repelled.'[14]

On the 9th elements of the 73rd Guards Rifle Division from Chistyakov's 25th Guards Rifle Corps weathered the terrible steel storm. In particular Colonel Davidenko's 214th Rifle Regiment, holding positions near the village of Krutoi Log, struggled to fight off 120 Panzers, including thirty-five Tigers. The 1st and 3rd battalions were almost swamped and they suffered terrible losses repelling their attackers. After twelve hours of fighting the 3rd Battalion was reduced from 450 men to just 150 and amongst the casualties was their commander, Captain Belgin. The guardsmen though claimed to have killed almost 1,000 Germans and destroyed thirty-nine tanks.

By 11 July Hoth's forces had only covered one third of the distance to Kursk. His largest penetration was toward Prokhorovka, having gained 35km in seven days of tough fighting. Vasilevsky and Vatutin now determined that the time was ripe to commit Rotmistrov's 5th Guards Tank Army and Zhadov's 5th Guards Army to a counterattack at Prokohotovka the following day. The fate of Citadel now hung in the balance.

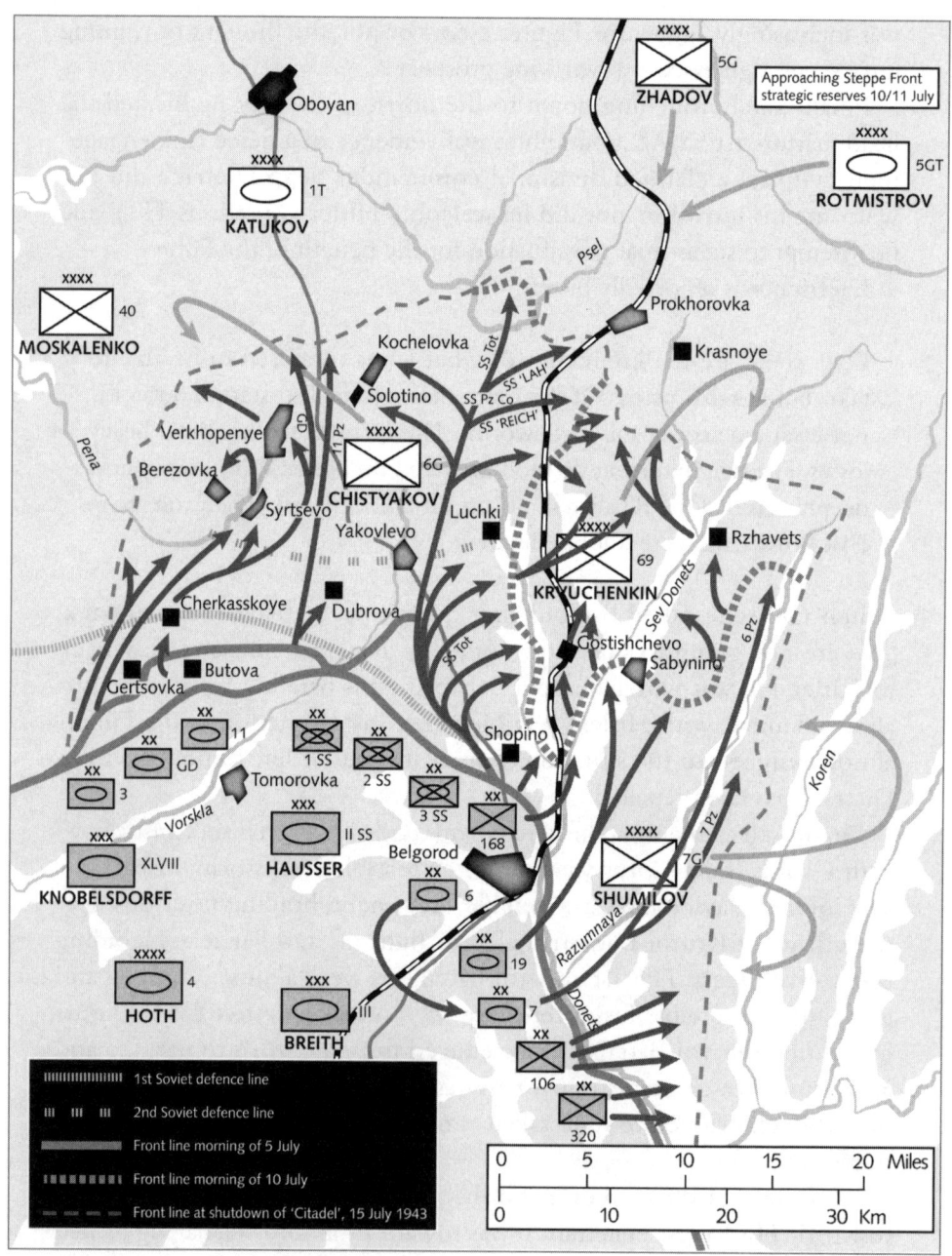

Manstein's Offensive, 5–15 July 1943.

The 1st SS had certainly suffered considerable attrition with its armour. Rudolf von Ribbentrop, the adjutant of the 1st SS Panzer Regiment, reported:

The losses of my 6th Company so far had been heavy. Of the twenty-two tanks which we had started on 5 July, only seven were still operational on the evening of 11 July. Fortunately, not all of these had been total losses, and a steady stream of repaired Panzer IVs was returning to the company.[15]

On the night of 11–12 July Breith's forces took a bridge over the Donets at Rzhavets. In theory this meant his Panzers would be in a position to swing to the left to help Hausser's assault on Prokhorovka. To prevent this happening Vatutin ordered the 11th and 12th Mechanised Brigades from the 5th Mechanised Guards Corps, plus the 25th Armoured Brigade from the 2nd Guard Corps to counterattack and protect Rotmistrov's flank.

After a week of relentless combat *Grossdeutschland* had been greatly weakened and the two flanking Panzer divisions were constantly being forced westward and eastward. They desperately needed a rest, as Mellenthin recalled:

On the morning of 12 July *Grossdeutschland* was assembled and concentrated astride the road south of Nowosselowka, waiting to launch the decisive advance to the north at first light on the 13th. The 12th of July was their first day without fighting; this breathing space was used to replenish ammunition and fuel and to carry out such repairs as could be effected in the forward area … news from the 3rd Panzer Division was not encouraging.[16]

Once Rotmistrov and Zhadov were moving to hold Prokhorovka and the Psel it meant that Hausser would inevitably run headlong into them. He could muster about 600 Panzers, while Breith to the right had more than 360. Rotmistrov's forces totalled some 850 tanks. At 08.30 Preiss' 3rd SS was to sweep to the west from the Psel as Wisch's 1st SS and Krüger's 2nd SS cut through to the south of the town across the area between the Psel and the Prokhorovka railway. This was good rolling tank country covered in wheat and rye.

Opposing them were the freshly arrived Soviet 2nd, 18th and 29th Tank Corps. The Soviet tankers knew they had to close as quickly as possible to stop the Tigers using their longer range guns, then a deadly dance of death would begin. Vasiliy Bryukhov, with the 2nd Tank Corps, was well aware of the challenge they faced, 'You are on the move, you look for targets, you spin around. A T-34/76 commander works like a circus artist … This requires full concentration, otherwise in combat he is done for.'[17]

On the morning of the 12th, under cover of the Luftwaffe and artillery bombardment, the SS Panzers in tight wedge formations sped forward to be met by Soviet rockets and shells. Mansur Abdulin and the 66th Guards Rifle Division went into action at daybreak, closely supported by their artillery, 'The roar of guns continued all day without pause. We infantrymen – surrounded by thick black smoke and covered in soot – looked like stokers, endlessly throwing coal into a furnace. Only the whites of our eyes and teeth were shining.'[18]

The summer heat added to the privations suffered by the infantry and tank crews. Many of the Soviet divisions were thrown into the fight tired and ill-prepared. General Baklanov's 13th Guards Rifle Division had been put on alert at midnight on 8–9 July to march to the Oboyan area. The following day one regiment lost seventy men to heatstroke; it was not a good start. That night they got just three hours sleep before pressing on. When they arrived at Oboyan they dug in, only to be ordered to march another 25km south.

Colonel Vavilov, a political officer with the division, grumbled bitterly:

At dawn on the 12th, we came to the start point, and at once entered the fighting, with two regiments. And didn't General Zhukov say: 'it is better not to begrudge a retreat of five or six kilometres than send tired men, with no ammunition, into battle!'[19]

All of a sudden, emerging from the smoke, Rotmistrov's tanks broke cover and charged past Prokhorovka. 'The sun came to our aid,' said Rotmistrov, who was directing the battle from a small hill to the south-west of the town. 'It picked out the contours of the enemy tanks and blinded the German tankmen … The appearance on the battlefield of a great number of our tanks threw the Germans into confusion.'[20]

Ribbentrop, with the 1st SS Panzer Regiment, was caught by surprise and they soon found enemy tanks amongst them:

We had no time to take up defensive positions. All we could do was fire. From this range every round was a hit, but when would a direct hit end it for us? Somewhere in my subconscious I realised that there was no chance of escape. As always in such hopeless situations, all we could do

was take care of what was at hand. So we knocked out a third, then a
fourth T-34, from distances of less than thirty metres.[21]

The fighting was brutal and at incredibly close quarter. 'A T-34 breaking through could not advance fifty metres without being turned into a
sieve,' said Rolf Erdhardt.[22] The Battle of Prokhorovka was soon absolute
mayhem. 'Burning T-34s ran into and over one another,' said Ribbentrop.
'It was a total inferno of fire and smoke, and impacting shells and explosions. T-34s blazed, while the wounded tried to crawl away to the sides.'[23]
Soviet losses were heavy. 'Within our main line of resistance there were
more than one hundred knocked-out Russian tanks.'[24]

'I took part in the battle of Prokhorovka,' recalled Vasiliy Bryukhov.
'Our task was to support the introduction of the 18th Tank Corps of the
5th Guards Tank Army into the battle … Our battalion was deployed with
the Psel River on its flank; the 170th Tank Brigade of the 18th Tank Corps
was deployed to the left of us.'[25]

Bryukhov's advance was held up by a ravine and they were forced to
swing to the left. As a result his brigade became entangled with the neighbouring 170th Brigade and the space between the mass of tanks went from
about 150m to under 20m. Having negotiated the ravine, Bryukhov and
his crew knocked out a Panzer III that suddenly appeared before them.
'Several minutes later,' said Bryukhov, 'a shell flew over, hitting us on the
side, and tore out an idler and the first roller … We leapt out, crawled into
a shell crater … we didn't take any further part in the action.'[26]

From his vantage point Rotmistrov saw that:

> The fighting in the Prohorovka area was exceptionally bitter. It was hard
> to make out who was attacking and who was defending. Hundreds of
> tanks were moving into battle. There was no room for manoeuvring.
> The tank men had to fire at point blank range. Built-up areas and domi-
> nating hills passed from hand to hand several times.[27]

Martin Steiger, commanding the 1st Panzer Company of *Totenkopf*'s
3rd SS Panzer Regiment, was involved in the horrors of this enormous
swirling tank melee:

> Ahead of us were the 'gully of death', the town of Prokhorovka, and the
> Psel River. None of us would forget that assault. The 'gully of death',
> so named by us because of the heavy losses, was to become everyone's

terrible memory. The crew of Sergeant Prenzl fell victim to a direct hit outside of its Panzer. We had barely crossed the Psel River and conquered its steep banks, barely taken position again above the gully, when the counterattacks by the Soviets began.[28]

Just before noon the 3rd SS was attacked by the 29th Tank Corps and the 33rd Guards Rifle Corps. It was vital that they hold their ground or they would open the flank of their sister divisions.

The strength and ferocity of Vatutin's reserves came as a shock to the Germans, who hoped they had fought the Red Army to a standstill. Steiger was amazed at the power of the counterattacks launched by Rotmistrov and Zhadov:

> They came in battalion and regiment strength. They came with whole brigades and divisions. They moved their guns in battery strength in front of the bridgehead and sent salvo after salvo into the riverbank and the occupied high ground. Tanks charged our lines in numbers that we had not experienced in such a small area during the Eastern campaign.[29]

The Soviet T-34 crews desperately slammed a 76.2mm tank round into the gun breech and fired as quickly as they could. Seconds later they expelled the hot, spent shell casing and rammed home another round – they did this over and over again. If you stopped you died. On the German side the Panzer III/IV, Panther and Tiger crews were doing the same. Tank rounds were stored in the immediate reach of the loader, but once they had been expended more rounds had to be retrieved from storage elsewhere in the tank. Tense seconds would follow while this happened.

Inside his Panzer IV, Ribbentrop found himself in just such a situation: 'All of our immediately available armour-piercing ammunition had been expended. Further ammunition had to be passed to the loader by the gunner, radio operator and driver. At this point remaining stationary was the surest means of being spotted and destroyed by the Russian tanks.'[30]

He and his crew had no choice but to retreat, turning their tank in the middle of the enemy armour swarming about them. They sped 50m to reach a reverse slope. Turning once more to give battle, they managed to sidestep a T-34 about to fire on them and shot it in the rear from just 10m, taking off the turret.

On both sides some crews ran out of armour piercing and had to rely on high explosive instead until they could break off and take on reloads.

Again Ribbentrop experienced this: 'Just then I heard my loader report: "No more armour-piercing available!" We had expended our entire supply of armour-piercing ammunition. All we had left on board at that point were high-explosive rounds, which were ineffective against the heavily armoured T-34s.'[31]

All they could do was use their machine guns to mow down the Soviet infantry, who were intent on blowing them up.

Abdulin's division was thrown into the battle: 'We moved at a furious pace, among burning tanks, exploding shells, and fire from every conceivable sort of weapon.'[32] He and his comrades quickly set about destroying German tanks:

> On 12 July, in just one encounter, Leonid Nochovny's [artillery] platoon destroyed five Tigers. One should not have the erroneous notion that gunners fire from some cover and from behind a firing line. No. In the majority of cases, if a cannon was not more than 152mm, it was used alongside the infantry, even though we often had to change our position, leaving the gunners to face the Nazis alone.[33]

The Soviet infantry also bravely set about the Panzers with grenades. Some men dug foxholes in front of their positions ready to jump out and surprise enemy tanks. Eighteen-year-old Kostia Martynov from Adbulin's unit did just this. While a machine-gunner scattered the tank's supporting infantry, Martynov hurled a bundle of grenades underneath it. Watching from their main position, Abdulin said, 'Then comes the powerful, defeating explosion. The Tiger loses its track and twitches, trying to resume its forward momentum. But having only one caterpillar, it turns and collapses on its side.'[34] Young Martynov sacrificed himself as he was unable to escape the blast. 'We found him,' lamented Abdulin, 'with blood flowing from his ears and his eyes almost falling out of their sockets.'[35]

In the meantime, Breith's troops were unable to cut through the Soviet blocking forces and when he finally managed this the following day it was too late. Breith's forces had tried but it had been at great cost. The 6th Panzer division was down to just forty-seven tanks, similarly the 19th Panzer Division had been reduced to just two companies and the 332nd Infantry Division had lost 3,700 men.[36]

Although the 1st SS and 2nd SS attempted to defeat the 18th Tank Corps, the latter was reinforced and Hausser could not break Rotmistrov's second echelon of reserves. There was no escaping that Hausser had been fought to a standstill by the end of the day and his divisions forced over to the defensive.

To achieve this feat Rotmistrov sacrificed more than half of his tank force and initially Stalin was furious until he learned the extent of the victory. 'The losses suffered by both sides were considerable and practically equal,' noted Rotmistrov. 'But the German advance was halted and the counterblow by our army's major forces was successful.'[37]

Hausser lost some 300 Panzers; those that could have been repaired were beyond help because Rotmistrov remained master of the battlefield. The countryside surrounding Prokhorovka was a massive tank graveyard. Almost everything had been incinerated. Rotmistrov said, 'More than 700 tanks were put out of action on both sides in the battle. Dead bodies, destroyed tanks, crushed guns and numerous shell craters dotted the battlefield.'[38] After touring the destruction he remarked, 'There was not a single blade of grass to be seen; only burnt, black and smouldering earth throughout the entire depth of our attack – up to eight miles.'[39]

Not long after, a Soviet biplane flew over the Prokhorovka battlefield to take photographs. It was a clear beautiful day without a cloud in the sky. On the ground it was a different matter. The aircraft crew saw a flat landscape scarred by multiple tank tracks gouged in the earth and littered in tank hulks. In one shot a Panzer lay to the left in the foreground, tellingly behind it some distance away was a T-34 facing the opposite direction. The Panzer had knocked out its opponent and got past only to be destroyed as well. The distance between the two was such that the tank crews could have shouted at each other. As the plane circled round, sightseers gathered about the Panzer looked up and waved hesitantly. For a moment they worried it was the Luftwaffe come to take revenge.[40]

# 13

# FLYING TANK BUSTERS

On 5 July the Luftwaffe performed miracles supporting Model and Hoth. To the north the Soviet early warning network between 04.25 and 11.00 hours logged 800 bomber missions conducted by General Deichmann's 1st Air Division, as well as some 200 fighter sorties. Although the Soviets had early warning radar and a version for tactical air control, it took them time to recover in the air from the early morning debacle over Belgorod and Kharkov.

Understandably, Zhukov, after all their preparations, was not happy about this and made his displeasure known. The commitment of so many fighters to the abortive raid left the Red Air Force struggling on both flanks of the salient. The two fighter corps assigned to defend the salient proved wholly unable to cope. Novikov not surprisingly held their commanders personally responsible.[1]

The Luftwaffe's bombers and dive-bombers attacked the Red Army's defensive positions and its extensive minefields with gusto. Anti-personnel bomblets were also showered over foxholes, trenches and exposed troop concentrations. General Deichmann was well aware of the carnage such weapons could cause:

On one occasion units of the division employed these bombs during an attack on a wooded area where Russian troops had assembled prior to an attack. Afterwards German troops entered the wooded area without encountering resistance and found what could be termed, in the truest sense, a 'dead man's wood'.[2]

Soviet infantry also feared the Luftwaffe's loitering spotter planes. 'German gunners keep incessantly shelling us,' said one soldier. 'The bastards fire as if they can see us!' They particularly hated the two-seater Henschel reconnaissance aircraft, which they called the 'hunchback'. 'This low-speed machine has only one engine,' added the soldier, 'and hovers over our positions to check how accurately the shells are falling …'[3]

As a result German spotter planes were made a priority target for the Red Air Force; they were to be shot down on sight. In particular, according to Soviet fighter ace Ivan Kozhedub, the Luftwaffe's main eye in the sky, the Fw 189 Eule short-range reconnaissance aircraft. This was used to pinpoint Soviet tanks by dropping violet flares and was considered to be highly effective.[4]

On the ground Soviet riflemen had been trained to shoot back at the Luftwaffe. One German pilot was horrified by the hot reception he received:

> They just blazed away with everything they'd got; machine guns, rifles, even pistols. The amount of iron in the air was indescribable. I swear, they would have thrown horseshoes at us, if they could have got them off the horses in time.[5]

Soviet anti-aircraft batteries similarly poured fire into the approaching bombers. Most of the guns were well dug in and concealed with cam-ouflage. They found the slower Stukas and Heinkel bombers easiest to target as they flew by. One battery under Lieutenant Barybin claimed four German aircraft. For the Stuka pilots it took courage to fly through the death-dealing bursts of flak, whilst hoping that enemy fighters were not about to swoop down and riddle their aircraft with cannon fire.

The Soviets had spent months preparing for this day. They had built dummy airfields, aircraft, artillery and defensive positions all designed to make the Luftwaffe waste their bombs. General Pukhov had ensured that his 13th Army headquarters was backed up with numerous auxiliary telephone lines and radio stations to ensure he could exercise command at all times, no matter what the enemy threw at him.

Among the attacking Stukas was Lieutenant Diekwisch with the 1st Stuka Group, operating from airfields at Orel. He was flying with the group commanded by Captain Friedrich Lang. Their targets were Soviet defences between Ponyri and Maloarkhangelsk. 'We were well aware how important it was for our armour that the initial air attack should be effec-tive,' said Lang.[6]

The Stukas were under great pressure to perform well, even though by this stage of the war they were obsolete in a dive-bombing role. Lang appreciated that 'Our relatively weak army units had to rely fully on the support provided by the Luftwaffe and expected every aircrew to do its best'.[7] The Stukas were required to compensate for the German inferiority in heavy artillery. Many field guns had been lost at Stalingrad while others were tied up in the Kuban bridgehead in the northern Caucasus.

Diekwisch's aircraft was carrying a camera and he photographed the moment they attacked exposed Soviet tanks on a road junction. Some of the bombs fell within metres of the tanks, creating huge craters.[8] Once their bombload was gone they turned home to reload, and along with the other Stuka units conducted up to six sorties that day. The ground forces could also call on the ground attack variant of the Focke-Wulf Fw 190 fighter, which was capable of delivering fragmentation bombs.[9]

That morning German fighters were preoccupied conducting restrictive bomber and Stuka escort missions. It was not until the afternoon that the first significant dogfights began to take place with their Soviet counterparts. Notably in the north the Luftwaffe's 51st Fighter Group, which had been issued with the newer model Fw 190, gained air superiority for the first few days. When the Fw 190 first went into combat in the autumn of 1941 it was soon dubbed the 'Butcher Bird' because of its performance and agility.

The enormous air battles fought over Kursk were just as ferocious as those fought on the ground. On 5 July above Rokossovsky's Central Front the Soviet 273rd and 279th Fighter Air Divisions had risen into the sky to establish air superiority. However, when these units under Colonels Fedorov and Dementiev attempted to attack the German bomber formations they were set upon by superior numbers. The 163rd Fighter Regiment recorded, 'Each Soviet fighter was countered by six to eight enemy fighters.'[10]

Amongst these enemy fighters was Hubert Strassl. The 24-year-old flight sergeant was an Austrian-born fighter ace who had been with 51st Group since 1941.[11] Strassl liked the Fw 190 as it was a forgiving aircraft. It functioned well on rough runways thanks to its wide-track undercarriage, which meant it was ideal for forward deployment. In contrast, the Bf 109 was a complete bone-shaker on rough ground. Its narrow-track undercarriage made it unstable when taking off or landing on forward airstrips, and accidents were a common occurrence. Once it in the air it was an enemy killer but no pilot wanted to become a crash casualty on the ground.

Strassl had slid forward his canopy and risen into the air with the rest of his squadron eager for a fight. He was soon adding to his existing score with four sorties flown that afternoon and evening. During these missions he claimed fifteen enemy aircraft and the following day another ten. Such claims, while perhaps exaggerated, seemed to indicate that the Red Air Force was once again not performing very well.

There was no hiding the fact that Soviet pilots were not being aggressive enough. Colonel Dementiev was frankly ashamed of their performance and almost accused them of cowardice:

> All our fighters carry out patrols about ten kilometres to the rear of the front line, unwilling to approach the forward edge of the battle area for fear of enemy anti-aircraft fire, and thus enable enemy bombers to wheel over their targets for hours.[12]

Rudenko's pilots supporting Rokossovsky's defences only managed 520 sorties on the first day of battle, although they had more than 1,000 fighter aircraft available. It was not until the following day that Rudenko ordered a huge fighter sweep to clear the Luftwaffe prior to Soviet ground attack aircraft and bombers setting about Model's ground forces. Rudenko acknowledged that their operations were 'more orderly ... with more purpose'.[13]

It was during this Red Air Force operation that the Luftwaffe's 54th Fighter Group lost their commander. The previous day fighter ace Major Reinhard 'Seppl' Seiler had shot down five enemy aircraft, pushing his total up to ninety-seven. On 6 July he had just clocked up his 100th kill by claiming an Airacobra when he was severely wounded and forced to bale out. Although he survived, his injuries were such that he was deemed unfit for further combat.

In the south the 8th Air Corps blazed the way for Hoth's Panzers. General Dessloch, commander of Luftflotte 4, had been explicit with his instruction. 'All units, including bomber units,' he said, 'are to engage tactical targets on the battlefield, destroying pillboxes and concentrated artillery.'[14]

While the bombers ranged behind Vatutin's lines the ground attack aircraft hit his defences, especially his anti-aircraft and anti-tank batteries. At 14.45 five groups of Stukas pounded a corridor 500m deep and 3km wide for ten minutes. It would take General Krasovski until 10 July to gain Soviet air superiority over the Belgorod–Oboyan highway. Khrushchev and Vatutin were photographed, binoculars in hand, watching the air battles over the Voronezh Front. While Khrushchev looked somewhat quizzical, Vatutin was grim faced.

General Seidemann, commanding the 8th Air Corps, knew exactly what was expected of him. His orders were clear:

> The main objective is to establish air superiority over the strike force and provide close air support to the 4th Panzer Army and Army Group Kempf. Special attention should be paid in focusing efforts over the breakthrough sector of the 2nd SS Panzer Corps.[15]

The Luftwaffe had detailed Focke-Wulf fighters to intercept Soviet fighters before they reached the front line, which meant on numerous occasions Soviet ground troops were left unsupported and exposed to air attack. In total the Fw 190s alone flew 522 sorties that were countered by 917 Soviet fighter combat missions.

The growing problem faced by the Luftwaffe was that it could not maintain its exhausting sortie rate or cope with the constantly changing and diverse targeting priorities. In contrast the Red Air Force's sortie rate gradually began to increase and Soviet aircraft began to roam up to 25km behind enemy lines.

Hans-Ulrich Rudel, sat at the controls of his gull-winged dive-bomber, turned to give his gunner the thumbs up. He then opened the throttle and their Ju 87 'Gustav' began to roll along the runway and rise up into the sky. Rudel was a longstanding combat veteran who had joined one of the first Stuka squadrons. He was later assigned to the 2nd Stuka Group *Immelmann*, named after a famous First World War fighter ace. Behind him his gunner cocked his machine gun and looked alert.

Model and Manstein both placed great faith in the Luftwaffe's dive-bomber forces, but in particular the 'Cannon Birds' armed with anti-tank weapons. These comprised Meyer's Henschel Hs 129 armed with an under-fuselage 30mm cannon and two 20mm cannon in the nose, plus Rudel's Junkers Ju 87G armed with 37mm cannon. They were also to cut a path for the Panzers.

The Junkers Ju 87G, nicknamed the *Panzerknacker* (tank cracker) or *Kanaonenvogel* (Cannon Bird), was armed with a pair of under-wing Flak 18 37mm cannon with twelve rounds per gun. This proved capable of destroying all but the heaviest Soviet tanks with its tungsten-cored rounds. Even the Soviet T-34 medium tank was not immune to the 'Gustav's' firepower.

Rudel had personally checked the two cannon pods slung beneath the wings of his Stuka. Each had a long ejector chute for spent shell cases once the rounds were fired from the magazine. It was important that these were not obstructed or they could cause fouling and jam the gun. Rudel was annoyed that, although the first production Ju 87G had been issued for combat in April 1943, he was flying the only new one. The rest were converted earlier models using existing airframes. Just after Stalingrad, Rudel had been recalled to Germany to form the first experimental anti-tank Stuka unit.

While Rudel was confident in his abilities he was concerned that his fighter escort stick very close. The Stuka was no longer really viable as a dive-bomber and was better restricted to low-level attacks; it could simply not hold its own against Soviet fighters. By 1943 those deployed on the Eastern Front were being severely mauled by the Red Air Force. On the 'Gustav' variant the heavy cannon only added to the aircraft's low speed and poor manoeuvrability.

The Henschel Hs 129 introduced in 1942 was first armed with a 30mm cannon early the following year. When it entered service great things were expected of this ground attack aircraft. Like the 'Gustav' it was nick-named the tank cracker but was never available in sufficient numbers. To the dismay of Bruno Meyer and his fellow tank buster pilots, they had discovered that the Henschel's radial engines were vulnerable to dust ingestion when operating from forward airfields. Also, serviceability of the aircraft was poor and it was unreliable. At the front Meyer's mechanics had informed him that the carburettor intakes were drawing dust into the cylinders, causing excessive wear. As a result engine failures were all too commonplace. This meant of his sixty-four aircraft only about fifty were ever available for operations.[16] It was not a good start.

By far the best Soviet ground attack weapon was the Ilyushin Il-2 Sturmovik, or 'Flying Tank', which first appeared in 1941. This was designed as a low-level close-support aircraft capable of defeating enemy armour and other ground targets. Following early teething problems it developed into one of the world's most potent ground attack aircraft and was armed with cannons, machine guns, rockets and bombs including anti-tank bomblets; with good cause the Germans dubbed it the *Schlächter* or 'Slaughterer'. The twin-engine Petlyakov Pe-2 was also a very versatile Soviet dive-bomber. This was used to bomb German supply lines.

To attack the Panzers' thinner rear armour Sturmovik pilots developed the 'Circle of Death'. They would circle around the enemy armour and peel off to make individual attack runs. When the run ended, they would rejoin their formation to wait for another turn. This kept the Germans under constant fire for as long as the Il-2s had ammunition left. It was a truly terrifying experience for the Panzertruppen battened down inside their tanks. The Panzers rocked violently as the Il-2 pilots sought to hit the engine deck, which had the thinnest armour. A direct hit could tear the engine out of the hull. However, this only worked if the German fighters were kept at bay.

Initial Soviet tactics intended to stop the Panzers at Kursk proved flawed and many Sturmoviks failed to get through to their targets. The Il-2s and Pe-2s were despatched in small groups lacking fighter escort that were easily picked off. This was quickly remedied by employing regimental size formations that were easier to escort and helped to break through thanks to weight of numbers. Despite the tactical problems, Soviet aircraft still made their presence felt. 'On the second day of the attack,' said General von Mellenthin, 'many tanks fell victims to the Red Air Force – during this battle Russian aircraft operated with remarkable dash in spite of German air superiority.'[17]

Risky Soviet low-level passes were soon abandoned in favour of dive-bombing at 1,000m at 30 or 40 degree angles. Bombs and rockets were delivered just 200 to 300m from a target, then it was saturated with cannon and machine-gun fire during repeated passes. Fine tuning these tactics though took several days before they began to show real results. While the Soviet fighters and dive-bombers were kept busy, the Soviet bombers were tasked with sealing off the German advances, which involved American-supplied Boston aircraft.

Bruno Meyer was on low-level patrol with a few of his temperamental tank busters on 8 July. General Kempf's divisions had not succeeded in clearing the Red Army from a belt of woodland to the north of Belgorod; its presence inevitably posed a threat to Hoth's eastern flank and the woods provided an ideal jump off point for a Soviet counterattack. The 8th Air Corps, expecting trouble, had ordered regular air reconnaissance of the area and its dive-bombers and anti-tank aircraft were put on notice to conduct air strikes at short notice.

Meyer, glancing to his right at the open country beyond the wood-land, spotted rank after rank of enemy tanks emerging from the trees. They were supported by Soviet riflemen. He radioed Mikoyanovka, reporting the presence of an enemy tank brigade to the west of Belgorod. Meyer signalled to the others to head for base, but decided that it would take too long to arm and refuel, and that the Soviet tanks would continue their advance unimpeded.

Instead he radioed his anti-tank force and ordered them to join him immediately. In less than fifteen minutes the first of his four squadrons had arrived and, directed by Meyer, the Henschels attacked the enemy tanks from astern and abeam. At the outset the brave or foolhardy Soviet tankers thought they would weather the Luftwaffe's storm and pressed on across the open landscape.

The Henschels swooped in, firing bursts of four or five rounds from their 30mm cannons. The recoil from this weapon vibrated through the cockpit but the pilots flew on. When the first of the tanks to be hit blew up the rest hesitated. The tank drivers opened their throttles and hurtled forward as fast as they could to escape their tormentors. Some zig-zagged but that risked bumping into each other.

The attacking squadron then circled to make another run. A second squadron was soon on the way and, while the first returned to base to refuel and rearm, it attacked the enemy tanks. The third and fourth squadrons also joined the fray. The Soviet infantry accompanying the tanks were hit by Major Alfred Druschel's Fw 190 fighter-bomber group. They dived in to deliver death-dealing fragmentation bombs.[18] It was not long before the countryside was dotted with burning tanks and dead infantry. The survivors turned tail and fled back into the sanctuary of the trees.

Reporting on the engagement, General Deichmann sang the praises of Meyer's tank buster forces:

> On 8 July, during the Citadel offensive, the 4th Group of 9th Ground Attack Air Wing repelled a surprise attack by a Russian armoured brigade against the rear flank of the 4th Panzer Army. Commanded by Captain Bruno Meyer, the 4th Group comprised of four squadrons each with sixteen Hs 129 aircraft; each aircraft was fitted with an Mk 101 30mm cannon. For about an hour the Group sent relays of aircraft to attack the Russian force, which was halted and then forced to withdraw. With many Russian tanks and other vehicles on fire, the German 4th Panzer Army continued its advance without interference.[19]

While this was a significant success, frustratingly the Luftwaffe could not be everywhere at once. On 7 July the 8th Air Corps was instructed to deploy almost half of its bombers and a third of its fighters north to the Orel salient to help Model's struggling 9th Army. This move inevitably weakened the Luftwaffe's efforts against the Soviet 2nd Air Army around Belgorod. It also weakened support for Hausser's SS Panzer Corps.

On the fourth day of the battle Hubert Strassl was in action to the south of Ponyri. Diving and weaving, he outmanoeuvred his adversaries, shooting down three more Soviet aircraft. Suddenly four Lavochkin fighters were bearing down on him and throttling forward he found himself losing height. One of his pursuers opened up with their guns, tearing apart one of his wings. Strassl had little choice but to bale out at less than 1,000ft, but tragically his parachute failed to open at such a low altitude and he plummeted to his death. In the first five days the 51st Fighter Group lost another four pilots. Fighter ace Major Rudolf Resch was also lost south of Ponyri on 11 July.

Having revised their tactics the Red Air Force's Il-2 and Pe-2 dive-bombers were soon wreaking havoc and destruction on the exposed Panzers. General von Mellenthin recalled:

> They swarmed over the battlefield from morning to night. Their heavily armoured Sturmoviks specialised in low-flying attacks and their pilots certainly showed plenty of dash and courage. Their night bombers operated singularly, and their main object seemed to be to disturb our sleep.[20]

Even Zhukov was moved to grudgingly note, 'Our air force managed to be considerably more effective, striking at tactical battle arrays and enemy columns, which were regrouping during the fighting.'[21]

Amongst those flying escort for the Soviet ground attack aircraft was Frenchman Major Jean Tulasne. He commanded the volunteer Free French Normandy unit flying Yak fighters. From 10–14 July they conducted 112 operational sorties and in that time claimed seventeen enemy aircraft for the loss of six pilots. Tulasne was amongst them. He was leading nine Yaks protecting Il-2 Sturmoviks when they were pounced on by a superior number of enemy fighters. Swamped by some thirty Fw 190s, they stood little chance of escape and were gunned down.

The Soviets devoted more than a third of their resources to gaining and holding control of the skies. While the Luftwaffe's efforts to support Citadel gradually got weaker the Red Air Force grew relentlessly stronger. By the end of 12 July the Germans had managed more than 16,000 sorties, the Soviets almost 22,700.

General von Mellenthin grudgingly accepted that the Red Air Force was improving, but he would not concede it was better than the Luftwaffe:

Certainly the degree of co-operation between air and ground forces kept improving all the time, and their technical inferiority gradually disappeared. Tactically they were always inferior, and their pilots were no match for our own.[22]

At this point Zhukov, supported by General Gromov's 1st and General Naumenko's 15th Air Armies, launched his counteroffensive with the Western and Bryansk Fronts. These were joined by General Rudenko's 16th Air Army on 15 July when the Central Front went over to the offensive. In just five days the 15th Air Army flew some 4,800 sorties while the 16th managed 5,000, more than half of which were conducted by Pe-2s and Sturmoviks against retreating German troops. The Luftwaffe was firmly on the defensive and all it could do was cover the ground forces.

# 14

# THE ZOO DISAPPOINTS

By late June 1943 around 200 rebuilt Panthers had been issued to 39th Panzer Regiment von Lauchert and the 1st Panzer Battalion of *Grossdeutschland* to create the 10th Panzer Brigade. This was assigned to 4th Panzer Army's 48th Panzer Corps. On paper the Panthers of this brigade formed the single most powerful armoured unit of all the Panzer forces committed at Kursk. For the Red Army this was a worrying development.

On unloading from the trains at Borisovka two Panthers immediately suffered engine fires and were write-offs. This was a warning of things to come. By 5 July, when Operation Citadel commenced, there were 184 operational Panthers but within two days this had fallen to just forty. Guderian's 'problem child' continued to be a big challenge.

Tank driver Gerd Küster felt that the preparation of the 51st and 52nd Panzer Battalions was a complete and utter shambles:

> We arrived for the battle with just two hours to spare. We were extremely tired and had to spend all the time available to us arming and servicing our Panther. We had received our tank just a week before and were still learning about its quirks. We were impressed with what we had learned but nervous as we had spent so little time training in her ...[1]

Küster and his crewmates were aware of some of the tank's shortcomings, but did not really understand its capabilities or limitations:

We knew all about the reliability issues – and were very aware that the engine could burst into flames – but what worried us most was a lack of 'feel' for the tank. How it would manoeuvre, where it could and couldn't go and the support that we would receive from the infantry and the air ...[2]

General von Mellenthin, Chief of Staff of 48th Panzer Corps, which had more than 300 Panzers and sixty assault guns available, noted '"*Grossdeutschland*" was a very strong [Panzergrenadier] division with a special organisation. It mustered about 180 tanks, of which 80 were part of a "Panther Detachment" commanded by Lieutenant Colonel von Lauchert, and the remainder were in the Panzer regiment.'[3]

Lauchert only reached *Grossdeutschland's* assembly area north of Moshchenoye on late 4 July. This meant that he missed the division's opening attack at 04.00 hours the following day. It rapidly became clear that, just as Guderian had warned, the Panthers and their crews were still not ready for combat.

When the 51st Panzer Battalion went into action Gerd Küster and his comrades were not at their best: He recalled with some bewilderment, 'I spent the night [4–5 July] refuelling, lugging shells and trying to overcome a steering problem ... We went into battle with weary eyes, splitting head-aches and not the faintest clue what the battlefield had in store for us.'[4]

Frustratingly, at 08.15 Lauchert's Panthers lurched forward only to lose at least four tanks to fuel leak fires. By this stage there must have been much swearing and cursing from the crews. Nonetheless, when 51st Battalion, under Captain Heinrich Meyer and 52nd, under Major Gerhard Tebe, finally deployed they covered an area some 500m wide and around 3km long.

Thanks to Soviet artillery, which had set fire to the rolling cornfields, *Grossdeutschland's* engineers were slow in breaching the Red Army's extensive and clearly deadly defensives. As a result, when the Panthers reached the 80m wide Berezovyi Ravine they were immediately held up. A number rumbled down to follow a cleared path, only to have their drives fail trying to get out the other side. Once again reliability was caus-ing operational problems.

In total about twenty-five Panthers found themselves immobilised in the ravine due to breakdowns, mines and the mud. As the tension rose so did the stress levels of the beleaguered crews, whose sense of annoyance was escalating. Desperately the drivers tried to back up but the Panthers did not want to reverse up the muddy banks. Engines began to overheat and drive sprocket teeth were damaged. When some of the Panthers attempted to shift westward they promptly ran into a Soviet minefield, causing yet more delay.

It was not until early afternoon that a better crossing had been established 1.5km to the west and thirty Panthers, fifteen Panzer Mk IVs and four battalions of infantry finally traversed Berezovyi Ravine. At Cherkasskoye the Panthers helped mop up Soviet resistance and thwarted a counterattack. The Panther Ausf D, lacking a ball-mounted hull machine gun (though a crude weapon port was provided), in the heat of battle had to rely on the coaxial machine gun mounted in the turret next to the main L/70 75mm armament for defence against infantry attack.

The Panther's performance on that opening day of the Battle of Kursk had been extremely disappointing. Mechanical failures aside, it showed up the lack of battalion level training and highlighted poor communication with the chain of command. On 6 July their performance was little better, with the regiment getting lost.

Near Alekseyevka *Grossdeutschland* ran into a T-34 tank regiment that was well dug in, thereby presenting a very low profile. Some 2km east of Cherkasskoye the Panthers blundered into Soviet mines and T-34s of the 14th Tank Regiment opened up on the Panthers' flanks at ranges of 1,000–1,200m. A platoon leader in 5th Company, 52nd Panzer Battalion by the name of Sergeant Gerhard Brehme had the dubious honour of commanding one of the very first Panthers to be knocked out by a T-34. Eventually the Panther's superior firepower and gunnery enabled Lauchert to extract his forces from the ambush. Once more though this episode highlighted a complete lack of experience on the part of the crews.

By the end of 6 July, 39th Panzer Regiment had lost nineteen tanks, having claimed only around a dozen T-34s. All in all it was not an auspicious start to the Panther's combat career. The following day, while trying to take Dubrova, the Panthers once again presented their side armour to the enemy, this time to dug in T-34s of the 16th Tank Regiment and 85mm guns of the 756th Anti-tank Battalion. When they ran into a minefield east of Syrtsev some fifteen Panthers were hit. Once more the Panther's L/70 gun got the better of the T-34s but at a cost of twenty-seven Panthers knocked out that day. The battlefield became known as the 'Panther cemetery at Dubrova'.

Guderian wanted to see first-hand how the Panther was performing and his worst fears were soon realised:

I visited both the attacking fronts during the time between 10th and 15th of July; I went first to the southern and then the northern area, and talked to the tank commanders on the spot. I there gained an insight into the course that events were taking, the lack of our men's experience in the attack and the weakness of our equipment. My fears concerning the premature commitment of the Panthers were justified.[5]

He reported the following regarding the Panther's disappointing debut:

Due to enemy action and mechanical breakdowns, the combat strength sank rapidly during the first few days. By the evening of 10 July there were only 10 operational Panthers in the front line. 25 Panthers had been lost as total write-offs (23 were hit and burnt and two had caught fire during the approach march). 100 Panthers were in need of repair (56 were damaged by hits and mines and 44 by mechanical breakdown). 60 percent of the mechanical breakdowns could be easily repaired. Approximately 40 Panthers had already been repaired and were on the way to the front. About 25 still had not been recovered by the repair service … On the evening of 11 July, 38 Panthers were operational, 31 were total write-offs and 131 were in need of repair. A slow increase in the combat strength is observable. The large number of losses by hits (81 Panthers up to 10 July) attests to the heavy fighting.

Guderian must have been deeply vexed at the breakdown rate, especially when the faults were only minor things. Combat losses were one thing but constant mechanical failures were clearly unacceptable.

Extravagantly, Colonel von Lauchert claimed that his Panthers destroyed 263 Soviet tanks from 5 to 14 July at ranges of 1,500–3,000m. In reality his command was ambushed three times by dug-in T-34s, often on the flanks, at ranges of less than 1,200m, which casts extreme doubt on the veracity of his claims. Although Hitler had categorically instructed that no Panthers were to fall into the Red Army's hands, seven were captured on 19 July and Guderian's fears came to fruition.

Once again the Tiger proved impervious to even the most determined attacker. After his opening engagement at Kursk, Tiger commander Will Fey recalled, 'We got out, smoked a cigarette, and marvelled that we had no losses. Both our machine guns were shot up. Other than that, we sustained only minor damage.'[6] Time and time again he and his crew engaged superior enemy numbers, but it was only a matter to time before they were overwhelmed. His tank came under attack from half a dozen T-34s and managed to destroy half of them:

> Then we heard an explosion and had no time to gather our wits. Headfirst, we dove out of the hatch, rolled backward, and pressed against the tracks. The long barrels of the enemy tank platoon sank hit after hit into our maimed Panzer, but miraculously it did not catch fire.[7]

While the Tiger proved a great success at Kursk, inflicting staggering losses on the Soviet tanks, there were simply too few of them. The 1st SS Panzer Regiment destroyed ninety tanks in the space of three hours on one day alone but still the enemy kept coming. While the crews now knew how to get the most out of the Tiger this did not make up for their limited numbers. Once the Soviet tankers closed in on them the Tigers' advantage of long range and thick armour was lost.

Likewise, at long range the Ferdinand proved to be deadly and tore great holes in the ranks of Soviet armour. T-34 tanks were reportedly knocked out at a range of more than 3 miles. While the Ferdinands of Major Steinwachs' battalion alone destroyed 320 Soviet tanks for the loss of thirteen of their number and the regiment as a whole claimed 502 tanks and another 100 vehicles, its' shortcomings rapidly became apparent. Many of them broke down, became stranded or were simply overrun by Russian infantry. After just four days of battle almost half of the eighty-nine Ferdinands committed to the attack were out of service due to technical problems or mine damage to the tracks and suspension.

Guderian was equally disappointed with the Ferdinand:

> Also the ninety Porsche Tigers, which were operating with Model's Army, were incapable of close-range fighting since they lacked sufficient ammunition for their guns, and this defect was aggravated by the fact that they possessed no machine-gun. Once they had broken into the enemy's infantry zone they literally had to go quail shooting with cannons. They did not manage to neutralise, let alone destroy, the enemy rifles and machine guns, so that the infantry was unable to follow up behind them. By the time they reached the Russian artillery they were on their own.[8]

Major Noak's crew had resorted to firing their MG34 machine gun down the barrel of the main armament in a desperate bid to keep the Soviet infantry at bay. It was a farcical situation. The few remaining Ferdinands were recalled to the factory and belatedly upgraded with a hull machine gun. Renamed 'the Elefant', they were then packed off to Italy and played no further part in any of the significant tank battles. Porsche was never asked to produce any more.

Following the Soviet counteroffensive at Belgorod the 52nd Panzer Battalion, with only twenty-seven operational Panthers and 109 under repair, was obliged to blow up seventy-two at Tomarovka and retreat. By the time they reached Akhtyrka just nine Panthers remained operational. A subsequent report on 20 July 1943 indicated forty-one Panthers were operational, eighty-five repairable, sixteen severely damaged and needing repair in Germany, fifty-six burnt out due to enemy action, and two that had been destroyed by engine fires. By 11 August 1943 the numbers of total write-offs had risen to 156, with only nine operational. The regiment was a shambles.

Major General von Mellenthin was dismissive of the Panther and felt it had done little to help 48th Panzer Corps or the elite *Grossduetschland*. 'The Panthers did not come up to expectations,' he complained, 'they were easily set ablaze, the oil and gasoline feeding systems were inadequately protected, and the crews were insufficiently trained.'[9] It is self-evident that the Panther's baptism of fire at Kursk, against Guderian's wishes, had been a complete and utter disaster. Mellenthin summed up Guderian's frustration after Kursk saying, 'The Panthers were still in their infancy and were a failure.'[10]

It was not long before Soviet sightseers came to view the carnage. All was quiet now that the battle was over and a group of men had come to view a stricken tank. The Germans had been driven from the battlefield so they were relaxed wearing side caps rather than helmets, nor were they wearing any field gear. Two of them were tankers or mechanics in their one-piece overalls, while the rest were in the standard Red Army trousers and tunics. They stood for a moment gazing up at their fallen foe, it was one of Hitler's new tanks, a Panther Ausf D. It lay abandoned on the open steppe, halted not far from a single lane track that led to a distant farm.

An almighty explosion had lifted the rear of the heavily armoured turret clear of the hull. It now rested at an awkward angle, revealing the fighting compartment, which had been obliterated by the blast. Tilting downwards, the front of the torn off turret rested on its mantlet on the right side of the hull. The barrel sloped down to the ground, the muzzle brake jammed against the hard-packed soil. Two sections of track shoes were strewn on the ground but these were discarded spares as the tank had not thrown its tracks.

Five of the men eagerly clambered on to the back of the tank. Their immediate source of interest was the engine compartment. One hopped on to the turret roof and, holding on to the commander's cupola, peered down on the engine deck, where two of his comrades were kneeling with two others standing either side. At the back of the tank, still on the ground, the three remaining men rummaged through the tank's left-hand storage pannier but found nothing of interest. None of them took any notice as a ninth man took a photograph to record the fate of Panther '312' for posterity.

Elsewhere they also took photographs of '434', which had once belonged to the 51st Panzer Battalion. Panther '433', captured intact, was hauled off for closer technical examination. Another completely decapitated Panther was inspected by an armed squad of Soviet infantry. Not only had the turret been ripped from the hull turret ring, the top and sides of the turret had been torn from its base plate. So much for the invincibility of the Nazis' new battle tank.

A captured German staff car hurtled down the road, its six Soviet occupants almost shaken to death. Having held the Germans at bay on the northern salient, inevitably it was not long before Soviet intelligence officers were hard at work assessing the new German weapons that had fallen into their hands. The car came to a stop, throwing up a cloud of dust. Just off to their right at the bottom of the bank was what they had come to see. The men climbed out of their vehicle, cameras and notebooks in hand.

Before them was one of the slab-sided Ferdinands, but with a difference. It had suffered such an enormous internal explosion that its massive superstructure had been blown skyward, flipping upside down as it did so and landing back with an almighty crash on top of the hull. Basic intelligence could be gleaned from this vehicle but again the interior was a complete mess. In contrast, Ferdinand '501', apart from throwing its left track, had been captured undamaged in a partially hull-down position. The crew had broken out their tools and the spare track shoes ready to conduct repairs, but with no way of defending themselves against marauding enemy infantry they had chosen to flee on foot instead. As a result '501' was quickly placed under armed guard ready for the Red Army's removal and technical analysis.

The field telephone rang in Rokossosky's HQ and a staff officer gave him a shout. After a brief discussion the marshal could not help getting involved in the sightseeing. He rounded up all his staff and they drove off with the air of a school outing. Parked under a tree stood a Ferdinand; like '501' it had shed its left track, exposing the drive sprocket and leaving it stranded. Led by Rokossovsky, about a dozen officers gathered around the beached monster. He climbed up on to the glacis plate and marvelled at the vehicle's tough armour plating. The front of the hull had received a direct hit, while two had been scored on the front of the superstructure to the right of the gun barrel. However, all three hits had been deflected, making barely any impression on the armour. Rokossovsky and his officers quickly came to the conclusion that the Ferdinand was just like the Tiger; at long range it was deadly, but once the Red Army's tanks had closed it struggled to escape its attackers.

Zhukov was equally dismissive of the impact of Guderian's zoo: 'This time the enemy had particularly relied on his Tiger and Panther tanks and the Ferdinand assault guns, apparently believing that these systems would stun the Soviet troops and they would not withstand their ramming impact. But this did not occur.'[11] Rotmistrov had little time for Guderian's zoo either, remarking, 'At the close of the battle, the Tiger tanks and Panther tank-destroyers – they were the pride of the Wehrmacht – were turned into heaps of twisted metal.'[12]

His heroic tankers had killed these enemy tanks from incredibly close ranges: 'We knew their vulnerable spots, so our tank crews were firing at their sides. The shells fired from very short distances tore large holes in the armour of the Tigers. Ammunition exploded inside them, and turrets weighing many tons were flung yards away.'[13]

The official Soviet account pointed out that the fighting conditions had favoured the Red Army, helping to neutralise the more powerful Panzers:

The close combat deprived the Tigers of the advantages which their powerful gun and thick armour conferred, and they were successfully shot up at close range by the T-34s. Immense numbers of tanks were mixed up all over the battlefield; there was neither time nor space to disengage and reform ranks. Fired at short range, shells penetrated front and side armour. There were frequent explosions as ammunition blew up … On the scorched black earth, smashed tanks were blazing like torches.[14]

In London, Churchill had watched the battle unfold with interest and noted, 'They gained no advantages to make up for their heavy losses, and the new "Tiger" tanks, on which they had counted for success, had been mauled by the Russian artillery.'[15] When Hitler was told that the Ferdinand and Tiger had fallen prey to Soviet anti-tank guns and dug-in T-34 tanks he flew into a rage. 'This all comes from not carrying out my orders!' he screamed, beating his fists upon the table.[16] Guderian's zoo had failed to win the day.

# PART FOUR

# STALIN STRIKES BACK

# 15

# VICTORY AT OREL

Hitler's generals feared it would happen and that it was only really a matter of time. While the fighting for Ponyri and Prokhorovka was still raging, Popov's Bryansk Front and Sokolovsky's Western Front launched Operation Kutuzov on 12 July. It was intended to drive Model from the Orel salient and trap as much of 2nd Panzer Army and 9th Army as possible. In the centre the plan was that Popov's 3rd, 61st and 63rd Armies would push directly west from the area of Novosil over the Susha River, cutting through the junction of the two German armies. This would enable Popov's 3rd Guards Tank Army to pass through Orel.

At the same time, to the north Sokolovsky's 11th Guards Army was to thrust south from the Belev area to crush the left shoulder of the German salient and allow Popov's 4th Tank Army to push through and cut off 2nd Panzer Army. On their left flank the 61st Army would attack Bolhov and push to the north-west of Orel. On the far right flank Sokolovsky's 1st Guards Army would head for Karachev and the 50th Army for Zhisdra.

The Soviet pincer would be completed by Rokossovsky's Central Front attacking the German right shoulder and pushing toward Komy. The problem he had was that his forces were regrouping and would not be ready until 15 July. This was to have an unforeseen benefit in that Model shifted a number of divisions northward to help stop Sokolovsky and Popov.

In principal Kutuzov was sound, but it had its flaws. Unfortunately Zhukov was not on hand to help as he was with Vatutin. He had been involved in the planning but the operation had not been as fine-tuned as some might have liked. Furthermore, Stalin was keen to get going and capitalise on Model's defeat as soon as possible.

The Soviet generals looking at their situation maps should have agreed that Sokolovsky ought to deliver the main blow heading for Karachev and Bryansk. The other two fronts would then simply conduct spoiling attacks to tie the defenders down. Once Sokolovsky was near Karachev, Rokossovsky could have attacked west of Komy and linked up with him, creating an enormous pocket of trapped Germans. Such a move would deliver a decisive blow.

Instead, Popov's frontal assault on well-prepared positions would not be easy and Rokossovsky's men were worn out. Plus, by attacking east of Komy his troops would run into some of Model's thickest defences. Rybalko's 3rd Guards Tank Army should not have been committed against Orel but rather supported Bagramyan's southern thrust alongside 4th Tank Army under Lieutenant General Badanov. It would be a long and hard slog to get to Orel.

After the fighting at Prokhorovka a lack of spare tanks meant some crews were redeployed to other units. Vasiliy Bryukhov and his friend, fellow tank commander Kolya Maximov, were sent to join Butkov's 1st Tank Corps on the Bryansk Front, which was tasked with liberating Orel. 'Kolya and I convinced our commanders not to split us up,' said Bryukhov, 'and we were sent together to the 1st Battalion of the 159th Brigade of this corps.'[1]

Frustratingly for Model and Kluge, their intelligence, derived from photo-reconnaissance and radio intercepts, had long warned them what to expect. Model's chain of command had been greatly eased as he had also been placed in command of 2nd Panzer Army following General Rudolf Schmidt's dismissal. In total he had half a dozen corps defending the Orel salient but his two Panzer corps were both tied up with Rokossovsky's Central Front.

The problem they had was a lack of resources to conduct counterattacks. Nonetheless, they had prepared considerable defences in depth, particularly in General Lothar Rendulic's 35th Corps sector. This was where the Soviet 63rd Army was to launch its assault. The Germans constructed more than half a dozen defensive lines that stretched all the way back to Bryansk, with the final one anchored on the Desna. Model knew he was playing for time whilst his men tried to complete the Hagen Line, which stretched right across the opening of the Orel salient. He also needed to keep the Red Air Force off the railheads at Bryansk because these were being used to replenish the army and the Luftwaffe following Citadel.

For the Soviet forces attacking directly toward Orel, their best hope was that their firepower would smash Model's defences to smithereens. General Sobennikov was in awe of their gunners:

> There had never been such a heavy concentration of Russian guns as against these defences; in many places the firepower was ten times heavier than at Verdun. The German minefields were so thick and widespread that as many mines as possible had to be blown up by the super-barrage, in order to reduce Russian casualties in the subsequent breakthrough.[2]

Kutuzov was preceded by an almighty artillery and air bombardment. Along the Bryansk Front more than 4,000 field guns and mortars let rip. Some fifteen minutes before the ground troops went in, Gromov and Naumenko's air armies dropped 3,500 high-explosive and fragmentation bombs on enemy artillery positions and strongpoints. The 11th Guards Army under General Bagramyan, reinforced by a number of tank units, surged forward, supported by the 4th Tank Army and the 11th Army.

Elsewhere events were having a direct impact on the fighting around the Kursk salient. On 10 July 1943 Hitler had been greeted with the news that the British and Americans had invaded Sicily. Although the Italian garrison was bolstered by tough German units, after Stalingrad Hitler had no faith in the fighting capabilities of the Italian Army. What this seemed to indicate to Hitler and his generals was that the Allies intended to open their long-awaited second front in Italy or the Balkans, not France. This suited Hitler as it would be easier to fight a defensive war in either regions, but it would mean a major redeployment of his forces.

German propaganda tried to hide what was going on. 'Low point of our mood on Friday,' wrote Jew Victor Klemperer on Sunday, 11 July in Dresden, 'Germany announces great successes at Kursk; high point on Saturday: Allied landing in Sicily.' He then added with a more despondent air, 'Will it be a second Dieppe, or will the Allies succeed this time ...'[3]

The very day after Kutuzov started in something of a panic on 13 July Hitler summoned both Kluge and Manstein to Rastenburg for an emergency meeting. Neither can have been very pleased as they were expecting a major Soviet counteroffensive at any moment. All was doom and gloom, everything they had fought for was slipping away. Manstein recalled, 'Field Marshal von Kluge reported that 9th Army was making no further headway and that he was having to deprive it of all its mobile forces to check the enemy's deep incursions into the Orel salient.'[4]

It was then that Hitler dropped his bombshell, as Manstein observed:

He opened the conference by announcing that the Western Allies had landed in Sicily and that the situation there had taken an extremely serious turn. The Italians were not even attempting to fight, and the island was likely to be lost ... the next step might well be a landing in the Balkans or Lower Italy.[5]

Looking at his field marshals, Hitler declared:

I must prevent that. And so I need divisions for Italy and the Balkans. And since they can't be taken from any other place, apart from the transfer of 1st Panzer Division from France to the Peloponnese, they have to be released from the Kursk Front. Therefore I am forced to stop Citadel.[6]

For a moment both field marshals were dumbfounded. 'Thus the very thing had come to pass of which I had warned Hitler in May,' said Manstein bitterly.[7] Kluge was supportive of this decision, saying, 'There could be no question of continuing with Citadel or resuming the operation at a later date.'[8] Manstein though was aghast:

I pointed out that the battle was now at its culminating point, and that to break it off at this moment would be tantamount to throwing a victory away. On no account should we let go of the enemy until the mobile reserves he had committed were completely beaten.[9]

However, Hitler would not be swayed, Citadel was off.

It was plain to the world that Hitler was taking a beating at Kursk. In Bucharest Mihail Sebastian was listening intently to the German news broadcasts. He was not fooled by the use of the word 'struggles', noting: 'It is the vocabulary of last winter.'[10]

Red Army progress was slow even when Rokossovsky joined the fight and his forces struggled to make much impression from their jump-off points at Olkhovatka, Ponyri and Malaorkhangelsk. By 18 July he and Popov had only achieved very modest gains, though Sokolovsky made better progress and was about 20km from Karachev. Despite this General Shtemenko of the General Staff recalled, 'Stalin was in a joyously jubilant mood'[11] because Hitler's summer offensive in the Orel–Kursk sector had completely collapsed.

The day before the gallant Bruno Meyer was almost killed; while on a mission in his Henschel tank buster he tangled with a Yak-9 fighter. Although his Hs 129 was a stable gun platform and provided good pilot protection, the French Gnome-Rhône engines were woefully underpowered. His plane was riddled with holes and he was unable to escape from the much faster Soviet aircraft. His opponent seemed to know the weak points on his aircraft and was firing accurately.

Taking a split second decision to bail out, Meyer yanked on the canopy release lever. The canopy shot off up into his airflow and hurtled backwards, crashing into the engine of the pursuing Yak. This undoubtedly saved his life. The impact was such that the enemy fighter caught fire and the pilot was forced to make an emergency landing. Meyer, once safely on the ground nearby, ran to claim his unexpected prize. To his surprise he found Lieutenant Antonina Lebedeva, a female pilot, dead at the controls.[12] There was nothing he could do for her.

Lebedeva's friend, Lieutenant Klavdiya Blinova, was also shot down.[13] She was part of a group of four Yak fighters escorting half a dozen Sturmoviks when they were intercepted by fourteen Fw 190s. One of the first to go was Blinova's escort leader, Senior Lieutenant Kuznetsov, who was killed in the ensuing dogfight.[14] A burst of cannon fire tore her aircraft to pieces. 'For some time, I was falling down together with the cockpit wreckage still squeezing tight the useless control column,' she said. 'I was not afraid. There was just one thought then: survive, survive!' Blinova struggled desperately to escape the remains of her aircraft and managed to jump free. Her parachute opened and she drifted down to be taken prisoner. On being asked her name she said she was Antonina Lebedeva.[15]

Meyer's Henschels, supported by Lieutenant Colonel Kupfer's Stukas, once more came to the rescue of the army on 19 July. A Soviet armoured brigade had moved to block the Bryansk–Orel railway at Khotynets to the east of Karachev. This threatened the only supply and reinforcement route for Kluge's 2nd Panzer Army and the 9th Army. It also endangered the entire German position at Orel. Model had no reserves available so it fell to the Luftwaffe to try and retrieve the situation.

To seal off this breakthrough the Luftwaffe summoned every available bomber, fighter-bomber and anti-tank aircraft. This was to be its last major concerted effort before its strength was dispersed across the Eastern Front. Many of the Luftwaffe units were close at hand, flying from Karachev. Meyer and Kupfer spent the whole day pursuing the scattered enemy tanks as they withdrew northwards. The Soviets were sent reeling, the Luftwaffe having single-handedly stabilised the situation, at least temporarily.

For the next two days the Luftwaffe maintained the security of the railway without any help from ground forces. Model was suitably impressed and grateful, signalling, 'For the first time in military history the Luftwaffe has succeeded, without support from the ground forces, in annihilating a tank brigade which had broken through.'[16]

Victor Klemperer wrote in his diary, 'Such a tortuous military bulletin that one could read the critical situation between the lines ... The military situation – I am listening to the radio again now – appears very depressing for Germany.'[17]

It was at this point that the partisans were called into all-out action. Moscow instructed on 14 July that the 'Rail War' should commence. Six days later they struck at the railways in the Bryansk, Orel and Gomel areas. During the night of 20–21 July they blew up some 5,800 rails; by the end of September they had destroyed another 11,200.[18] These attacks inevitably disrupted the withdrawal of German personnel and equipment from the occupied towns and cities.

Stalin was buoyed by the General Staff report that had been submitted to him on the night of 24 July. According to their figures, during 5–23 July Hitler's forces lost 70,000 men killed, 2,900 tanks destroyed or disabled, along with 195 self-propelled guns. In addition they claimed 1,392 German planes, more than 5,000 motor vehicles and 844 field guns.[19] Hitler's two Army Groups actually recorded 50,000 casualties for this period. In Stalin's mind a fundamental milestone had just been passed.

Shtemenko and Antonov were summoned to draft Stalin's congratulatory order of the day. When they had finished reading their first effort Stalin dictated an important addition with evident pride: 'Thus the legend that in a summer offensive the Germans are always successful, and that Soviet troops are compelled to retreat, is refuted.'[20] The Wehrmacht's reputation for being invincible had been truly overturned. He then looked at his generals and said, 'That must be mentioned, Goebbels and all the Germans have been maintaining that legend ever since the winter defeat at Moscow.'[21]

The following day Stalin got even more good news. The Axis alliance was coming apart. On 25 July Mussolini was ousted by Marshal Badoglio and that opened the prospect of the Italians defecting. German troops would definitely be needed to occupy northern Italy to stop the Allies pushing up into Austria and the Balkans. 'Palermo fallen – the Italian report candid,' wrote Victor Klemperer. 'The German one so obscure that one can draw conclusions about the reliability of German reports from the Eastern Front – the Russian offensive in the East is continuing.'[22]

When Kluge met Hitler on 26 July, the Führer told him that in order to free up troops for deployment to Italy he and Manstein must fall back to the Hagen Line on the Dnieper. Field Marshal von Kluge was dismayed, pointing out that he would be unable to 'fall back to a position which is practically non-existent'.[23] He stated he would be obliged to continue fighting east of the river while the half-started defences were completed. Until that time he could not release any of his forces. When Hitler pressed him Kluge said, 'The earliest time for occupying the Hagen Line would be in about four weeks.'[24] They did not have a month and Hitler was annoyed by this unhelpful response, stating, 'Well, we just can't wait as long as that. We must free troops before then.'[25] Hitler's generals were sceptical that the ill-prepared Hagen defences would hold.

Rybalko had still not got to Orel but the Red Army had taken a swathe of territory, eliminating the Germans' first layer of defences. One of the first towns to be liberated was Mtsensk to the north-east of Orel; it was in a terrible state. The surrounding countryside had not been cultivated and thistles and weeds had taken over. War correspondent Vasily Grossman, heading south, saw, 'In Mtsensk, grass growing in the ruins of houses, the blue sky was looking through the empty eye sockets of windows and torn-off roofs'.[26] It had once been home to 20,000 people, but when journalist Alexander Werth arrived with the Red Army there were just 200.

Although the Germans had departed, danger lurked everywhere. The surrounding area was riddled with mines. Werth and his companions were greeted in town by a colonel: 'He talked of new delayed-action mines found in German dug-outs. Contraptions in which acid eats through the metal; some take two months to blow up. And there were also booby-traps, plenty of them.'[27]

The summer weather only added to the soldiers' woes, as Evgeni Bessonov recounted:

It was unbearably hot on those August days of 1943 in the Orel area, and we mostly moved on trucks during the night. There was a huge amount of dust on the roads, and our feet sank into it as if it were cotton. By morning we were all covered with [a] thick layer of dust.[28]

Once the Red Army was pushing on Orel the Red Air Force began dropping leaflets calling on Russian collaborators, be they policemen or

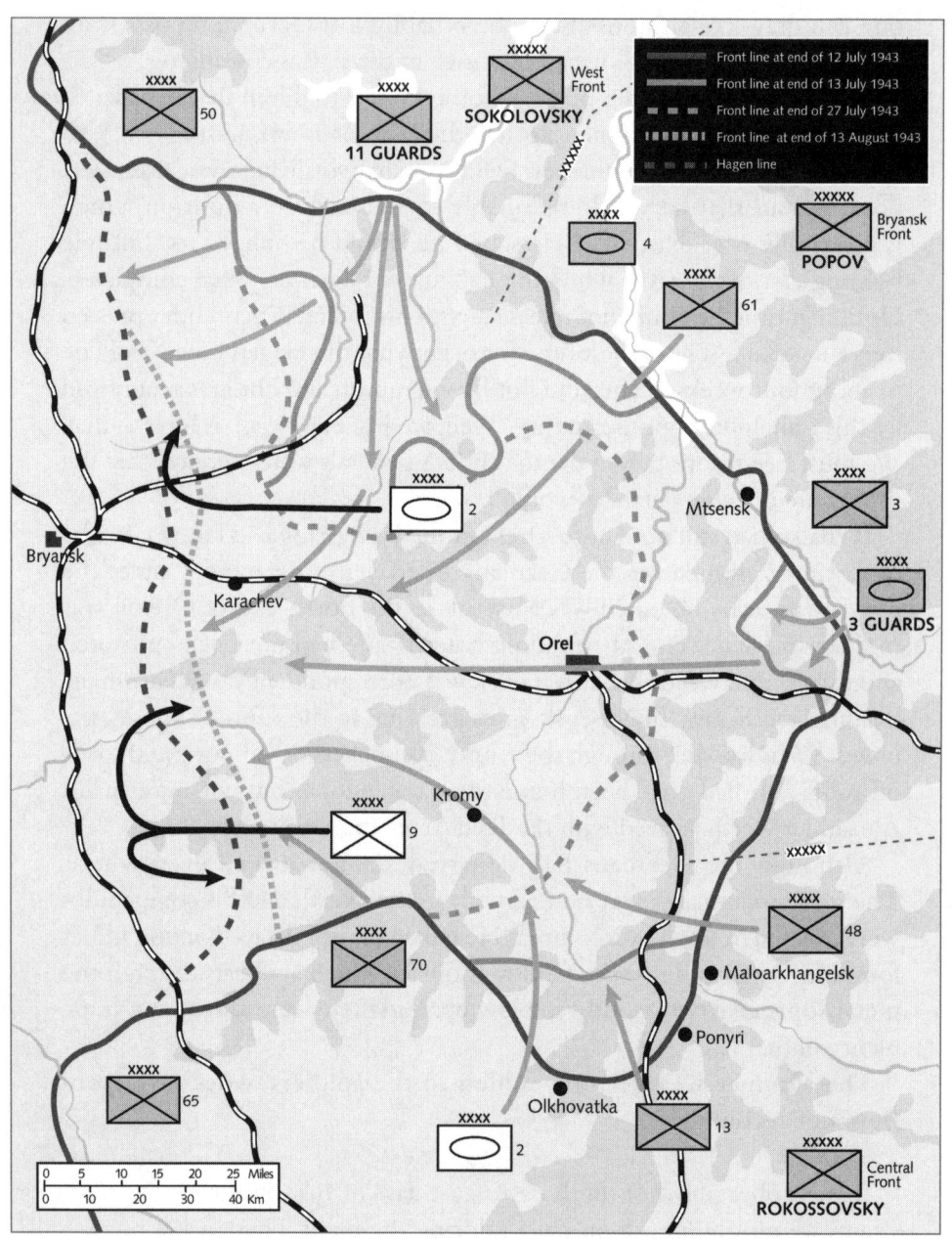

Operation Kutuzov, 12 July–18 August 1943.

local militia members, to join the partisans and turn their guns on the Germans. Few accepted this offer as they doubted they would be granted a long-lasting amnesty. Those who had taken part in the Germans' brutal anti-partisan operations knew they could expect little leniency.

Much to his fury, Hitler had no choice but authorise a fighting withdrawal to the half-completed Hagen Line in front of Bryansk. However, three of Popov's units – the 5th, 129th and 380th Rifle Divisions – did not liberate Orel until 5 August. Despite General Gorbatov's 3rd Army doing a good job, it was not strong enough to trap the German forces in the Orel area and was reliant on Sokolovsky to cut them off.

'Last night the Germans withdrew altogether,' wrote Nikolai Belov. 'This morning we arrived in the western outskirts of the city. The whole of Orel is in flames. The population is greeting us with exceptional joy. The women are weeping with joy.'[29]

General Sobennikov was one of the first into Orel, along with an armoured car broadcasting patriotic music:

Yes, I drove into Orel in the morning of the 5th. You can imagine the dawn, and the houses around still blazing, and our guns and tanks driving into town, covered with flowers, and the loud speaker bellowing The Holy War, and old women and children running among the soldiers, and pressing flowers into their hands and kissing them.[30]

Resistance was not over though as German tanks and self-propelled guns prowled the streets. In some of the buildings German sub-machine-gunners and snipers remained behind. General Gurtiev was gunned down on his arrival.

Grossman also got himself to Orel:

We reached Orel on the afternoon of 5 August by the Moscow high-way … Almost all villages between Mtsensk and Orel were burned … Red-cheeked girls, traffic controllers, were standing at all the crossroads, smartly waving their red and green little flags. A day or two would pass, and Orel would start coming back to life …[31]

The city before the war had some 114,000 inhabitants; after almost two years of German occupation there were just 30,000 remaining. Werth observed:

Many had been murdered; many had been hanged in the public square – that very square where there were now new graves of the first Russian tank crew that had broken into Orel, and also of General Gurtiev, of Stalingrad fame, who had been killed here the morning the Russians fought their way into the city.[32]

Before withdrawing the Germans systematically destroyed anything of use in Orel; in particular they tore up the railway line. Werth, who had been at Stalingrad only six months earlier, had seen the damage there, which could be repaired. In contrast, at Orel he noted, 'The Germans had used a special engine which, as it went along, destroyed both rails and sleepers. To use any railways in these newly-liberated territories, the Russians had to rebuild them practically from scratch.'[33]

Across the Orel salient the withdrawing German troops indulged in a wanton orgy of destruction as part of their scorched earth policy. 'In an attempt to turn the area around Orel into a wilderness,' observed Evgeni Bessonov, 'the enemy burnt entire villages during his retreat, putting everything that he could to the torch.'[34]

Werth soon found evidence of German atrocities at Orel prison: 'The Gestapo firing squads would visit the prison twice a week. Besides these, many others had been murdered at Orel; some had been publicly hanged as "partisans" in the main square.'[35] Despite the efforts of Soviet artillery, Red Army sappers still cleared some 80,000 mines in the Orel area.

Stalin was clearly pleased with Kutuzov's progress because in an unprecedented move he left Moscow on 3 and 5 August to visit the headquarters of Sokolovsky's Western Front and that of Voronov's Kalinin Front. This was the only time during the war that he travelled to an active theatre of operations. In reality he only got as far as Yuknov and the generals were obliged to see him there. Stalin made use of 'an unsightly little dacha',[36] which looked as if it was going to be used for a propaganda film.

When Zhukov and Vasilevsky pressed Stalin to reinforce Sokolovsky's left flank, the Soviet leader said he wanted the Germans driven from the Orel salient as 'soon as possible' and that the enemy should be surrounded once they were 'more debilitated'.[37] Zhukov soon regretted they did not press their point more strongly because a chance to annihilate the retreating Germans was lost. 'The slow development of the counteroffensive on all three fronts,' complained Zhukov, 'gave the enemy the opportunity to regroup his troops, move in fresh forces from other areas and withdraw the troops from the Orel area.'[38]

Model's resistance was tenacious and the Red Army struggled to fight its way forward much more than 4km a day. Evgeni Bessonov was with the 4th Tank Army serving with the 49th Mechanised Brigade and his battalion was tasked with taking a heavily defended hill. 'That was my baptism of fire,' he recalled. 'The enemy first opened up with machine gun fire from the hill and then launched a concentrated mortar barrage on us.'[39] He and his comrades taking shelter in a ravine dug in frantically. A second attack got the same treatment. They got to the barbed-wire entanglements but had no wire cutters and had to withdraw.

The following day Bessonov was dismayed by the performance of their supporting tanks:

In the daytime, after an unimpressive artillery preparation and with the support of three T-34 tanks, we again assaulted the enemy's trench and were again thrown back. The tanks were knocked out because of the failure of the crews; they had abandoned the tanks before they were knocked out and so the tanks kept rolling empty towards the enemy … I never again saw such a shameful episode in the whole war.[40]

The day after, Bessonov's unit was bombed by the Luftwaffe from dawn until dusk. The Red Air Force was a no show and the German bombers pounded their anti-aircraft guns into silence. 'That was my first experience of such a heavy air raid,' said Bessonov. 'It was pure hell; it is hard to find a comparison for it. You are just lying in your foxhole and waiting for death …'[41] German artillery and mortar fire added to the destruction and he had to overcome the urge to run away.

When their battalion commander, Senior Lieutenant Terenti Kozienko, arrived he accused them of lying about the barbed wire. Miraculously, Bessonov's company did not suffer any fatalities but a dozen men were wounded and shell-shocked. They never did capture the hill and were redeployed to fight elsewhere. Later, the brigade was broken up to provide combat replacements.

Bryukhov almost burnt to death during Kutuzov:

Somewhere between Orel and Bryansk my tank was hit and caught fire. I yelled: 'Abandon the machine!' and grabbed the edges of the hatch chute to pull myself up and out – but the interphone plug was tightly stuck in the socket, and when I moved upwards, it jerked me back into the seat. My gunloader leapt out of my hatch, then I managed to escape and follow him. The helmet saved me – it didn't burn well, which is why I got scorches only on my face and hands, though so severely that they were covered in blisters.[42]

In order to hold the Red Army at bay, on 12 August Hitler finally woke up to the need for a static defensive line running the entire length of the Eastern Front. This was in reluctant recognition of his weakening manpower. Soon after the failure of Citadel, General Zeitzler saw Hitler and recommended they must now create an East Wall, or Panther Line, extending from Narva near the Baltic down the Dnieper to the Sea of Azov near Melitopol. This had remained nothing but a line on the map as once again Hitler refused to permit any construction work to begin.

An entire month was wasted, though some field commanders had taken matters into their own hands and began to prepare some defences in their rear areas. Belatedly the Führer ordered his three army groups to commence fortifying the massive Panther Line. His generals knew it was too late and an impossible task. There was little concrete or barbed wire to be had and slave labourers began building poorly located earthworks that were almost useless. Tank traps and trenches were unlikely to do much to slow the Red Army. The barrier of the Dnieper was of limited tactical value because it could only be held until such time as it froze.

Hitler's manpower situation was critical. The German infantry divisions had fewer than 1,000 combatants each while the Panzer divisions were down to about forty-five tanks each. This permitted no defence in depth with no reserves, all of which made a mockery of the Hagen and Panther Lines. They were of far greater propaganda value to the likes of Goebbels than offering any great military utility.

Ten days after the liberation of Orel three Soviet rifle divisions fought their way into Karachev. Lend-Lease armour was involved in the fighting. 'We have some British and American tanks there,' said General Sobennikov, 'but not many.'[43] Later, Bessonov and the 4th Tank Army were placed in reserve in the Karachev area. By 18 August the Red Army was level with the Hagen Line and the German Orel salient had been completely cleared. 'After the end of the Orel operation, the battalion,' said Bessonov, 'had just 28 or 30 officers left, among them five company commanders, ten platoon leaders and thirteen staff officers – the remaining sixteen were either dead or wounded.'[44]

As far as General Deichmann was concerned it was his 1st Air Division that saved Kluge's two armies:

In a series of heavy air attacks the Luftwaffe succeeded in preventing a Russian breakthrough, though on several days this was threatened. These delaying operations enabled German ground commanders to make gradual withdrawals in some semblance of order, to straighten the front lines.[45]

The 6th Air Fleet had been reinforced to such an extent that General Greim reported he 'could not support further units'.[46] Certainly the Luftwaffe did everything it could to help 9th Army and 2nd Panzer Army escape, dropping more than 20,000 tons of bombs. Deichmann noted:

> The air division, whose actions resolved several critical situations, flew a total of 37,421 sorties. It shot down 1,735 enemy aircraft, 1,671 by fighter action. For the loss of only 64 planes. In addition the air units put out of action 1,100 tanks, 1,300 wheeled and tracked motor vehicles and other vehicles, and numerous artillery batteries.[47]

His command reported that during this period its pilots were flying up to six missions a day.

# 16

# KHARKOV LIBERATED

On 12 July, Stalin telephoned Zhukov and instructed him to fly south to take charge of coordinating the Voronezh and Steppe Fronts. It may have been that Stalin was getting uneasy about the ferocity of the fighting at Prokhorovka and was secretly fearing that Manstein was going to cut his way through to Kursk. If that happened then Vatutin's armies were in danger of becoming trapped. Sending Zhukov also implied a vote of no confidence in Vatutin, but Zhukov was quick to jump to his defence, saying he 'was a highly erudite and steadfast commander'.[1]

Zhukov though understood that Model had exhausted his resources and that he could help elsewhere:

> I arrived at the command post of the Voronezh Front on 13 July, and the Commander of the Steppe Front, General Konev, was also there. On the evening of that day I met Vasilevsky at the command post of the 69th Army. The Supreme Commander had sent him to the South-western Front to organise the offensive operations there which were to begin when the Voronezh and Steppe Fronts went over to the counteroffensive.[2]

Zhukov was greatly heartened after their briefing. He felt that Manstein must be at breaking point and that they should capitalise on Rotmistrov and Zhadov's successful counterattacks before launching Operation Rumantsyev. They were fighting a battle of attrition that he was confident the Red Army could win:

Fierce, bloody battles were being fought on all sectors of the Front, and hundreds of tanks and self-propelled guns were going up in smoke. Clouds of dust and smoke hung above the battlefield. This was the turning point in the fighting on the Belgorod sector.[3]

Despite Hausser's mauling at Prokhorovka, General von Knobelsdorff's 48th Panzer Corps did not give up. At 06.00 on 14 July, *Grossdeutschland* was ordered to attack once more but not northwards, rather to the west. This was in response to 3rd Panzer Division having been driven from Berezovka and forced to give up Hill 247 just to the north of the town. *Grossdeutschland* reached 3rd Panzer that afternoon. However, Mellentin noted despondently, 'By the evening of 14 July it was obvious that the timetable of the German attack had been completely upset.'[4]

On the Voronezh Front the intensity of the fighting meant that the Red Army had to bide its time until it struck back with full force. Zhukov knew that Manstein's troops had been fought to a stop and had spent their offensive power just as Model had in the north:

Drained of their life blood and having lost their faith in victory, the Nazi forces gradually changed over to defensive operations. On 16 July, the enemy finally halted the attack and began to withdraw his troops in the rear to Belgorod. On 17 July, the withdrawal of the enemy troops was discovered, however, units still engaged with our forces offered dogged resistance.[5]

Mansur Abdulin with Zhadov's 5th Guards Army pressed south:

Starting from Prokhorovka, our 32nd Guards [Rifle] Corps was constantly engaged in action with the German SS Divisions, *Totenkopf*, *Grossdeutschland* and *Das Reich*. We also had encounters with the Russian Liberation Army of the traitor, General Vlasov. Vlasov's men knew they were doomed but fought desperately. We did not take them prisoner.[6]

Bizarrely, some farming went on even in the midst of the battle. Abdulin noted:

Early one morning we saw a field, on the German side, something strange and mysterious. The whole meadow was covered with enormous sheaves of wheat! We were just trying to imagine why the Nazis would want to mow wheat during the night and assemble it in such order, when their artillery began shelling No Man's Land.[7]

Although the Soviet armies maintained their pressure around the German Prokhorovka penetration, they were understandably exhausted. Casualties were high and their ammunition had been spent. This situation enabled Manstein by 23 July to conduct a fighting withdrawal to the defences in front of Gertsovka, Tomarovka and Belgorod, his original start line. The western part of the salient was held by Hoth's battered 4th Panzer Army, while to the east lay Kempf's forces. The SS Panzer Corps was withdrawn to the south-west of Kharkov. If Manstein could not hold the salient then the Kharkov–Sumy railway formed a logical stopline.

At Belgorod General Erhard Raus was not a happy man. Reports flowing into his HQ about the withdrawal from Prokhorovka indicated that his 11th Corps would soon be in the firing line from two directions. Now that Vatutin was pressing in from the north and Konev from the east his troops were in a very exposed position. Once Hausser and Breith had withdrawn to the west of Belgorod there was every chance that Konev or Malinovsky would pierce the German salient to the south of the city. If the rest of Army Detachment Kempf did not withdraw it faced every prospect of being cut off and surrounded.

In Moscow the *Red Star* newspaper was jubilant about the situation, reporting, 'The liquidation of the German offensive in the east in the summer of 1943 was a mighty blow to Hitler. The collapse of his ally, Mussolini, is another blow.' Stalin would have smiled as he read, 'The jackal had boundless greed, but his teeth were rotten … And now he has been forced to abandon his post of Dictator …'[8]

Stalin had been disparaging about Churchill and Roosevelt's intention to invade Sicily. He could see little value in such an operation, but now it was having a far greater political impact. The effect on the Axis allies was not something that Hitler could ignore. The alliance had been pushed to the limit thanks to the losses incurred at Stalingrad and now this.

In Berlin in his office in the Propaganda Ministry Goebbels was feeling decidedly despondent. He felt as if all his efforts to galvanise the nation following Stalingrad had come to nothing despite invoking 'total war'. Nazi Germany was enduring yet another defeat. 'We are doing too much on the military and too little on the political side of the war,' he confided in his diary at the end of July. 'At this moment, when our military successes are none too great, it would be a good thing if we knew how to make better use of the political instrument.'[9]

For the Germans in the Belgorod salient the situation was extremely frustrating. Mellenthin summed up their predicament, saying:

Fourth Panzer Army was informed that the SS Panzer Corps would be withdrawn immediately for operations in Italy, while the 4th Panzer Corps was told to release *Grossdeutschland* and send it to the assistance of Field Marshal von Kluge's Army Group Centre. In the circumstances it was impossible to hold our gains in the Kursk salient ...'[10]

Understandably Stalin wanted to launch the Belgorod counteroffensive immediately, but it would take at least a week for his forces to recuperate and re-equip. Zhukov grumbled, 'the Supreme Commander was pressing us to start the operation'.[11] He was wary that they not be forced into starting before everything was ready; in the past Stalin's rash decisions had caused the Red Army grievous harm. Zhukov cautioned:

A well calculated and prepared offensive should guarantee a definite breakthrough of the enemy's defences in tactical and operational depth, and such an assault should also provide the right conditions for subsequent operations.[12]

Zhukov was particularly concerned about the condition of the 1st Tank and 6th and 7th Guards Armies, which had sustained heavy losses. They needed reinforcing. After 'a great deal of trouble' Zhukov and Vasilevsky finally persuaded Stalin to acquiesce to the delay. This though gave the Germans time to prepare their defences, especially around Belgorod and Kharkov. In particular, their tough SS armoured units were ready to counterattack when the time came.

Under the code name Operation Rumyantsev, Vatutin's Voronezh and Konev's Steppe Fronts were to push the Germans from their Belgorod salient with the ultimate aim of liberating Kharkov. Vatutin was to deliver the main blow south toward Valki and Novaya Vodolaga. Konev would strike west toward Belgorod. These forces were to bypass Kharkov from the west and at that point the South-Western Front would join the offensive, throwing General Gagen's 57th Army toward the city. On Vatutin's far right his 38th and 40th Armies were to attack toward Graivoron and Trostyanets.

Zhukov spent the evening before their offensive commenced with General Managarov, commander of the 53rd Army. After supper Managarov played his accordion. 'My tiredness disappeared immediately,'[13] recalled Zhukov, who had always wanted to learn how to play this instrument. 'So, it began on 3 August ...'[14]

In the early hours the Red Army unleashed a deadly deluge upon the German defences. For three nerve-shredding hours almost 6,000 field guns and mortars pounded the enemy's fortifications. They were joined by Goryunov's and Krasovski's bombers. Then at 08.00 hours the guns began to range into the German rear areas.

General N.K. Popel witnessed the devastation of the opening battle:

> During three hours our artillery batteries and bombers loosened the ground, mixed it with pieces of concrete blocks, logs, iron core, and the bodies of enemy soldiers. In the meantime our tanks got to the very front-line … and in this moment we stood straight in the trench and eagerly watched the T-34 tanks overtaking each other, the squadrons of the lightning-like attack aircraft and the bombers spreading their wings in the skies above us.[15]

Preceded by 'artillery music' and the bombers, the 5th and 6th Guards Armies stormed forward and broke through. That afternoon the 1st and 5th Guards Tank Armies rolled into the breach and fought their way forward to a depth of up to 35km. The Steppe Front facing the Germans' Belgorod defences struggled to advance and only managed about half this distance.

That day the exhausted Luftwaffe conducted 569 sorties, but it was swamped by the Red Air Force, which mounted 2,671 combat missions. The 5th Air Army, using bomber groups of up to 100 aircraft, pounded the first echelon of the German defences. The 2nd Air Army, flying in much smaller formations of about a dozen, attacked the second. To stop the Germans bringing up reserves and to silence their anti-aircraft batteries to the north-west of Belgorod, General Krasovski sent two waves of bombers at 12.10 and at 18.00.

Captain A.V. Vorozheikin, with the 728th Fighter Regiment, was involved in a dogfight over Tomarovka, west of Belgorod. He remembered:

> I just managed to rush out of the ball of fire and smoke, and immediately spotted the German fighter nearby. I quickly approached and fired with a burst with my cannon. The enemy dashed aside, I followed him. My second burst was followed by another and I saw the hits, but felt that I hurried – it was not a deadly fire.[16]

The enemy pilot Vorozheikin was up against was experienced enough to take very effective evasive action. Vorozheikin was concerned that he would be taken by surprise if he pressed home against his elusive quarry:

... the Messerschmitt started to make wide rolls and I couldn't get him into the crosshairs of my gunsight. Of course I could try to catch him in such manoeuvres, but I should not be carried away. Being concerned about another enemy pair, I dropped the agile Messerschmitt, and looked around for another target ...[17]

The following day, once Vatutin's forces were beyond Belgorod, the Germans had little choice but to withdraw, which permitted Konev to advance much more quickly. Kruchenkin's 69th Army advanced from the north, while the 7th Guards Army pushed from the south-east and at the same time the 1st Motorised Corp enveloped Belgorod from the west.

Raus' corps consisted of two infantry divisions, though in reality it was now little more than an ad hoc battle group drawing men from half a dozen divisions. He had insufficient troops to hold Belgorod and had little choice but to give it up. To his relief, General Kempf ordered him to retreat toward Kharkov. His men withdrew to prepared positions between the Donets and Lopan rivers to the north of Kharkov. These though were soon compromised and his men were once more heading south.

Half a dozen Soviet rifle divisions fought their way toward Belgorod. Then at 06.00 on the morning of 5 August, the same day as Orel was being retaken, elements of the 89th Guards, 305th and 375th Rifle divisions reached the city. 'The 270th Guards Rifle Regiment of the 89th Guards Rifle Division was the first to break into the city ...'[18] noted Zhukov. According to Red Army figures, the Germans left behind 3,000 dead.[19]

'Belgorod had suffered less from the shelling than one would have expected,' observed Werth during a tour of the newly liberated city, 'and there were many people about.' Driving south he witnessed where the true damage had been done:

> The rich farm country between Belgorod and Kharkov was, however, cultivated only to the extent of about forty per cent – which was different from the Western Ukraine. But in 1943 this area was already very near the front line, and the Germans didn't bother.[20]

Stalin was delighted and in his Order of the Day issued to the front commanders said, 'For excellent offensive operations I express my thanks to all the troops commanded by you who took part in the operations to liberate Orel and Belgorod.'[21] He was in a celebratory mood. 'General Antonov and I were summoned to Supreme Headquarters,' said Shtemenko. 'We set out at once, taking our maps, reference notes, and documents, as usual. The members of the Supreme Headquarters were all there.'[22]

Upon arrival they were flummoxed to be asked by Stalin if they read history. Before they could answer he said:

> If you had read, you would know that in ancient times, when troops won victories, all the bells would be rung in honour of the commanders and their troops ... We're thinking of giving artillery salutes and arranging some kind of fireworks in honour of the troops who distinguished themselves and the commanders who led them.[23]

They all agreed that it was a very good idea, though only Stalin had the authority to order a salute in the capital. He summoned the Kremlin military commandant and asked him how many guns were in the Kremlin. The officer was slightly panicked as this was the last thing he had expected Stalin would want to know. He hazarded a rough guess and said 120. Stalin instructed him to conduct a twelve-salvo salute with 'all available guns'[24] to mark the occasion. When the commandant checked his inventory he found that there were 124 guns in working order so to be on the safe side he employed them all that evening.

To avoid panicking the capital's inhabitants a communiqué was issued to Yurii Levitan, the announcer on Moscow state radio. However, once these salutes became common practice Comrade B.S. Pusin, the director of the state radio network, was instructed that the communiqués should not be read out more than a minute before the guns started firing. 'It was the war's first artillery salute in honour of a Red Army Victory,' said Zhukov with some pride. 'The morale of the soldiers rose sharply as a result, and their faces radiated joy, gallantry and confidence in their own strength.'[25]

Just as in the Orel salient, the Germans destroyed everything they could in the Belgorod salient. Abdulin witnessed the devastation at first hand:

> After a series of battles, the Germans retreated but began burning everything in their path. Villages and fields were set ablaze ... We marched through endless smoke. We seized two large villages, Tomarovka and Borisovka, where storehouses of tobacco were set on fire; everyone had his share of tobacco smoke, whether he was a smoker or not![26]

By this stage the 7th Guards, 53rd and 69th Armies needed 35,000 replacements and Zhukov was urging that the 57th Army be signed over to Konev.

Zhukov also wanted 335 replacement tanks, 90 fighters, 60 ground-attack aircraft and 40 dive-bombers. All this gave clear indication of the heavy losses they had suffered. He signalled Stalin, outlining their plans and requesting the battle replacements.

On 7 August the 1st Tank Army and elements of the 6th Guards Army took Bogodukhov to the west of Kharkov. At Graivoron the Germans tried to extricate three infantry divisions and Schmidt's 19th Panzer Division. They were bombed by the 2nd Air Army, then attacked by Trofimenko's 27th Army. The Messerschmitt Bf 109 played its part. That day fighter ace Captain Günther Rall, piloting such an aircraft, achieved his 175th victory to the west of Belgorod.[27] Many new Soviet fighter pilots undertaking their first combat learned the hard way that the Messerschmitt fought in the vertical while the Focke-Wulf struck from the dive. Four days later the 1st Tank Army cut the Kharkov–Poltava railway line.

By now the Red Army had cleared much of the Belgorod salient running north-west to south-east through Boromlys–Akhtyrka–Koteleva–Valki but the Germans were still holding Kharkov. When General Werner Kempf, commanding Army Detachment Kempf, requested permission to abandon the city on 12 August, Manstein agreed. In response Hitler insisted it be held and Manstein replaced Kempf with General Otto Wöhler and Kempf's former command became the German 8th Army. Hitler was worried that the loss of Kharkov would damage his prestige with Turkey, which while neutral was pro-Nazi. In the spring the Turkish commander in chief had inspected Kempf's defences, pronouncing them 'impregnable'.

Raus reached Kharkov on the 12th. Once Soviet troops cut the Kharkov–Poltava rail link his position in Kharkov would be seriously jeopardised. Despite the presence of large numbers of administrative and logistical personnel in the city, Raus could only muster 4,000 infantrymen. In addition, ammunition was precariously low. Thanks to the Battle of Kursk the intense fighting had consumed half of what had been set aside for the end of August and early September. As a result the supply depot in Kharkov had five train-loads of spare Panzer tracks but not much else.

In the meantime, to alleviate some of the pressure the 2nd SS, 3rd SS and 5th SS Panzergrenadier Divisions counterattacked in the Akhtyrka area south of Trostyanets and at Valki south of Bogodukov. The Soviets claimed that Manstein managed to mass seven Panzer and motorised divisions with 600 tanks supported by four infantry divisions.[28]

This attack forced back both the 1st Tank and 6th Guards armies so Rotmistrov's armour was brought forward to help out. *Wiking* did all it

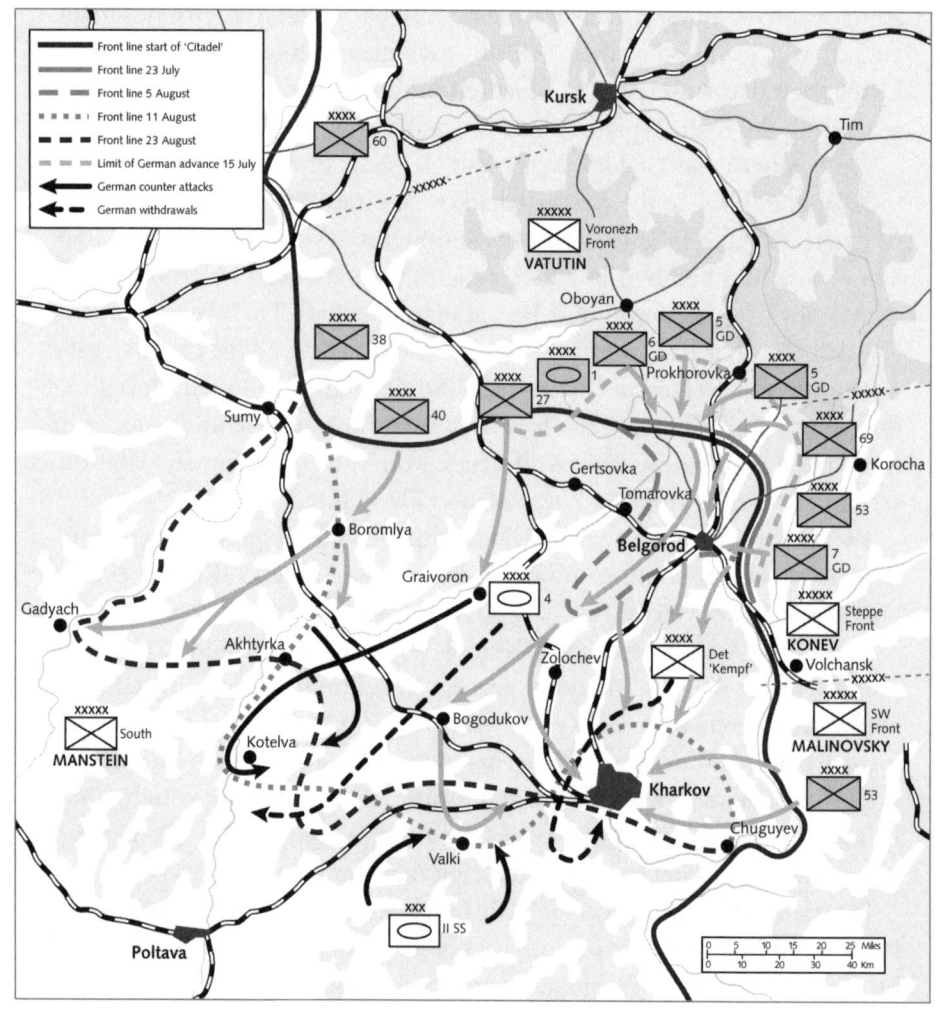

Operation Rumantsyev, 3–23 August 1943.

could to blunt the Red Army's attack. On 13 August 1943, Kurt Eggers, former editor of the Waffen-SS's newspaper, died commanding a Panzer. His tank suffered a direct hit and he was killed instantly. Eggers' loss was felt throughout the SS.[29] Fighting against the Soviet 1st Tank and 5th and 6th Guards armies lasted for a week.

In Germany all was not well with the Luftwaffe. On 13 August the Wiener Neustadt aircraft factories were bombed by an American daylight raid. Afterwards General Jeschonnek, Chief of the Air Staff, was harangued by Hitler for an hour. Four days later the Americans attacked the ball-bearing factories at Schweinfurt and the Messerschmitt complex at Regensburg. Although the Luftwaffe shot down sixty American bombers, Jeschonnek found himself being held personally responsible for the enemy penetrations so far into Germany.

The RAF also struck the Peenemünde rocket facility that night. Jeschonnek ordered 200 fighters assemble over Berlin, which were promptly shot at by their own flak. In the meantime, 750 scientists and workers were killed in the bombing of Peenemünde. British scientist Dr R.V. Jones, who had worked for a time at Bletchley Park and helped coordinate the raid, recalled:

> … shortly after midnight Jeschonnek had been called on the telephone by an infuriated Göring, because of the battle between the anti-aircraft guns and the nightfighters over Berlin. It was too much for Jeschonnek; by nine o'clock on the morning of the following day he had not emerged from his room.[30]

It was the final straw for Jeschonnek, who was sick to death of being made a scapegoat for Göring's failures. The exhausted Luftwaffe had done everything it could at Stalingrad and Kursk, but had still been held partly responsible for both defeats. He scribbled a note: 'It is impossible to work with Göring any longer. Long live the Führer!'[31] Unholstering his service pistol, he then shot himself in the head. He was found by his unfortunate secretary.

At Kharkov the mood in General Raus' new headquarters cannot have been a happy one, but to be fair German generals had found themselves in this type of situation on innumerable occasions and had still turned the tables on the enemy. Raus was actually Austrian and was an experienced pair of hands, having commanded the 6th Panzer Division during the early part of the war.

Raus, examining his maps, anticipated that the Red Army would attempt to cut off Kharkov by breaking through the defensive arc to the west of the city. He therefore rushed every anti-tank gun and 88mm flak gun to the high ground on the northern edge of the precarious bottleneck, which would have to be kept open to facilitate an escape route for withdrawing units.

By now Mangarov's 53rd Army was pressing in from the north-east and south-east on the German defenders at Kharkov. Under Senior Lieutenant Petrishchev a company of just sixteen men from the 299th Rifle Division took Hill 201.7 in the Polevoi area of the city. After two-thirds of his men were cut down Petrishchev rallied the survivors and cried, 'We may die, but we shall not retreat!'[32] Despite German counterattacks they clung to the hill until the rest of the division fought its way to them.

Enveloping Kharkov involved forces under the command of Gagen, Mangarov, Kruchenkin, Shumilov and Rotmistrov. In the forefront of the push from the north were two infantry corps including Major General Kozlov's 33rd Guards from Zhadov's 5th Guards Army. A total of ten rifle divisions were involved in overcoming the German defences around Ukraine's second city.

To try to prevent the Panzers moving forward to bolster the inadequate defences at Kharkov, between 6 and 17 August 1943 Soviet bombers conducted 2,300 sorties against trains and railway stations. Close air support missions accounted for up to 80 per cent of the daily sorties. For the German Army so used to the Luftwaffe setting about the Red Army it now found the tables turned. Large numbers of bombers hit German rear areas, targeting airfields, roads, railways plus supplies and reserves struggling to reach the front. Anything that moved was bombed and strafed. It was a sobering experience for German convoys caught in the open.

The Luftwaffe did everything it could to stem the tide of the Red Army. During 19 and 20 August the 8th Air Corps flew almost 1,800 sorties, by which time some units were running out of bombs.

Despite the efforts of the Red Air Force, the German defences were reinforced by the welcome and timely arrival of Panzers from the 2nd SS, giving Raus ninety-six Panthers, thirty-five Tigers and twenty-five Sturmgeschütz III assault guns. All of these were capable of giving Soviet tanks a very bloody nose. The Red Army began to mass for its attack on 20 August and was promptly set upon by the Luftwaffe's Stuka dive-bombers. General Raus witnessed, 'A horrible picture of death and destruction!'[33]

He recalled the ferocity of the air attack:

Dark fountains of earth erupted skyward and were followed by heavy thunderclaps and shocks that resembled an earthquake. These were the heaviest, two-ton bombs, designed for use against battleships, which were all that Luftflotte 4 had left to counter the Russian attack. Soon all the villages occupied by Soviet tanks lay in flames.[34]

Despite the devastation Soviet tanks continued to advance through the broad cornfields, emerging on the east–west highway several hundred metres from Raus' main defences. Initially his Panthers held the T-34s at bay, but weight of numbers got them to the Germans forward battle positions.

Raus had a surprise for them, as he noted:

Here a net of anti-tank and flak guns, Hornet 88mm tank destroyers, and Wasp self-propelled 105mm field howitzers trapped the T-34s, split them into small groups, and put large numbers out of action. The final waves were still attempting to force a breakthrough in concentrated masses when Tigers and StuG III self-propelled assault guns, which represented our mobile reserves behind the front, attacked the Russian armour and repulsed it with heavy losses.

The 5th Guards Tank Army alone lost 184 T-34s that day. In total the Red Army had 450 tanks destroyed during the Belgorod–Kharkov offensive.

Having expended their last resources, the German position at Kharkov was now completely compromised. Manstein was forced to abandon battered Kharkov for a second time on 22 August. The retreating Germans blew up their remaining ammunition and fuel dumps and set fire to parts of the city to slow down the advancing enemy. Although the Luftwaffe and Panzers had done all they could to stop the Soviets, with their ammunition and strength spent there was little more they could do. To insist that the garrison remain at their posts was simply a waste of valuable manpower.

Once Soviet aerial reconnaissance spotted the Germans withdrawing from Kharkov toward Poltava the air force flew 1,300 sorties against the retreating columns. The roads soon became choked with blazing vehicles. The German rearguard fought desperately to hold open the escape corridor as troop convoys sped to safety. Despite repeated Soviet attacks and attempts to cut them off, Raus and his 11th Corps fought their way back to the Dnieper.

At the Luftwaffe's Kharkov-Rogan air base organised chaos broke out. The resident units had just an hour to evacuate everything because no one had warned them that the Red Army was coming down the Kharkov road. They were only alerted when an exhausted infantry rearguard marched past heading westward. Aircraft and personnel were frantically flown out to an airfield north of Poltava. Miraculously there were no losses and the aircraft were soon in the air attacking Soviet tank columns again.

One of the pilots flying with the 1st Ground Attack Group evacuated from Rogan was amazed how disaster had been averted:

> Our ground crews were magnificent. We were flying from first light until late evening. Our main task was to attack Ivan's armour and his supply lines. Our local success was colossal, but we couldn't stop the overall momentum of the advance.[35]

Following the evacuation of Kharkov's surrounding airfields most of the Luftwaffe units withdrew to bases near Dnepropetrovsk, Kremenchug and Mirogorod to help hold the Dnieper Line. This deployment was driven by Hitler's intention to hold on to the Crimea, but at the same time exposed the northern flank of the Ukrainian salient. This soon became apparent to Soviet aerial reconnaissance.

The following day Konev's men drove in to Kharkov and were 'enthusiastically welcomed by the inhabitants'.[36] Shortly after, Commissar Khrushchev and the other generals were photographed touring the city centre – once more he had something to be thankful for. Climbing out of his staff car, Khrushchev took his hat off and looked up at the surrounding buildings with a big grin upon his face. When he had been photographed with Apanasenko and Rotmistrov in mid-July his expression had been one of deep concern. Now a sense of relief flooded over him. They had done it. The disaster at Kharkov the previous year had at least been partially expunged.

The propaganda and public relations value of this achievement did not go to waste, as Zhukov recalled:

> A city-wide rally was promptly held, with representatives of the Soviet Army and the government and Party organizations of the Ukraine on the speakers' stand. The rally proceeded with a great show of enthusiasm as the working people of Kharkov celebrated their liberation.[37]

After the rally a dinner was held for the senior generals and politicians. As a treat the famous opera singer Ivan Kozlovsky sang for them, performing Russian and Ukrainian songs. 'His heartfelt performance moved everyone present to tears,' said Zhukov. 'He sang for a long time, and all of us who had missed good vocalists for so many months were very grateful to him.'[38]

Kharkov's liberation was considered a much greater victory than Belgorod and Orel, so at 21.00 on 23 August, 224 guns fired twenty salvos that rumbled noisily out across a jubilant Moscow. This set a rather tiresome precedent for the Soviet General Staff. 'We had no respite from the phone calls of Army Group commanders,' complained Shtemenko, 'who demanded salutes for almost every inhabited point that was taken.'[39] Stalin's order of the day ended with his usual refrain, 'Death to the German invaders!'

Shortly afterwards, Alexander Werth visited newly liberated Kharkov. 'This was a hideous experience,' he wrote, 'for, as we travelled at night in a number of jeeps from Valuiki to Kharkov, one of them struck a mine and three of our travelling companions were killed.'[40] Werth was shaken by this terrifying incident and especially by the loss of handsome young Soviet press officer Kozhemiako, who he had found to be charming and great fun. 'He spoke perfect English, though he had never been abroad,' recalled Werth. 'Had he lived he would almost certainly have rapidly climbed to the top of the diplomatic ladder.'[41]

On 25 August Vatutin's forces dug in ready for a new offensive that would take them to the Dnieper. The Belgorod salient had been completely liberated.

# 17

# HITLER'S BITTER HARVEST

There was no hiding the fact that Hitler's Wehrmacht had been outfought at almost every turn. General von Mellentin was full of grudging praise for the performance of the victorious Red Army:

> The Russian High Command had conducted the Battle of Kursk with great skill, yielding ground adroitly and taking the sting out of our offensive with an intricate system of minefields and anti-tank defences. Not satisfied with counterattacking in the salient, the Russians delivered heavy blows between Orel and Bryansk … Citadel had been a complete and most regrettable failure.[1]

Nonetheless, he could not help himself indulging in hand wringing and self-recrimination. It was heresy to think that the Panzers had been outmatched:

> Nineteen-hundred and forty-three was still a year of apprenticeship for the Russian armour. The heavy German defeats on the Eastern Front were not due to superior Russian tactical leadership, but to grave strategic errors by the German Supreme Command, and to the vast Russian superiority in numbers and material.[2]

Zhukov, Rokossovsky, Vatutin, Rotmistrov and the other Soviet generals would have begged to differ; meticulous planning and preparation had given them victory. Theirs had been a well thought out strategy, unlike the Germans' confused dithering.

'This major battle of the Great Patriotic War ended in the taking of Kharkov on 23 August 1943,' said Zhukov. 'Our troops displayed exceptional courage and mass heroism, and military skill in the fighting near Kursk.'[3]

Khrushchev was delighted that the Red Army had scored another decisive victory. He was also at pains to point out that it did not have any help this time:

> Our detractors used to say that the only reason we were able to defeat Paulus's colossal army at Stalingrad was that we had the Russian winter on our side. They had said the same thing about our defeat of the Germans outside Moscow in 1941. Ever since Russia turned back Napoleon's invasion, people claimed that winter was our main ally. However, the Germans couldn't use this excuse to explain their defeat at the Battle of the Kursk Salient in 1943. They fired the first shot; they chose the time, place, and form of battle. All the cards were in the hands of Hitler and his cutthroats.[4]

He was right about the weather. However, Khrushchev conveniently avoided acknowledging that Hitler had walked into a trap that had been carefully set up by Zhukov, Rokossovsky and Vatutin. It was what Zhukov had dubbed 'deliberate defence' and it required Hitler to trigger it.

Stalin was ecstatic that the detailed planning of his generals had paid off. There was always the danger that they had underestimated the Wehrmacht and overestimated the capabilities of the Red Army. He had not been let down. General Shtemenko, Stalin's Chief of Operations, succinctly summed up the situation: 'The German command's schemes to regain the initiative were demolished for good at the battle of Kursk. The Nazi offensive strategy had collapsed completely.'[5]

After fifty days of fighting Zhukov reported that Hitler had lost thirty divisions, including seven armoured divisions as these units had lost more than half their manpower. He claimed, 'The overall losses sustained by the enemy amounted to approximately 500,000 men, 1,500 tanks, including a large number of Tiger and Panther tanks, 3,000 guns, and more than 3,700 aircraft.'[6] There is no way to verify these figures and Zhukov makes no mention of Red Army losses.[7] Some 100,000 officers and men were awarded orders and medals for their role.

Khrushchev inevitably saw the victory at Kursk in ideological terms, saying, 'It was decisive in determining the defeat of Hitlerlite Germany and the ultimate triumph of our Soviet Army, our ideology, and our Communist Party.[8] He took great satisfaction from his involvement, adding, 'I'm not without certain human weaknesses, including pride, and I'm certainly pleased to have been a member of the Military Council for the fronts involved in the huge battle which the Red Army waged at Stalingrad and Kursk.'[9] Stalin had no cause to menace him this time.

In early September alarming news reached Berlin that a small Allied landing had taken place in Italy opposite Sicily at Reggio di Calabria. Hitler's generals were mindful that this was not the Allies' main effort and withdrew their forces northwards in anticipation of another attack. Less than a week later the Allies landed at Salerno and Taranto. The Italian government began to clamour for an armistice and Hitler took over the country.

Hitler was shaken by the loss of his ally Mussolini and the Allies' invasion of mainland Italy. In his darkest hours he began to fear that victory on the battlefield was unachievable. Propaganda Minister Goebbels was summoned to see the Führer at Rastenburg on 10 September. He found Hitler worried about the critical situation on the Eastern Front and concerned about an Allied invasion in the west. The prospect of a two-front war weighed heavily with Hitler. His resources were already stretched to the limit. Goebbels observed:

> The depressing thing is that we haven't the faintest idea as to what Stalin had left in the way of reserves. I doubt very much whether under these conditions we shall be able to transfer divisions from the East to the other European theatres of war.[10]

Goebbels broached the idea of a negotiated peace. He thought that Stalin was a more practical politician than Churchill, so might be more approachable. Hitler clung to the hope that the Americans and British, alarmed by the Soviet Union's victories, would side with Germany to fight Bolshevism. Goebbels felt because Churchill was an old anti-Bolshevik he might come round to a more conciliatory stance with Germany's National Socialism.

Hitler though could not forgive the terrible damage wrought on Germany's cities by Britain and America's bomber offensive. To the German people, although the news was bad from Russia and Italy, these events were hundreds of miles away. Likewise, they had no real feeling for how Hitler's U-boat campaign was going in the Atlantic. In Germany there was no hiding the British attacks by night and the American ones by day. Hitler resolutely refused to tour any of his bombed cities, it was just too painful.

Thirteen days later Goebbels met with Hitler again and once more they discussed the possibility of negotiating their way out of the war. Hitler made it clear he would rather negotiate with Stalin, but as the Soviet leader now had the advantage there was little incentive for him to enter into talks. Goebbels warned that they had to do something:

> Whatever may be the situation, I told the Führer that we must come to an arrangement with one side or another. The Reich has never yet won a two front war. We must therefore see how we can somehow or other get out of a two-front war.[11]

More than ever Hitler desperately needed a victory over Stalin that would put him in a stronger negotiating position. However, the Wehrmacht was simply not in a position to do that thanks to the losses incurred at Kursk. Quite remarkably, Hitler, after all his agonising over conducting Operation Citadel, seemed to simply ignore his defeat at Kursk. Instead he devoted his energies to rescuing Mussolini and securing the situation in northern Italy and the Italian-occupied areas in the Balkans. The loss of Italy risked unravelling the Axis alliance and that posed a far greater threat than Kursk. He successfully conducted a bloodless coup, creating a puppet state in German-occupied Italy. This left the Allies facing a hard slog up through Italy and for the time being secured his Western Front.

Meanwhile, Hitler's armies continued to give ground on the Eastern Front. A month after the liberation of Kharkov, a fourth major city was set free. Some 300 miles to the north-west, on 25 September the Red Army rolled triumphantly into Smolensk. This positioned it ready for the liberation of Minsk and Byelorussia. In the south, by the end of the month Hitler's armies had withdrawn to the Dnieper River. There they had built a defensive line running from Zaporozhe on the bend of the river down to the Sea of Azov.

Crucially, Hitler had lost control of the industrial heartland of the Donets Basin and the German 17th Army now faced being trapped in the Crimea. The Führer insisted it stay put. Hitler and his generals hoped that the Red Army would regroup. Instead, during the first week of

October they crossed the Dnieper to the south-east and north of Kiev, which was liberated on 6 November. Hitler's forces were also losing the battle for the skies over Germany and the Battle of the Atlantic. His U-boats had failed to prevent the vast numbers of troops and quantities of supplies that were coming across the Atlantic ready for the Allies' assault on Fortress Europe in 1944.

The Red Army's success at Kursk was not so much holding Hitler's Citadel offensive, but liberating the German-held Belgorod and Orel salients. It was these victories that confirmed the tide of the war on the Eastern Front had been turned once and for all. Although the mauled Wehrmacht escaped to fight another day it had been unable to stop the liberation of the two key cities, nor retake them. Hitler was disappointed that Himmler's Waffen-SS had not carried the day to the south; even a partial victory would have been something on which to cling.

Kursk was little more than a risky gamble for Hitler. He felt he had no choice but to attack the Soviet salient. He could not sit and do nothing while the Red Army grew stronger. Zeitzler, determined to avenge Stalingrad, worked hard to convince Hitler that a limited offensive at Kursk could result in a major victory if the Red Army was trapped and defeated inside the salient. This though ignored the presence of the Steppe Front, which would have been poised to open the pocket and trap the Germans against Kursk. Even if Hitler's forces had reach Kursk he had nothing with which to exploit such a success.

The Führer deliberately ignored his intelligence and the warnings from his generals that he should not underestimate the strength of the dug-in Red Army. 'With the Kursk offensive I wanted to reverse fate,' said Hitler. 'I would never have believed the Russians were so strong ...'[12] Yet he had been warned time and time again.

Hitler chose not to heed Manstein's advice that they should conduct an 'elastic defence' because in the Führer's mind this represented nothing more than a fighting retreat. Yet even at this stage Hitler could quite easily have traded space in order to create a better defensive line that could have enabled his generals to fight on ground of their own choosing.

General Warlimont summed up Hitler's terrible dilemma:

> Perhaps his eventual consent to the execution of this attack was mainly due to the fact that, otherwise, he could not have evaded the necessity for a deliberate strategic retreat in the East on a large scale. To consider such a possibility, however, was contrary to his creed ...[13]

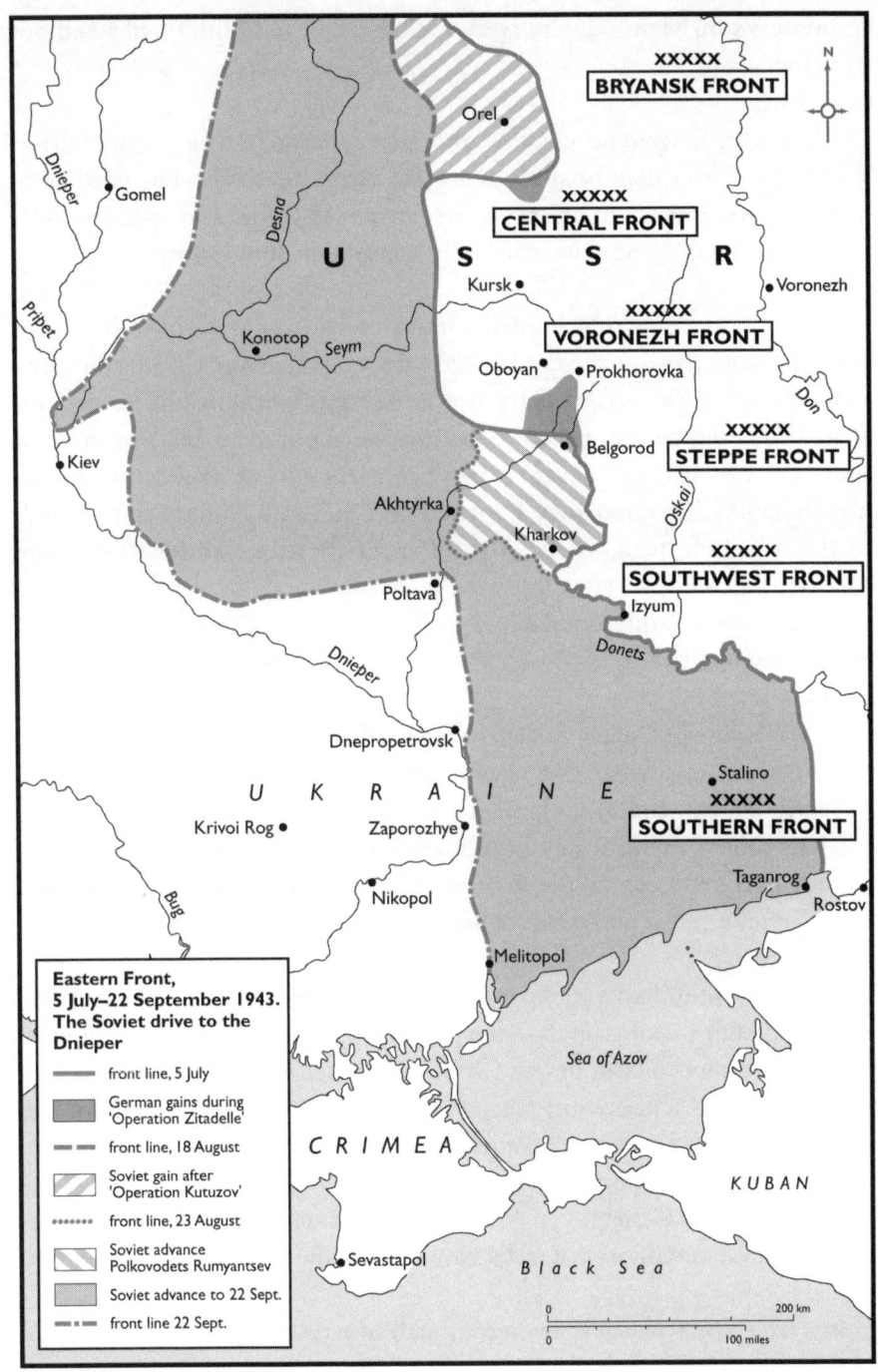

Stalin's gains by the end of September 1943.

Rommel's son, Manfred, observed that his father felt Hitler had acted out of desperation:

> My mother has told me that my father later expressed the view that Hitler realised in 1943 that the war was lost. Yet the more the disasters piled up and the more criticism he saw directed at himself the more desperately he clutched at every straw and tried to persuade himself of victory.[14]

Operation Citadel had been such a straw.

While Hitler may have felt backed into a corner over Citadel, he convinced himself that Guderian's zoo could deliver the result he desired. What he failed to accept was that they were not available in sufficient numbers, nor had the design faults been ironed out. It did not matter how many Soviet tanks they knocked out, there was simply not enough of them. In addition, many of the Panzer divisions' older tanks were simply outclassed.

Guderian was understandably very bitter because all his hard work had been thrown away:

> By the failure of Citadel we had suffered a decisive defeat. The armoured formations, re-formed and re-equipped with so much effort, had lost heavily in men and in equipment and would now be unemployable for a long time to come. It was problematic whether they could be rehabilitated in time to defend the Eastern Front … From now on the enemy was in undisputed possession of the initiative.[15]

Guderian himself had a lucky escape, not from the Red Army but Allied bombers. After picking up dysentery on the Eastern Front, he accepted an offer from Speer to convalesce at an inn in upper Austria. He and his wife had just arrived when word reached them that their home in Berlin had received a direct hit during an air raid.

'With the failure of our supreme effort, the strategic initiative passed to the Russians,' agreed General von Mellenthin. He was also in complete agreement with Guderian over the fatal blow their armoured units had suffered:

> It is true that Russian losses were much heavier than German; indeed tactically the fighting had been indecisive. Fourth Panzer took thirty-two thousand prisoners and captured or destroyed more than two thousand tanks and nearly two thousand guns. But our Panzer divisions – in such

splendid shape at the beginning of the battle – had been bled white, and with Anglo-American assistance the Russians could afford losses on this colossal scale.[16]

Colonel Gehlen, with an air of resignation, wrote, 'Operation Citadel was the last German attempt at a strategic offensive in the Russian campaign. With its failure the tide of the war in Russia finally turned against us. The German Army was forced on to the defensive and never regained the initiative.'[17] Gehlen felt that, because he had been a naysayer and a harbinger of doom that after Kursk, Hitler had simply ignored his assessments. 'We produced intelligence digests, and showed which enemy moves were considered most probable,' said Gehlen. 'But the more our predictions were confirmed by subsequent events, the less Hitler as supreme commander was inclined to heed our reports.'[18]

Zhukov put their victory down to superior preparation, numbers and the quality of the troops. He claimed the Red Amy had a 20 per cent superiority in tanks, 40 per cent superiority in manpower and aircraft and 90 per cent more guns and mortars. Hitler did not have the resources to attack on a broad front and his narrow attacks on the shoulders of the Kursk salient initially gave him a distinct advantage. However, once the Red Army began to commit its in-depth defensive forces their superiority soon became apparent.

On the very vexed issue of Lend-Lease equipment, Zhukov was quick to refute it had contributed to the Red Army's material superiority and their victory at Kursk. 'I do not wish to deny this completely,' he said, 'and make out that this aid did not exist. It did help the Red Army and the war industry to a certain extent, but, all the same, is should not be regarded as more significant than it actually was.'[19]

In contrast, Zhukov was fulsome in his praise of the role played by Soviet partisans in the Battle of Kursk:

The 'railroad war' carried out by the guerrillas of Byelorussia, Smolensk, and Orel oblasts and the Dnieper valley was especially effective in cutting enemy supply lines. The guerrillas blew up trains, stations and yards and provided the Soviet command with intelligence data that enabled it to assess the strategic situation and enemy intentions ...[20]

This was only partly true. There were ammunition shortages but the partisans never came close to strangling Army Group Centre during Citadel or preventing the withdrawal of 2nd Panzer Army and 9th Army from the

Orel salient. Likewise in the south, while they were troubling to Army Group South, they did little to disrupt German operations in the Belgorod salient. They were a glorified nuisance. Their greatest role was undoubtedly intelligence gathering, which was probably far more harmful to the German war effort than their military activities.

Despite the remarkable Soviet victory not all Stalin's generals involved were feted as heroes. Vatutin came under criticism for not anticipating the direction of Manstein's main blow soon enough. He was accused of dissipating his forces over a 164km-wide defensive zone, which permitted the Germans to penetrate as far as Prokhorovka. Zhukov refuted this, arguing that Vatutin's 6th and 7th Guards Armies, which bore the brunt of the Germans' southern offensive, were backed by all the reserve artillery and tank formations. He pointed out that 'In the sectors of the 38th and 40th Armies the artillery density was negligible, and these armies had very few tanks'.[21] Likewise, the 69th Army was holding the junction between the two Guards armies. In addition, the weight of the attack against Vatutin's defences had been heavier involving five German corps, whereas Rokossovsky had initially been attacked by three corps.

Essentially Kursk was four separate battles. Firstly, the Citadel operations fought at Ponyri and Prohorovka, which was the defensive phase for the Red Army, which ended on Rokossovsky's Central Front on 12 July and Vatutin's Voronezh Front on 23 July. Kutuzov and Rumyantsev were fought as two further separate battles. Zhukov was critical of how their subsequent counteroffensives were handled. He blamed Konev's Steppe Front for the delay in the later operation:

> Troops near Belgorod did not start their offensive until 3 August, twenty days after the Central, Bryansk and Western fronts.
>
> These three fronts required less time for preparation because their offensives had been planned and all supplies provided during the defensive stage of the battle. The forces near Belgorod required more time because the troops of the Steppe Front lacked a fully worked-out plan when they were drawn into the counteroffensive. Having been kept in the Supreme Headquarters reserve, they were not familiar with their precise objectives, their jumping-off areas or the specific enemy forces they were supposed to engage.[22]

This was unfair as Konev's forces had previously been the Reserve Front so were not as battle-tested as the others. Besides, Vatutin's Voronezh

Front was the main striking force but it had been exhausted holding the Germans at Prokhorovka. Nonetheless, Zhukov did acknowledge, 'The counteroffensive of the Voronezh Front forces was launched under more difficult conditions than the attack around Orel.'[23] He also accepted that the piecemeal use of the Steppe Front during the defensive phase had weakened it before it went over to the offensive.

Finally, just how much value did Stalin gain from his spies in Britain and Switzerland? While their espionage work was exciting and dangerous, the answer is very little. By the time decrypted intelligence reached Moscow it was often days, if not weeks, out of date. John Cairncross, Leo Long and Anthony Blunt liked to think they were instrumental in changing the course of the war. This was a deluded view. Sándor Radó and Rudolf Roessler were fed information direct from the German High Command, but whether this was better than the intelligence gained from the Lorenz decrypts at Bletchley is unknown. The Soviet leader had numerous sources of intelligence and his spies were just one small part of his vast information-gathering network.

Churchill's understandable reluctance to reveal the source of his intelligence inevitably did little to enhance its credibility with the Kremlin. Furthermore, by the time intercepts had been decrypted units were often long gone, having been redeployed elsewhere. Stalin got much better intelligence from his partisans behind enemy lines monitoring German-controlled airfields, railways and roads. Likewise the Red Army ran its own radio intercept operations and the Red Air Force conducted regular photographic reconnaissance flights.

Nonetheless, the role of Enigma- and Lorenz-derived intelligence passed to Stalin officially or unofficially should not be completely dismissed. If Moscow was never ready to acknowledge the part played by Lend-Lease equipment, then it was certainly never going to accept it won the war thanks to British- and American-supplied intelligence.

Codebreaker Captain Jerry Roberts was in little doubt that intelligence supplied by Bletchley Park played a vital part in shortening the war and hastening Hitler's final defeat. He pointed out that Churchill 'gave the Russians full details of the plans three months before the battle took place and allowed them to deploy the maximum number of tanks and win the Battle of Kursk'.[24] Until his dying day Roberts championed the unsung heroes of Bletchley:

> Most people in Britain are unaware of the Kursk story and its enormous significance, and of the major contribution made by the Lorenz decrypts

to its successful outcome. I wonder whether the Russian authorities ever realised the importance of the help that Britain had given. Few people in the world will be aware of the facts of the Lorenz story, which Britain kept secret for more than sixty years after the war.[25]

It is very notable that Khrushchev and Zhukov said they were tipped off that Citadel was about to commence against both the Central and Voronezh Fronts by prisoners captured just hours before. It is completely improbable that lowly privates from the German Army and the Waffen-SS would be privy to such information. Even if they were, it seems a convenient coincidence that the two fronts received the same warning at about the same time from the same type of source.

It may be that Zhukov and Khrushchev wanted a plausible reason for opening fire before Hitler attacked. Could it be that Stalin and his high command already knew the exact day and hour that Operation Citadel was due to commence. This is more than likely; was this knowledge derived from Bletchley's intelligence? It is impossible to tell. Besides, Stalin would never have acknowledged such timely assistance. Ultimately the battle had been brewing for months and for the Red Army it was just a case of sitting tight until such time as Hitler chose to attack. Certainly a man with secret documents stuffed down his trousers was not really going to have much bearing on such events.

While the Battle of Stalingrad marked the peak of Hitler's attempts to crush the Soviet Union, the failure of his 1943 summer offensive and Stalin's massive counteroffensive put an end to any hopes he had of being anything more than on the defensive on the Eastern Front. General Halder, former Chief of Staff to the German Army, wrote despairingly:

> Towards the end of 1943 at the latest it had become unmistakably clear that the war had been lost …
>
> By the sacrifice of German blood and the cost of exposing the homeland to the enemy Air Forces, the war could still be kept going for a little longer. But were the results to be gained by such a course worth the sacrifice?[26]

The fall of Mussolini and the Allied landings in Italy proved an unwelcome drain on Hitler's stretched resources. It also made Kursk an irrelevance to Hitler in the face of the Allies' impending second front. The situation became much worse following the D-Day landings in France the following year. After Kursk, strategically Hitler was left just playing for time on the Eastern Front. He hoped the Wehrmacht could contain things until winter brought the fighting to a halt once again. That would give it time to rebuild and re-equip. By the following summer the Wehrmacht was still not in a position to conduct a large-scale offensive. Stalin was and his Red Army reached Warsaw, and despite some temporary setbacks was soon on the road to Berlin. All this was thanks to their hard-fought victory at Kursk.

'The victory at Kursk,' Hitler had said, 'must shine like a beacon to the world.' Kursk did shine out to the world but not for the reasons he had naively hoped for.[27] Despite his seeming indifference to Operation Citadel just four days before it commenced, he stated:

> The defeat that Russia will suffer as a result of this offensive must in the immediate future wrest the initiative from the Soviet leadership and may decisively influence developments … the success of this great battle of 1943 will decide more than any ordinary battle.[28]

They were prophetic words.

# EPILOGUE

# NO SWORD OF KURSK

The Red Army was rightly proud of its achievements at Kursk, seeing it as 'one of the greatest operations of the Second World War'. Unfortunately, after the ill-feeling over Lend-Lease, the Allies' treatment of the Soviet victory subsequently fuelled further deep resentment between London and Washington on one hand and Moscow on the other.

Deliberately or otherwise, Churchill and Roosevelt underplayed the Red Army's success at Kursk by recognising Stalingrad as the key turning point of the war. Churchill, with Roosevelt in attendance, at the end of 1943 in Tehran presented Stalin with the highly ornate specially commissioned Sword of Stalingrad. It was inscribed, 'To the steel-hearted citizens of Stalingrad, a gift from King George VI as a token of the homage of the British People.'[1] Another snub was plain to see, it congratulated the citizens not the Red Army or Stalin's leadership.

Although the gift was well intended, to someone as cynical and manipulative as Stalin he undoubtedly saw hidden meaning in it. As his name translates to 'Man of Steel' he was probably flattered by the reference to 'steel-hearted' and shed a tear on acceptance of the bejewelled weapon. The ceremony though was marred by one of his generals dropping the sword with a loud clatter. The following year Roosevelt presented the city with a commemorative scroll and whilst it recognised the defenders it spoke of Stalingrad being a 'turning point in the war'.[2] A similar scroll was also presented to the people of Leningrad to mark their heroic resistance.[3] There were no such accolades for the victors of Kursk.

In the years that followed the resentment over how Britain and America viewed Kursk grew. The Soviet official history recorded with some bitterness:

> After the war many bourgeois historians sought to belittle the signifi-
> cance of the Red Army victory in the summer of 1943. Some of them
> regard the battle in the Kursk Salient as an ordinary, commonplace
> episode of the Second World War. Others either completely ignore it
> or speak of it vaguely. However, the significance of this massive battle
> cannot be obscured, much as it is impossible to conceal … the thrashing
> received by the Nazi generals.[4]

Who needed a Sword of Kursk when you had so soundly thrashed Hitler's armies? Where the Soviets were concerned, at Stalingrad they had won the battle, while at Kursk they had won the war.

# DRAMATIS PERSONAE

## Americans

Cassidy, Henry: Head of Associated Press.
Kerr, Walter: Correspondent for the *New York Herald Tribune* based in Moscow.
Roosevelt, Franklin D.: US President from 1933 until his sudden death in April 1945. He sponsored the Lend-Lease Act that Congress passed in 1941, which permitted America to help its allies with almost everything they needed except for troops. The latter changed after the Japanese attack on Pearl Harbor.
Standley, Admiral William H.: US Ambassador to Moscow.

## British

Blunt, Anthony: Soviet mole working for MI5.
Cairncross, Captain John: Spy working for Soviet military intelligence at Bletchley Park.
Churchill, Winston: British Prime Minister and Minister of Defence from May 1940 until July 1945. He offered Stalin every assistance despite his anti-Bolshevik stance.
Foote, Allan: Spy working for Soviet military intelligence in Lucerne, Switzerland.
Long, Intelligence Officer Leo: Spy working for Soviet military intelligence at the War Office.

Macintyre, Captain: Commander of the escort cruiser HMS *Scylla*, which sailed with the Arctic convoys.

Oakeshott, Arthur: Reuters special correspondent who sailed with the Arctic convoys.

Roberts, Captain Jerry: Codebreaker at Bletchley Park working on the German Lorenz cipher system.

Werth, Alexander: Correspondent for *The Sunday Times* based in Moscow.

White, Yeoman: Royal Navy sailor on HMS *Scylla*.

# French

Tulasne, Major Jean: Commander of the volunteer Normandy Squadron serving with the Red Air Force.

# Germans*

Balck, General Hermann: Commander of *Grossdeutschland* Panzergrenadier Division.

Bormann, Martin: Head of Party Chancellery (succeeding Rudolf Hess). One of Hitler's closet advisors and became his Private Secretary.

Brehme, Sergeant Gerhard: Platoon commander 5th Company, 52nd Panzer Battalion.

Canaris, Admiral Wilhelm: Chief of Amtsgruppe Ausland/Abwehr (intelligence in Oberkommando der Wehrmacht, or Command of Armed Forces) 1938–44.

d'Alquen, Colonel Günther: Editor of *The Black Corps*, the official newspaper of the Waffen-SS.

Deichmann, General: Commander of Luftwaffe's 1st Air Division, 6th Air Fleet.

Diekwisch, Lieutenant: Pilot with 1st Stuka Group.

Eggers, Colonel Kurt: Former Editor of *The Black Corps*. Killed in action with the 5th SS.

---

* Correct terminology always poses a problem. Throughout the text I refer to the 'Russians' as Soviets simply because this encompasses the numerous nationalities within the Soviet Union. The Germans in their newsreels referred to them as Bolsheviks or Soviets while the troops generically called them 'Russkies' or Russians. The Soviets tended to refer to the Germans as fascists or Nazis, though they included Austrians and other nationalities in their ranks.

Eggers, Traute Kaiser: Kurt's wife.

Erhardt, Rolf: Tank driver with 1st SS Panzergrenadier Division.

Fellgiebel, General Erich: Chief of signals for the army and OKW.

Frantz, Captain Peter: Commander of *Grossdeutschland*'s assault artillery detachment.

Gehlen, Colonel Reinhard: Head of intelligence on the Eastern Front.

Goebbels, Dr Joseph: Nazi Minister for Propaganda.

Göring, Reichsmarschall Hermann: Reichsminister for Air, Reichsminister for the five-year plan and Commander in Chief of the Luftwaffe.

Grossmann, General: Commander of 6th Infantry Division.

Guderian, General Heinz: Inspector General of Armoured Forces, answering directly to Hitler.

Günsche, SS-Major Otto: One of Hitler's military adjutants.

Halder, General Franz: Chief of Army General Staff 1 November 1938 to 24 September 1942, succeeded by General Zeitzler.

Hausser, General Paul: Commander SS Panzer Corps.

Heusinger, General Adolf: Head of Army Operational Planning.

Himmler, Reichsführer-SS Heinrich: Head of the Schutz-Staffel and the Waffen-SS.

Hitler, Adolf: Became German Chancellor in 1933 and by the outbreak of the war was also head of state and supreme commander of the armed forces. He made himself personally responsible for the conduct of the war.

Hörnlein, General Walter 'Papa': Balck's successor, commander *Grossdeutschland* Panzergrenadier Division.

Hoth, Colonel General Hermann: Commander of 4th Panzer Army.

Jeschonnek, General Hans: Luftwaffe Chief of Staff, answering directly to Hitler, although technically subordinate to Göring.

Jodl, General Alfred: Head of Armed Forces Operational Staff throughout the war and Field Marshal Keitel's deputy.

Jungenfeld, Colonel Baron Ernst von: Commander 656th Panzerjäger Regiment.

Keitel, Field Marshal Wilhelm: Chief of High Command of the Armed Forces (Oberkommando der Wehrmacht [OKW]) throughout the war.

Kleist, Field Marshal Ewald von: Commander of Army Group A.

Klemperer, Victor: Jewish academic living in Dresden who kept a diary throughout the war. He avoided the concentration camps because he was married to a non-Jew.

Kluge, Field Marshal Günther von: Commander of Army Group Centre.

Knobelsdorff, General: Commander of 48th Panzer Corps.

Kupfer, Lieutenant Colonel: Commander of 2nd Stuka Group.

Küster, Gerd: Panther tank driver with 51st Panzer Battalion.

Lang, Captain Friedrich: Pilot with 1st Stuka Group.

Lauchert, Major Meinrad: Commander of 39th Panzer Regiment.

Linge, SS-Major Heinz: One of Hitler's military adjutants.

Lubbe, General: Commander of 2nd Panzer Division.

Magold, Captain Hans: Commander of *Grossdeutschland*'s assault gun battalion.

Manstein, Field Marshal von: Commander Army Group South.

Mellenthin, General von: Chief of Staff of 48th Panzer Corps.

Meyer, Captain Bruno: Commander Luftwaffe 4th Anti-Tank Group.

Milch, Air (Field) Marshal Erhard: Air Inspector General in charge of air-craft production, answering to Göring.

Model, Colonel General Walter: Commander of 9th Army.

Morell, Dr Theodor: Hitler's physician.

Noak, Major: Commander of 654th Panzerjäger Battalion, 656th Panzerjäger Regiment.

Porsche, Dr Ferdinand: Designer of the Ferdinand heavy tank destroyer.

Raus, General Erhard: Commander of 11th Corps.

Ribbentrop, Rudolf von: Adjutant of 1st SS Panzer Regiment.

Roessler, Rudolf: German exile working for Soviet intelligence in Switzerland.

Rosenberg, Alfred: Reichsminister for Occupied Eastern Territories.

Rudel, Colonel Hans-Ulrich: Tank-busting dive-bomber commander.

Scheller, General: Commander of 9th Panzer Division.

Schleiben, General: Commander of 18th Panzer Division.

Schneider, Christian: German émigré working for Soviet intelligence in Switzerland.

Seidemann, General Hans: Commander of 8th Air Corps.

Seiler, Major Reinhard 'Seppl': Commander of 54th Fighter Group.

Simon, General Max: Commander of 3rd SS Panzergrenadier Division *Totenkopf*.

Speer, Albert: Professor of Architecture. Succeeded Fritz Todt as Reichsminister for Armaments in 1942.

Steiger, Martin: Commander of 1st Panzer Company, 3rd SS Panzer Regiment.

Steinwachs, Major: Commander of 653th Panzerjäger Battalion, 656th Panzerjäger Regiment.

Strachwitz, Colonel Graf: Commander of *Grossdeutschland's* Panzer Regiment.

Strassl, Flight Sergeant Hubert: Fighter ace with 51st Fighter Group.

Thomale, General Wolfgang: Chief of Staff to General Heinz Guderian.

Wisch, Theodor: Commander 1st SS Panzergrenadier Division
  *Leibstandarte Adolf Hitler.*

Wulf, Grenadier 1st Class E: Soldier with the 332nd Infantry Division.

Zeitzler, General Kurt: Chief of the Army General Staff answering
  directly to Hitler.

## Axis Allies

Antonescu, Field Marshal Ion: Romanian dictator.

Horthy, Admiral: Hungarian dictator.

Keyneres, Milklós: Hungarian fighter pilot serving with the Luftwaffe.

Mussolini, Benito: Italian dictator who by 1939 had already been in power
  for thirteen years. That year he concluded a pact with Hitler. He was
  ousted from power on 25 July 1943 for his poor conduct of the war.

## Russians

Abdulin, Mansur: Soldier with 193rd Guards Rifle Regiment, part of
  66th Guards Rifle Division.

Anisimov, General: Logistics commander for Voronezh Front.

Antipenko, General: Logistics commander for Central Front.

Badanov, General: Commander of 4th Tank Army.

Baklanov, General: Commander of 13th Guards Rifle Division.

Baksov, Colonel: Commander of 67th Guards Rifle Division.

Barybin, Lieutenant: Anti-aircraft battery commander.

Belgin, Captain: Commander of 3rd Battalion, 214th Rifle Regiment.

Belov, Nikolai: Rifleman.

Bessonov, Lieutenant Evgeni: Junior officer with the 49th Mechanised
  Brigade, 4th Tank Army.

Bilaonov, Captain Pavel: Abdulin's regimental commanding officer.

Blinova, Lieutenant Klavdiya: Pilot with 65th Guards Fighter
  Aviation Regiment.

Bryukhov, Lieutenant Pavolich: Tank commander with 2nd Tank Corps.

Chistyakov, General: Commander of 21st Army.

Chuikov, General: Commander of 62nd Army at Stalingrad.

Davidenko, Colonel: Commander of 214th Rifle Regiment.

Dement'ev, Pyotr: Deputy Commissar for Aircraft Production.

Gagen, General: Commander of 57th Army.

Gorsky, Anatoli: John Cairncross' spymaster in London.

Grossman, Vasily: Special correspondent for *Red Star* military newspaper.

Gubkin, Georgi: Officer with 4th Rifle Company, 184th Rifle Division.

Khrulev, General: Chief of Red Army Rear Services and Transport.

Khrushchev, Leonid: Nikita's son, killed in action.

Khrushchev, Nikita: Political Commissar and Ukrainian Communist Party boss.

Kirichenko, Senior Sergeant Petr: Tank commander with 159th Tank Brigade.

Knorring, Oleg: Photographer for *Red Star* military newspaper.

Kosykh, Major General: 16th Air Army liaison officer to 13th Army.

Kozhedub, Ivan: Soviet fighter ace.

Kozhemiako: Press officer.

Kozienk, Senior Lieutenant Terenti: Battalion commander of 49th Mechanised Brigade, 4th Tank Army.

Kozin, General: Commander of 52nd Rifle Division.

Kozlovsky, Ivan: Famous opera singer.

Krasovski, General Commander of 2nd Air Army.

Kuznetsov, Senior Lieutenant: Pilot with 65th Guards Fighter Aviation Regiment.

Lebedeva, Antonina: Pilot with 65th Guards Fighter Aviation Regiment.

Levitan, Yurii: Announcer on Moscow state radio.

Lipasvsky, Major: TASS correspondent.

Malinin, Lieutenant General: General Rokossovsky's Chief of Staff.

Managarov, General: Commander of 53rd Army.

Martynov, Kostia: Rifleman with 193rd Guards Rifle Regiment, part of 66th Guards Rifle Division.

Molotov, Vyacheslav: Soviet Foreign Minister.

Morozov, Alexander: Chief tank designer.

Nekrasov, Colonel: Commander 52nd Guards Rifle Division.

Nochovny, Lieutenant Leonid: Artillery platoon commander, 66th Guards Rifle Division.

Novikov, Air Marshal: Commander of Red Air Force.

Pantyukhov, Lieutenant Colonel: Regimental commander with 52nd Rifle Division.

Paton, Yevgeny: Soviet engineer who introduced electric welding to tank production, protégé of Khrushchev.

Petrishchev, Senior Lieutenant: Served with 299th Rifle Division.

Popov, General: Commander of Bryansk Front.

Pukhov, General: Commander of 13th Army.

Rokossovsky, General: Commander of Central Front.

Rotmistrov, General Pavel: Commander of 5th Guards Tank Army.

Rudenko, General: Commander 16th of Air Army.

Rukosuyev, Colonel: Commander of 3rd Anti-Tank Artillery Brigade.

Rybalko, General: Commander of 3rd Guards Tank Army.

Seid-Mamedova, Senior Lieutenant: Pilot with 586th Fighter Regiment.

Shtemenko, General: Red Army Chief of Operations.

Simutenkov, Senior Lieutenant: Dive-bomber pilot.

Sokolovsky, General: Commander of Western Front.

Stalin, Joseph: Soviet dictator and supreme commander. He became a Marshal of the Soviet Union in 1943 and Generalissimo in 1945.

Studets, Lieutenant General: Commander of 17th Air Army.

Vasilevsky, General: Chief of General Staff.

Vatutin, Lieutenant General: Commander of Voronezh Front.

Vavilov, Colonel: Political Officer of 13th Guards Rifle Division.

Voronov, Lieutenant Colonel: Political officer of 52nd Rifle Division.

Vorozheikin, Captain: Pilot with 728th Fighter Regiment.

Yakovlev, Alexandr: Soviet aircraft designer responsible for Yak fighters.

Yenshin, General: Commander of 307th Rifle Division.

Yepishev, Alexei: Ukrainian Communist Party Representative.

Zhadov, General: Commander of the 5th Guards Army.

Zhukov, Marshal Georgi: He became Chief of General Staff in January 1941 and was appointed C-in-C of the Russian western front in October 1941. In August 1942 he also became Deputy Commissar for Defence or Deputy Supreme Commander, answering directly to Stalin.

# SOVIET ORDER OF BATTLE, 5 JULY 1943

## Central Front

General of the Army Konstantin Rokossovsky

13th Army: Lieutenant General Pukhov

15th Rifle Corps
8th Rifle Division
74th Rifle Division
148th Rifle Division

17th Guards Rifle Corps
6th Guards Rifle Division
70th Guards Rifle Division
75th Guards Rifle Division

18th Guards Rifle Corps
2nd Airborne Guards Rifle Division
3rd Airborne Guards Rifle Division
4th Airborne Guards Rifle Division

29th Rifle Corps
15th Rifle Division
81st Rifle Division
307th Rifle Division

Anti-Tank & Artillery Units (4th Artillery Corps)
3rd Anti-Tank Artillery Brigade

13th Anti-Tank Artillery Brigade
5th Artillery Division
11th Mortar Brigade
22nd Mortar Brigade

**48th Army: Lieutenant General Romanenko**

42nd Rifle Corps
16th Rifle Division
73rd Rifle Division
137th Rifle Division
143rd Rifle Division
170th Rifle Division
202nd Rifle Division
399th Rifle Division

**60th Army: Lieutenant General Chernyahovsky**

24th Rifle Corps
42nd Rifle Division
112th Rifle Division

30th Rifle Corps
121st Rifle Division
141st Rifle Division
322nd Rifle Division
Independent 55th Rifle Division

**65th Army: Lieutenant General Batov**

18th Rifle Corps
69th Rifle Division
149th Rifle Division
246th Rifle Division

27th Rifle Corps
37th Guards Rifle Division
60th Rifle Division

181st Rifle Division
193rd Rifle Division
194th Rifle Division
354th Rifle Division

70th Army: Lieutenant General Galanin

28th Rifle Corps
102nd Rifle Division
106th Rifle Division
132nd Rifle Division
140th Rifle Division
162nd Rifle Division
211th Rifle Division
280th Rifle Division

2nd Tank Army: Lieutenant General Rodin

3rd Tank Corps
16th Tank Corps

16th Air Army: Air Marshal Rudenko

3rd Bombing Air Corps
6th Mixed Air Corps
6th Fighter Corps

Independent Formations
4th Artillery Corps (assigned to 13th Army)
Independent 9th Tank Corps
Independent 19th Tank Corps

## Voronezh Front

General of the Army Nikolai Vatutin

6th Guards Army: Lieutenant General Chistyakov

22nd Guards Rifle Corps
67th Guards Rifle Division
71st Guards Rifle Division
90th Guards Rifle Division

23rd Guards Rifle Corps
51st Guards Rifle Division
52nd Guards Rifle Division
375th Rifle Division
Independent 89th Guards Rifle Division

7th Guards Army: Lieutenant General Shumilov

24th Guards Rifle Corps
15th Guards Rifle Division
36th Guards Rifle Division
72nd Guards Rifle Division

25th Guards Rifle Corps
73rd Guards Rifle Division
78th Guards Rifle Division
81st Guards Rifle Division
Independent 213th Rifle Division

38th Army: Lieutenant General Chibisov

50th Rifle Corps
167th Rifle Division
232nd Rifle Division
340th Rifle Division

51st Rifle Corps
180th Rifle Division
240th Rifle Division
Independent 204th Rifle Division

40th Army: Lieutenant General Moskalenko

4th Rifle Corps
161st Rifle Division
206th Rifle Division
237th Rifle Division
52nd Rifle Corps
100th Rifle Division
219th Rifle Division
309th Rifle Division
Independent 184th Rifle Division

69th Army: Lieutenant General Kruchenkin

48th Rifle Corps
107th Rifle Division
183rd Rifle Division
307th Rifle Division

49th Rifle Corps
111th Rifle Division
270th Rifle Division

1st Tank Army: Lieutenant General Katukov

6th Tank Corps
31st Tank Corps
3rd Mechanised Corps

2nd Air Army: Air Marshal Krasovski

1st Assault Air Corps
1st Bombing Air Corps
4th Fighter Air Corps
5th Fighter Air Corps

Front Assets
35th Rifle Corps
92nd Guards Rifle Division

93rd Guards Rifle Division
94th Guards Rifle Division
Independent 2nd Guards Tank Corps
Independent 3rd Guards Tank Corps

## Steppe (Reserve) Front

Colonel General Konev

5th Guards Army: Lieutenant General Zhadov

32nd Guards Rifle Corps
6th Airborne Guards Rifle Division
13th Guards Rifle Division
66th Guards Rifle Division

33rd Guards Rifle Corps
9th Airborne Guards Rifle Division
95th Guards Rifle Division
97th Guards Rifle Division
Independent 42nd Guards Rifle Division

5th Guards Tank Army: Lieutenant General Rotmistrov

5th Guards Mechanised Corps
29th Tank Corps

27th Army: Lieutenant General Trofimenko
47th Army: Lieutenant General Ryzhov
53rd Army: Lieutenant General Mangarov

5th Air Army: Colonel General Goryunov

3rd Fighter Air Corps
7th Fighter Air Cops
7th Mixed Air Corps
8th Mixed Air Corps

Front Assets
3rd Cavalry Corps
5th Cavalry Corps
7th Cavalry Corps
1st Guards Mechanised Corps

4th Guards Tank Corps
10th Tank Corps
18th Tank Corps

# GERMAN ORDER OF BATTLE, 5 JULY 1943

## Army Group Centre

Field Marshal von Kluge

9th Army: Colonel General Model

20th Army Corps: General Freiherr von Roman
45th Infantry Division: Major General Freiherr von Falkenstein
72nd Infantry Division: Lieutenant General Müller-Gebhard
137th Infantry Division: Lieutenant General Kamecke
251st Infantry Division: Major General Felzmann

23rd Army Corps: General Freissner
78th Assault Division: Lieutenant General Traut
216th Infantry Division: Major General Schack
383rd Infantry Division: Major General Hoffmeister

46th Panzer Corps: General Zorn
7th Infantry Division: Lieutenant General von Rappard
31st Infantry Division: Lieutenant General Hossbach
102nd Infantry Division: Major General Hitzfeld
258th Infantry Division: Lieutenant General Hocker

47th Panzer Corps: General Lemelsen
2nd Panzer Division: Lieutenant General Lubbe
9th Panzer Division: Lieutenant General Scheller
20th Panzer Division: Major General von Kessel
6th Infantry Division: Lieutenant General Grossmann

41st Panzer Corps: General Harpe
18th Panzer Division: Major General von Schlieben
86th Infantry Division: Lieutenant General Weilding
292nd Infantry Division: Lieutenant General von Kluge

Luftflotte 6: Colonel General von Greim
1st Air Division: Major General Deichmann

# Army Group South

Field Marshal von Manstein

Army Detachment Kempf: General Kempf

11th Army Corps: General Raus
106th Infantry Division: Lieutenant General Forst
320th Infantry Division: Major General Postel

42nd Army Corps: General Mattenklott
39th Infantry Division: Lieutenant General Loeweneck
161st Infantry Division: Lieutenant General Recke
282nd Infantry Division: Major General Kohler

3rd Panzer Corps: General Breith
6th Panzer Division: Major General Hünersdorff
7th Panzer Division: Lieutenant General Freiherr von Funck
19th Panzer Division: Lieutenant General Schmidt
168th Infantry Division: Major General de Beaulieu

4th Panzer Army: Colonel General Hoth

2nd SS Panzer Corps: SS–General Hausser
1st SS Panzergrenadier Division *Liebstandarte Adolf Hitler*:
SS–Brigadeführer Wisch
2nd SS Panzergrenadier Division *Das Reich*: SS–Major General Krüger
3rd SS Panzergrenadier Division *Totenkopf*: SS–Brigadier Priess

48th Panzer Corps: General Knobelsdorff
3rd Panzer Division: Lieutenant General Westhoven
11th Panzer Division: Major General Mickl
Panzergrenadier Division *Grossdeutschland*: Lieutenant General Hörnlein
167th Infantry Division: Lieutenant General Trierenberg

52nd Army Corps: General Ott
57th Infantry Division: Major General Fretter-Pico
255th Infantry Division: Lieutenant General Poppe
332nd Infantry Division: Lieutenant General Schaeffer

Reserve
24th Panzer Corps: General Nehring
5th SS Panzergrenadier Division *Wiking*
17th Panzer Division

Luftflotte 4: General Dessloch
8th Air Corps: General Seidemann
1st Flak Corps: General Reiman

# GERMAN PANZER DIVISIONS AT KURSK – MAIN COMBAT UNITS

2nd Panzer Division
2nd Panzer Reconnaissance Battalion
3rd Panzer Regiment
2nd Panzergrenadier Regiment
304th Panzergrenadier Regiment
38th Panzerjäger (Tank Destroyer) Battalion
74th Artillery Regiment
273rd Flak (Anti-Aircraft) Battalion

3rd Panzer Division
3rd Panzer Reconnaissance Battalion
6th Panzer Regiment
3rd Panzergrenadier Regiment
394th Panzergrenadier Regiment
39th Panzerjäger Battalion
75th Artillery Regiment
314th Flak Battalion

6th Panzer Division
6th Panzer Reconnaissance Battalion
11th Panzer Regiment
4th Panzergrenadier Regiment
114th Panzergrenadier Regiment
41st Panzerjäger Battalion
76th Artillery Regiment

298th Flak Battalion

7th Panzer Division
7th Panzer Reconnaissance Battalion
25th Panzer Regiment
6th Panzergrenadier Regiment
7th Panzergrenadier Regiment
42nd Panzerjäger Battalion
78th Artillery Regiment
296th Flak Battalion

9th Panzer Division
9th Panzer Reconnaissance Battalion
33rd Panzer Regiment Prince Eugene
10th Panzergrenadier Regiment
11th Panzergrenadier Regiment
50th Panzerjäger Battalion
102nd Artillery Regiment
287th Flak Battalion

11th Panzer Division
11th Panzer Reconnaissance Battalion
15th Panzer Regiment
110th Panzergrenadier Regiment
111th Panzergrenadier Regiment
61st Panzerjäger Battalion
119th Artillery Regiment
277th Flak Battalion

18th Panzer Division
18th Panzer Reconnaissance Battalion
18th Panzer Regiment
52nd Panzergrenadier Regiment
101st Panzergrenadier Regiment
88th Panzerjäger Battalion
88th Artillery Regiment
208th Flak Battalion

19th Panzer Division
19th Panzer Reconnaissance Battalion
27th Panzer Regiment
73rd Panzergrenadier Regiment
74th Panzergrenadier Regiment
19th Panzerjäger Battalion
19th Artillery Regiment
272nd Flak Battalion

20th Panzer Division
20th Panzer Reconnaissance Battalion
21st Panzer Regiment
59th Panzergrenadier Regiment
112th Panzergrenadier Regiment
92nd Panzerjäger Battalion
92nd Artillery Regiment

# GERMAN PANZERGRENADIER DIVISIONS AT KURSK – MAIN COMBAT UNITS

Panzergrenadier Division *Grossdeutschland*
*Grossdeutschland* Panzergrenadier Reconnaissance Battalion
*Grossdeutschland* Panzer Regiment
*Grossdeutschland* Fusilier Regiment
*Grossdeutschland* Panzergrenadier Regiment
*Grossdeutschland* Panzerjäger Battalion
*Grosstdeutschland* Sturmgeschütz Battalion
*Grossdeutschland* Artillery Regiment
*Grossdeutschland* Flak Battalion

1st SS Panzergrenadier Division *Leibstandarte Adolf Hitler*
1st SS Panzergrenadier Reconnaissance Battalion
1st SS Panzer Regiment
1st SS Panzergrenadier Regiment
2nd SS Panzergrenadier Regiment
1st SS Panzerjäger Battalion
1st SS Sturmgeschütz Battalion
1st SS Artillery Regiment
1st SS Flak Battalion

2nd SS Panzergrenadier Division *Das Reich*
2nd SS Panzergrenadier Reconnaissance Battalion
2nd SS Panzer Regiment
3rd SS Panzergrenadier Regiment *Deutschland*
4th SS Panzergrenadier Regiment *Der Führer*
2nd SS Panzerjäger Battalion
2nd SS Sturmgeschütz Battalion

2nd SS Artillery Regiment
2nd SS Flak Battalion

3rd SS Panzergrenadier Division *Totenkopf*
3rd SS Panzergrenadier Reconnaissance Battalion
3rd SS Panzer Regiment
5th SS Panzergrenadier Regiment *Thule*
6th SS Panzergrenadier Regiment *Theodor Eicke*
3rd SS Panzerjäger Battalion
3rd SS Sturmgeschütz Battalion
3rd SS Artillery Regiment
3rd SS Flak Battalion

# SOVIET ORDER OF BATTLE, 12 JULY 1943

## Operation Kutuzov

*Western Front*
General of the Army: General Sokolovsky
11th Army
11th Guards Army
50th Army
1st Air Army

*Bryansk Front*
General of the Army: General Popov
3rd Army
3rd Guards Tank Army
4th Tank Army
61st Army
63rd Army
15th Air Army

*Central Front*
General of the Army: General Rokossovsky
2nd Tank Army
13th Army
48th Army
65th Army
70th Army
16th Air Army

# SOVIET UNITS INVOLVED IN THE LIBERATION OF OREL, 5 AUGUST 1943

5th Rifle Division
129th Rifle Division
380th Rifle Division

# SOVIET UNITS INVOLVED IN THE LIBERATION OF KARACHEV, 15 AUGUST 1943

16th Guards Rifle Division
84th Guards Rifle Division
238th Rifle Division
369th Rifle Division

# SOVIET ORDER OF BATTLE, 3 AUGUST 1943

## Operation Rumyantsev

*Voronezh Front*
General of the Army: Vatutin
1st Tank Army
5th Guards Tank Army
5th Guards Army
6th Guards Army
27th Army
38th Army
40th Army
2nd Air Army

Supreme Command Reserves
4th Guards Army

*Steppe Front*
General of the Army: Konev
7th Guards Army
53rd Army
69th Army
1st Mechanised Corps
5th Air Army

*South-Western Front*
General of the Army: Malinovsky
57th Army
17th Air Army

# SOVIET UNITS INVOLVED IN THE LIBERATION OF BELGOROD, 5 AUGUST 1943

89th Guards Rifle Division
93rd Guards Rifle Division
94th Guards Rifle Division
111th Rifle Division
305th Rifle Division
375th Rifle Division

# SOVIET UNITS INVOLVED IN THE LIBERATION OF KHARKOV, 23 AUGUST 1943

15th Guards Division
28th Guards Rifle Division
84th Rifle Division
89th Guards Rifle Division
93rd Guards Rifle Division
116th Rifle Division
183rd Rifle Division
252nd Rifle Division
299th Rifle Division
375th Rifle Division

# NOTES

## Introduction

1 Khrushchev, *Khrushchev Remembers*, p.208.

2 Ibid.

3 Grossman, *A Writer at War*, p.225.

4 Abdulin, *Red Road from Stalingrad*, p.82.

5 Bessonov, *Tank Rider*, p.33.

6 Ibid.

7 Yakovlev describes this uncomfortable meeting in Bialer, *Stalin and His Generals*, pp.381–2. It is also referenced in Axell, *Russia's Heroes*, pp.56–7, Boyd, *The Soviet Air Force Since 1918*, p.197 & Montefiore, *Stalin The Court of the Red Tsar*, p.400. Translations vary but the general gist remains the same, both Yakovlev and Dement'ev were wrong-footed by Stalin at this meeting despite being well aware of the problem with the fighters.

8 See Quarrie, *Hitler's Teutonic Knights*, p.192 & Williamson, *Waffen-SS Handbook 1933–1945*, pp.56–7.

9 D'Alquen first edited *The Black Corps* during the late 1930s, he later became head of the Army Propaganda Department though Himmler continued to make use of his services until the very end of the war. See Reitliger, *The SS Alibi of a Nation*, pp.16 & 389.

10 Guderian, *Panzer Leader*, p.310.

11 Mellenthin, *Panzer Battles*, p.261.

12 Ibid.

13 Ibid.

14 Eberle & Uhl, *The Hitler Book: The Secret Dossier Prepared for Stalin*, p.115. This dossier was mainly based on the interrogations of Otto Günsche and Heinz

Linge. The first served as one of Hitler's adjutants while the other was head of his personal household, so both were very close to the Führer. However, they were commenting from memory.

15  Ibid., p.114.
16  *War Illustrated*, 30 October 1942, p.317.
17  Ibid.
18  Smith, *Station X*, pp.163–4. The Soviets codenamed Cairncross 'Liszt' due to his passion for music. Before the war while working for the Treasury in a section dealing with the General Post Office he had passed the Soviets information on Bletchley Park's intercept sites, which included Beaumanor Hall, London and Scarborough. This was also of concern for the out-stations in Cairo, Colombo, Mombasa and Singapore.
19  See Mckay, *The Lost World of Bletchley Park*, pp.40–1, which reproduces some of the memos dealing with these problems and claimed the loss rate of crockery was five times that of a Royal Navy warship.
20  Andrew, *The Defence of the Realm*, p.173.
21  McKay, *The Secret Life of Bletchley Park*, p.236.
22  Andrew, *The Defence of the Realm*, p.280.

# 1: Training at Saratov

1  Once Stalin had recovered from the shock of Hitler's invasion in 1941, he re-evaluated his strategy and made reconstructing his tank fleet a national priority. He established the People's Commissariat for Tank Production and new tank plants sprang up east of the Ural Mountains, in particular Uralmashzavod, the Ural Machine-Building Plant, and Chelyabinsk Tractor Factory. Stalin's answer to America's Detroit Tank Arsenal was Tankograd at Chelyabinsk, which produced a staggering 18,000 tanks and self-propelled guns.

In 1942 Soviet factories produced 24,670 tanks, of which almost 60 per cent were T-34s. Even allowing for continual combat losses, by mid-1943 the Red Army had almost 10,000 operational tanks and self-propelled guns. By comparison American tank building went from just 330 in 1940 to 29,500 at its peak in 1943. The Detroit Tank Arsenal, which was constructed from scratch, in 1940–45 accounted for 25 per cent of all America's tanks – producing more than 25,000 vehicles. A good introduction to this topic is by Tim Bean and Will Fowler, *Russian Tanks of World II: Stalin's Armoured Might*, Hersham: Ian Allan, 2002 and Dr Matthew Hughes & Dr Chris Mann, *The T-34 Tank*, Staplehurst: Spellmount, 1999.

2  Khrushchev, *Khrushchev Remembers*, p.117.
3  Ibid.
4  Ibid.

5   Roberts, *Lorenz*, p.130. Bletchley Park broke the Lorenz cipher system in early April 1943 and Churchill almost immediately began to warn Stalin. Quite how much heed Stalin took of these warnings and whether he benefitted from them is subject to endless debate.

6   Khrushchev, *Khrushchev Remembers*, p.118.

7   Zhukov, *Reminiscences and Reflections*, Vol. 2, p.146.

8   Werth, *Russia at War*, p.562.

9   Zhukov, *Reminiscences and Reflections*, Vol. 2, p.146.

10  Khrushchev, *Khrushchev Remembers*, p.226.

11  Werth, *Russia at War*, p.569.

12  Bessonov, *Tank Rider*, p.44.

13  Merridale, *Ivan's War*, p.186.

14  Drabkin & Sheremet, *T-34 in Action*, pp.128–9 & Bryukhov, *Red Army Tank Commander*, p.21.

15  A T-34/76 tank platoon comprised three tanks with a total of twelve crew. This was led by a lieutenant with sergeants commanding the other two tanks. A company consisted of three platoons totalling ten tanks and forty-two crew led by a senior lieutenant. A Soviet tank battalion had thirty-one tanks and 180 men and was commanded by a captain or major. The battalion included repair, transport and medical support units.

16  Bryukhov, *Red Army Tank Commander*, pp.24–5.

17  Ibid., pp.26–7.

18  Merridale, *Ivan's War*, p.186.

19  Ibid., p.178. Slesarev may have been writing in such positive terms for the benefit of the Communist Party censors.

20  Ibid., p.186.

21  Shtemenko, *The Last Six Months*, p.6.

22  Ibid.

23  Stalin, *On the Great Patriotic War of the Soviet Union*, p.59.

24  Ibid.

## 2: Abdulin and Friends

1   Eberle & Uhl, *The Hitler Book*, p.104.

2   Ibid.

3   Abdulin, *Red Road from Stalingrad*, p.84.

4   Reitlinger, *The SS Alibi of a Nation*, p.196.

5   Messenger, *Hitler's Gladiator*, p.116.

6   Ibid., p.115.

7   Abdulin, *Red Road from Stalingrad*, p.72.

8   Ibid., p.85.

9   Ibid., p.87.

10  Bessonov, *Tank Rider*, p.30.

11  Ibid., pp.32–3.

12  Abdulin, *Red Road from Stalingrad*, p.89.

13  Bessonov, *Tank Rider*, pp.44–5.

14  Muñoz, *Wehrmacht Rear Guard Security in the USSR 1941–1945*, pp.47–8, and Cooper, *The Phantom War*, pp.133–4.

15  Slepyan, *Stalin's Guerrillas*, p.90.

16  Zhukov, *Reminiscences and Reflections*, Vol. 2, p.150, and Minasyan, *Great Patriotic War of the Soviet Union*, p.458. Both quote the same figures and Zhukov almost certainly drew on the Russian language version of the latter. For more information on Hitler's numerous types of security forces deployed to the Eastern Front see Gordon Williamson, *German Military Police Units 1939–45*, Oxford: Osprey, 1989, Kevin Conley Ruffner, *Luftwaffe Field Divisions 1941–45*, Oxford: Osprey, 1990, and Peter Abbott and Eugene Pinak, *Ukrainian Armies 1914–55*, Oxford: Osprey, 2004. These provide a good introduction to what was effectively a separate war fought behind German lines using mainly second rate units. Not surprisingly, in many instances discipline was very lax, resulting in atrocities.

17  Operation Harvest Home 2 (Erntefest II) along the Minsk–Slutsk road took place 28 January–9 February 1943. Operation Cormorant (Kormoran) to secure the railway was carried out during 22 May–20 June 1943. Harvest Home 1 was against enemy forces west of Ossipovchi 18–27 January 1943. A very comprehensive guide to these regular anti-partisan security operations is available in Chris Chant's excellent *The Encyclopaedia of Codenames of World War II*, London: Routledge & Kegan Paul, 1986. At almost 350 pages with detailed entries throughout, this book is clearly the result of a vast amount of research. It is an invaluable reference aid.

18  Operation Marksman (Freischütz) was carried out during May and June 1943 to little avail. The previous summer 2nd Panzer Army had conducted Operation Woodpecker (Grünspecht) against partisans in the area south of Bryansk. See Chant.

19  Cooper, *The Phantom War*, p.134.

20  Führer War Directive No.46 *Instructions for intensified action against the Banditry in the East*, 18 August 1942. Trevor-Roper, *Hitler's War Directives 1939–1945*, p.197.

21  Ibid., p.199.

22  Gehlen, *The Gehlen Memoirs*, p.100.

23  Shtemenko, *The Last Six Months*, p.6. A Soviet Front is roughly equivalent to a British Army Group.

## 3: Digging Fortress Kursk

1   Zhukov, *Reminiscences and Reflections*, Vol. 2, pp. 155–6.
2   Ibid., p. 158.
3   Suvorov, *Inside the Soviet Army*, p. 14.
4   Ibid.
5   Bialer, *Stalin & His Generals*, p. 350.
6   Zhukov, *Reminiscences and Reflections*, Vol. 2, p. 159–60.
7   Abdulin, *Red Road from Stalingrad*, p. 89.
8   Zhukov, *Reminiscences and Reflections*, Vol. 2, p. 179.
9   Axell, *Russia's Heroes*, p. 194.
10   Abdulin, *Red Road From Stalingrad*, p. 91.
11   Grossman, *A Writer at War*, pp. 229–30.
12   Ibid., p. 229.
13   Merridale, *Ivan's War*, p. 178.
14   Abdulin, *Red Road from Stalingrad*, p. 88.
15   Merridale, *Ivan's War*, p. 178.
16   Zhukov, *Marshal Zhukov's Greatest Battles*, p. 232.
17   Merridale, *Ivan's War*, p. 188.
18   Ibid.


## 4: Gifts from Uncle Sam

1   Kerr, *The Russian Army*, p. 128.
2   Archangel was one of the capital cities of Stalin's Gulag system, as it lay on the route to Solovetsky, Kotlas, Kargopollag and the other northern prison camps. This meant that there was no shortage of slave labourers to work in the regions ports and mines. Applebaum, *GULAG*, p. 511.
3   Service, *Stalin: A Biography*, pp. 461–2.
4   Bruce, *Second Front Now!*, p. 102.
5   Ibid., p. 103.
6   The PQ convoys were outbound, QP homebound, both suffered attacks by bombers and U-boats. They ran from August 1941 to September 1942. These were followed by a second series JW/RA that ran from December 1942 until the end of the war. The convoys were postponed between July and September 1942, and again between March and November 1943.
7   See Bernard Edwards, *The Road to Russia: Arctic Convoys 1942*. Hitler's War Directive No. 36 issued on 22 September 1941 ordered, 'It is the task of the Navy to attack enemy supplies moving to Murmansk even in the winter, and

particularly at times when air operations are more or less crippled.' Trevor-Roper, *Hitler's War Directives 1939–1945*, p.158.

8  Kerr, *The Russian Army*, p.128.

9  The Arctic convoys ran from August 1941–May 1945, during which time 105 merchant ships and twenty-three escort vessels were lost, including two light cruisers. Almost 3,000 British and American sailors gave their lives. Edwards, *The Road to Russia*, pp.196–7.

10  Kerr, *The Russian Army*, p.128.

11  Werth, *The Year of Stalingrad*, pp.34, 37, 41–2.

12  Hammerton, *The War Illustrated*, 30 October 1942, p.317.

13  Ibid., p.318.

14  Galante, *Hitler Lives – and the Generals Die*, p.174.

15  Bormann, *Hitler's Table-Talk*, p.708. These remarks were made on 19 June 1943.

16  Churchill, *The Second World War*, Vol.V, p.229.

17  These consisted of 375 British Hurricanes and 285 American Airacobras and Kittyhawks. Werth, *Russia at War*, p.657.

18  Ibid.

19  Zhukov, *Reminiscences and Reflections*, Vol. 2, p.96.

20  The initial squadron consisted of fourteen French pilots and fifty-eight mechanics. Minasyan, *Great Patriotic War of the Soviet Union*, p.188.

21  Kerr, *The Russian Army*, p.129.

22  Khrushchev, *Khrushchev Remembers*, p.225.

23  Hilton, *Hitler's Secret War in South America*, pp.3–5.

24  Bekker, *The Luftwaffe Diaries*, p.349.

25  Werth, *Russia at War*, p.567.

26  Kerr, *The Russian Army*, p.131.

27  Werth, *Russia at War*, p.565.

28  Bean & Fowler, *Russian Tanks of World War II*, p.145 & 149.

29  Gehlen, *The Gehlen Memoirs*, p.68.

30  Werth, *Russia at War*, p.569.

31  These were supplied both as the USAAF A-20B and RAF Boston III bomber variants. At Kursk they were flown by the 221st and 244th Bomber Divisions.

32  Kerr, *The Russian Army*, p.131.

33  Werth, *Russia at War*, p.569.

34  American lend-lease supplies including 'tractors, trucks, steam shovels and tools' were sent to the Gulag to be used by the political prisoners. Likewise, much of the clothing sent was issued to the camp administration. When the Americans questioned why Soviet miners at Kolyma were wearing US Army issue boots their hosts claimed these had been bought using cash. If the press had got hold of this it would have sparked yet another diplomatic row. Applebaum, *GULAG*, p.400.

35  Khrushchev, *Khrushchev Remembers*, p.226.

36  Many of the prisoners had never seen canned meat before and were very grateful for the supplement to their meagre rations. They also used the empty cans to make every day utensils. Applebaum, *GULAG*, p.400.

37  Werth, *Russia at War*, p.611.

## 5: Shadow of Stalingrad

1   Beevor, *Stalingrad*, p.380.

2   Dated 14 January 1943, sent from Stalingrad by military field mail. Binns and Wood, *The Second World War in Colour*, pp.146–7.

3   Beevor, *Stalingrad*, p.399.

4   Security Service, 'Reports from within the Reich, 4 February 1943', No.356. This also noted that public estimates for men lost at Stalingrad ranged from 60,000 to 300,000 with the assumption that most had been killed. Understandably, people were fretting over the fate of prisoners taken by the Red Army. Binns and Wood, *The Second World War in Colour*, pp.147–8.

5   Rutherford, *Hitler's Propaganda Machine*, p.118.

6   Propaganda Minister Dr Joseph Goebbels, along with the Wehrmacht High Command, had oversight of the armed forces Propaganda Companies (Propaganda Kompanien), whose members were known as PK-reporters for short. In 1941 some 300 film reporters were trained at Goebbels' State Film Institute and the Hansa School in Berlin. Goebbels instructed reporters to use German-made cameras. Official military pictures taken at the front were submitted to the Nazi-run Picture Press Bureau. Like their SS counterparts, these propaganda companies were assigned to units as and when they were needed. Due to combat losses there was always a shortage of cameramen and photographers, which led to the recruitment of amateur photographers. See Herbert Kraft, 'Colour Photography during the Second World War', in *The Onslaught The German Drive to Stalingrad*, pp.189–90.

7   Rutherford, *Hitler's Propaganda Machine*, p.177.

8   Toland, *Adolf Hitler*, p.734.

9   Ibid.

10  Ibid., p.735.

11  The Berlin Sportaplast arena built in 1910 could hold up to 14,000 people.

12  Rutherford observes, 'For Goebbels everything was premeditated and calculated. It was an exercise in sheer histrionics executed with the skill of the actor who knows how to render his audience silent at one moment so that not a single cough is heard and at another to rock them with laughter.' *Hitler's Propaganda Machine*, p.53.

13  Roland, *The Secret Lives of the Nazis*, p.84.

14 Toland, *Adolf Hitler*, p.735.

15 Liddel Hart, *The Other Side of the Hill*, pp.316–7 & Manstein, *Lost Victories*, p.443.

16 Ibid., Liddel Hart, p.317.

17 Weitz, *Hitler's Diplomat*, p.291.

18 Speer, *Inside the Third Reich*, p.333. Speer noted that General Halder, Zeitzler's predecessor, 'was a quiet, laconic man who was probably always thrown off by Hitler's vulgar dynamism and thus gave a rather hapless impression'.

19 Guderian, *Panzer leader*, p.442.

20 Mussolini had deployed some 230,000 troops to the Eastern Front, of which 95,000 were missing. Around 25,000 of these had been killed in action, while 70,000 had been captured, 20,000 of them died marching to the Soviet camps and 40,000 died in the camps. Farrell, *Mussolini A New Life*, p.362.

21 Liddell Hart, *The Other Side of the Hill*, p.319.

## 6: Citadel Too Late

1 The Battle of Grunwald (Tannenberg) in 1410.

2 See Geoffrey Evans, *Tannenberg 1410/1914*, p.5.

3 For a fuller account of the Second Battle of Tannenberg see Max Hastings, *Catastrophe Europe Goes to War 1914*, pp.259–85. It was also memorably commemorated by Russian writer Alexander Solzhenitsyn in his epic novel *August 1914*.

4 Mellenthin, *Panzer Battles*, p.313.

5 Eberle & Uhl, *The Hitler Book*, p.117.

6 General Fellgiebel was chief of signals for the Army and OKW from 1940–44 and 1942–44 respectively. As General of the Communication Troops he had encouraged the introduction of Enigma encryption. He was executed as one of the 20 July 1944 bomb plotters. Seaton, *The German Army 1933–45*, p.103.

7 Every day OKW's communications centre despatched more than 3,000 teleprinter messages, which as they were sent by secure land line were unencrypted. Two female teleprinter operators sent spent ribbons via courier to Roessler in Switzerland. According to Radó, they received some 4,500 top secret messages and 800 special reports by this method. Hastings, *The Secret War*, p.188.

8 Bullock, *Hitler: A Study in Tyranny*, p.705 citing *The Goebbels Diaries*, pp.274–5. Mussolini was in a poor position to defend his homeland. By 1943 he had lost 200,000 men killed or captured from the 5th and 10th Armies in North Africa. In December 1942 the 230,000-strong Italian 8th Army had collapsed on the Eastern Front contributing to Hitler's defeat at Stalingrad. Mussolini had another 580,000 men bogged down in the Balkans fighting Albanian and Yugoslav partisans, comprising the ill-equipped Italian 2nd and 9th Armies with

sixteen divisions and fifteen Blackshirt Legions based in Western Yugoslavia. By September 1943 the Italian Army had twenty-one divisions in mainland Italy, although half of these were of poor quality, four in Sardinia and another thirty-six overseas. For more on Italian security operations in Yugoslavia during 1943 see Milovan Djilas, *Wartime*, London: Martin Secker & Warburg, 1977.

9   Farrell, *Mussolini :A New Life*, pp.356–7 & 371.

10  Eberle & Uhl, *The Hitler Book*, p.116. Günsche was paraphrasing Hitler from memory so the wording may not be accurate but the sentiment was clear.

11  Ibid.

12  Ibid.

13  Guderian, *Panzer Leader*, p.306.

14  The source of this signal is Zhukov, who offers no explanation of its provenance. It is quite possible that it came via the 'Lucy' and 'Dora' spy rings. Zhukov, *Reminiscences and Reflections*, Vol. 2, pp.153–4.

15  According to General Warlimont, Zeitzler 'exercised much pressure on Hitler in favour of the Kursk attack'. Liddell Hart, *The Other Side of the Hill*, p.320.

16  Guderian, *Panzer Leader*, p.307.

17  Manstein, *Lost Victories*, p.447.

18  Guderian, *Panzer Leader*, p.307.

19  Khazanov, *Air War over Kursk*, p.7.

20  During the spring of 1943 renegade General Andrei Vlasov toured the Eastern Front acting as if he were Stalin's successor and this had rattled the German authorities. In April he was returned to prison camp and threatened with the Gestapo if he did not moderate his behaviour.

21  Gehlen, *The Gehlen Memoirs*, p.103.

22  Some writers assumed that Hitler's generals were all of one voice when it came to Operation Citadel. Mark Arnold-Forster in his book *The World at War*, which accompanied the award-winning Thames Television series, on p.143 states, 'The attack on the Kursk salient was scheduled to begin in May. For once Hitler and all his generals were in agreement,' when this plainly was not true.

23  Gehlen, *The Gehlen Memoirs*, p.103.

24  General Thomale's brother-in-law was Graf von Schwerin von Schwanenfeld, an Abwehr officer, who was one of the key individuals involved in the 20 July 1944 bomb plot to kill Hitler. Guderian always maintained he knew nothing of the attempted coup. Neither Guderian nor Thomale were implicated and Guderian went on to become Chief of the General Staff. See Bernd Freytag von Loringhoven, *In the Bunker with Hitler*, p.67 and Guderian, *Panzer Leader*, pp.338–50.

25  Guderian, *Panzer Leader*, pp.308–9.

26  Ibid.

27  Ibid., p.309.

28 Ibid.

29 Loringhoven, *In the Bunker with Hitler*, p.67.

30 Liddell Hart, *The Rommel Papers*, pp.426–7. Manfred, Rommel's son, presumed his father was referring to the war as a whole as Rommel was jobless at the time. He also felt his father thought they could force their enemies to the negotiating table rather than achieve total victory. Nonetheless, tantalisingly Rommel may have been referring to Citadel.

Kenneth Macksey in *Rommel: Battles and Campaigns*, p.190, contends that Manfred was wrong and that Rommel was referring to taking charge of an army group with which to occupy Italy. I am not convinced by this line of argument as General Zeitzler had no real say over this area of operations and Hitler was at the time preoccupied with preparations for Citadel. Also Manfred says his father had no specific assignment when these meetings took place.

31 Galante, *Hitler Lives – and the Generals Die*, p.175.

32 Ibid.

33 German newsreels loved the Stuka. Wherever the dive-bombers were deployed they invariably had a cameraman with them. From North Africa to the Eastern Front the Stuka always featured in the movie news shown in German cinemas. Stirring Wagnerian soundtracks accompanied the wailing aircraft as they hurtled toward their targets. Audiences were taken on a roller coaster ride when, seated behind the pilot, they suddenly dropped from the sky before jerking upwards as the bombs were released. The ground became peppered in great billowing smoke clouds caused by the blasts. The message was clear: no one could survive such a deluge. In the public's mind the Stuka came to symbolise Nazi invincibility as much as the Panzer.

34 See Paul Dunn (dir), *World War II Through German Eyes: The Russian Front Late 1943*, 2017. These German military exercises were probably already scheduled as part of the Citadel preparations, nevertheless the Turkish delegation were clearly impressed by what was on show.

35 The Turkish government took note not only of Hitler's defeat at Stalingrad but also his significant withdrawal from the Soviet Caucasus in early 1943. This clearly signalled his attempts to capture the vital oil fields at Grozny and Baku had singularly failed. Had Hitler got to Tbilisi, the capital of Soviet Georgia, south of the Caucasian mountains he would have been within striking distance of the Turkish border. He had hoped such an achievement might encourage Turkey to join the Axis. Only his remaining military presence in the Kuban bridgehead signalled to Ankara that his Caucasus campaign was not entirely at an end.

36 Galante, *Hitler Lives – and the Generals Die*, p.179.

37 Ibid., p.178.

38 Ibid., pp.178–9.

39  Bormann, *Hitler's Table-Talk*, p.708.

## 7: **Hitler's Armoured Fist**

1   Reichsführer Heinrich Himmler created the Waffen-SS from Hitler's personal protection squad. Lacking military experience, Himmler surrounded himself with highly able generals. Despite wearing a uniform, he was not a military man but a civilian. Unlike many of his Nazi contemporaries, he was not a veteran of the First World War. His main ability was choosing skilled subordinates who made the SS look good. In addition, he was a highly efficient organiser, which tragically for Europe's Jews included the Final Solution.

2   A Nazi anthem commemorating a stormtrooper killed in a 1920s street battle.

3   Quarrie, *Hitler's Teutonic Knights*, p.28.

4   Ibid. This comparison was wholly unfair in light of how poorly equipped the Italian Army was on the Eastern Front.

5   Guderian, *Panzer Leader*, p.303.

6   Good accounts of the rise of these premier divisions can be found in Michael Sharpe and Brian L. Davis' *Leibstandarte Hitler's Elite Bodyguard* and *Das Reich Waffen-SS Armoured Elite*, Hersham: Ian Allan, 2002 and 2003. Likewise, Gordon Williamson's *The SS: Hitler's Instrument of Terror*, London: Sidgwick & Jackson, 1994, and *Waffen-SS Handbook 1933–1945*, Stroud: Sutton, 2003, are good introductory guides to the many facets of the SS.

7   Guderian, *Panzer Leader*, p.298.

8   Ibid., p.281.

9   Deichmann, *Spearhead for Blitzkrieg*, p.130. He was present as Commanding General 1st Air Division.

10  Toland, *Adolf Hitler*, p.736.

11  Ibid.

12  Irving, *The Rise and Fall of the Luftwaffe*, p.202.

13  Toland, *Adolf Hitler*, p.728.

14  Ibid., p.736.

15  Irving, *The Rise and Fall of the Luftwaffe*, p.224.

16  Khazanov, *Air War over Kursk*, p.87.

17  The Junkers Ju 87G known as the 'Gustav' entered service in the autumn of 1942 armed with two 37mm cannons in pods mounted outboard of the main landing gear on the hardpoints normally used to carry bombs.

18  The Hs 129B-2/R1 was armed with two nose-mounted 20mm cannon and two 13mm machine guns. The R2 had an additional 30mm MK 103 cannon under the fuselage. The R3 was armed with a 37mm BK 3.7 gun but lost the two machine guns.

19 The initial tests were with the 30mm MK 101 but the MK 103 offered a higher muzzle velocity and twice the rate of fire. The Rechlin test and evaluation establishment was at Mecklenburg.

20 This unit formed part of the 9th Ground Attack Wing. Bekker, *The Luftwaffe Diaries*, p.378. In fact they were assigned to the 1st and 2nd Ground Attack Wings, see Khazanov, *Air War over Kursk*.

21 Deichmann, *Spearhead for Blitzkrieg*, p.118.

## 8: Guderian's Zoo

1 Mellentin, *Panzer Battles*, p.258.

2 Ibid., p.259.

3 Lucas, *War on the Eastern Front 1941–1945*, p.153.

4 Loringhoven, Bernd Fretag von & d'Alançon, François. *In the Bunker with Hitler*, pp.32 & 34. For those interested in a more detailed history of *Grossdeutschland*'s development, Michael Sharpe and Brian Davis' *Grossdeutschland Guderian's Eastern Front Elite*, Hersham: Ian Allan, 2001, has much to recommend it.

5 Speer, *Inside the Third Reich*, p.336.

6 Ibid., p.335.

7 Guderian, *Panzer Leader*, p.307. As highlighted in the introduction, Guderian, Thomale and Speer did everything they could to rectify the production problems with the Panther tank. These were largely of Hitler's own making. Hitler, however, saw Guderian's and Speer's reasoned arguments as nothing more than excuses.

8 Ibid., p.453.

9 Ibid., 294. When Guderian first met Speer he observed he was 'a most enthusiastic follower of Hitler's' but as the war progressed Speer did not hesitate to speak his mind to Hitler'.

10 Speer, *Inside the Third Reich*, p.325.

11 Ibid., p.324.

12 Ibid., p.325. Speer is inaccurate in his memoirs when he describes the Tiger's weight increasing from 50 to 75 tons, the production model was 56 tons. Likewise, the Panther was not 48 tons, but 3 tons lighter.

13 Ibid., p.326.

14 Galante, *Hitler Lives – and the Generals Die*, p.174. The Soviets were developing the SU-152 assault gun in response to the Tiger tank. This was armed with a 152mm howitzer that could penetrate 110mm of armour.

15 Ibid.

16 Ibid., p.175.

17 Manstein, *Lost Victories*, p.447.

18 Speer, *Inside the Third Reich*, p.369.

19  Eberle & Uhl, *The Hitler Book*, p.116.

20  Ibid. Günsche may have said this simply to impress his interrogators as it was not true. Less than 100 Ferdinands were available.

21  Khrushchev, *Khrushchev Remembers*, pp.210–1.

22  Abdulin, *Red Road from Stalingrad*, p.89.

23  Hastings, *The Secret War*, p.188.

24  Gehlen, *The Gehlen Memoirs*, pp.86–7.

25  This unfounded allegation was based on Bormann running a radio transmitter network that was sending fake messages to Moscow – with Hitler's full support. After the war Gehlen claimed that Bormann had escaped to the Soviet Union and had been a Soviet spy, whereas he actually died during the battle for Berlin.

26  McKay, *The Secret Life of Bletchley Park*, p.232.

27  Churchill, *The Second World War*, Vol.V, p.229.

28  Interestingly, some historians also subsequently referred to 'the new Tiger tank' when they actually meant the Ferdinand. For example, Philip Warner, *World War Two, The Untold Story*, London, Bodley Head, 1988/London: Cassell, 2002. p.222 uses this expression and goes on to say, 'Although the Tigers were unequalled at engaging targets at long distances, they had no machine guns for dealing with close-quarter attacks.' The Tiger I had machine guns in both its hull and turret, the Ferdinand did not.

29  Klemperer, *To the Bitter End*, p.231.

30  Roberts, *Lorenz*, p.130.

## 9: A Flawed Plan

1   *The War Illustrated*, 22 January 1943, p.482.

2   Gehlen, *The Gehlen Memoirs*, p.83.

3   Ibid.

4   Craddock, *Know Your Enemy*, p.21.

5   Churchill, *The Second World War*, Vol.V, p.229.

6   McKay, *The Secret Life of Bletchley Park*, p.237. Captain Jerry Roberts MBE was the last surviving Bletchley codebreaker until his death in 2014. His memoirs, *Lorenz: Breaking Hitler's Top Secret Code at Bletchley*, were published by The History Press three years later. Roberts was adamant that Bletchley intelligence was instrumental in helping the Red Army.

7   Quite remarkably, Cairncross gave the Soviets 5,832 documents between 1941 and 1945. However, he made Gorsky's job extremely difficult because he either 'borrowed' documents for the Soviets to film or copied extracts by hand. Neither of these were very efficient, nonetheless John Cairncross was

eventually presented with the Order of the Red Banner by Moscow for his efforts. Hastings. *The Secret War*, p.355.

8   Werth, *Russia at War*, p.658.

9   Ibid.

10   Ibid.

11   Manstein, *Lost Victories*, p.445.

12   *The War Illustrated*, 5 February 1943, p.515.

13   The first battle for Kharkov was in October 1941, when the Germans captured the city; the second in May 1942 saw the Red Army fail to liberate it and the third in February 1943 when the Red Army briefly retook Kharkov only to be pushed out again in mid-March 1943.

14   Zhukov, *Reminiscences and Reflections*, Vol. 2, p.146.

15   Chaney, *Zhukov*, p.250.

16   Ibid., p.251.

17   Ibid.

18   The first echelon German infantry divisions were assessed to comprise the 26th, 68th, 323rd, 75th, 255th, 57th, 332nd, 167th and one unidentified. The Panzer divisions were identified as *Grossdeutschland*, 6th, 11th, 1st SS, 2nd SS and 3rd SS. Zhukov, *Reminiscences and Reflections*, Vol. 2, p.158.

19   Bialer, *Stalin & His Generals*, p.382.

20   Ibid., p.381.

21   Ibid., p.382.

22   Brookes, *Air War over Russia*, p.125.

23   Mellenthin, *Panzer Battles*, p.262.

24   On 22 April 1943 Soviet bombers attacked the Luftwaffe's strategic reconnaissance bases at Orsha and Orsha-South, destroying the recon aircraft. This left Army Group Centre with only a single recce unit.

25   These totalled more than eighty dug-in tanks. Seaton, *Stalin as Warlord*, p.186.

26   Eberle & Uhl, *The Hitler Book*, p.117.

27   Liddell Hart, *The Other Side of the Hill*, p.318.

28   Gehlen, *The Gehlen Memoirs*, p.82.

29   Ibid., pp.82–3.

30   Ibid., p.82.

31   Ibid., p.83.

32   Burleigh, *The Third Reich a New History*, p.510. The source for this visit is unclear and Manstein himself makes no mention of the episode in his memoirs. This is odd as he thought very highly of Marshal Antonescu. The official reason for his flight to Bucharest on 2 July 1943 was to present Antonescu with a Golden Crimea Shield for his services in the Crimea campaign the previous year. Manstein may have been pleased to see the Romanian leader but the trip was an unwanted distraction at a very critical time and he departed the

following day. See Melvin, *Manstein: Hitler's Greatest General.*

33 Jewish writer Mihail Sebastian, who was living in Bucharest at the time, did not pick up on Manstein's presence and made no reference to it in his diary. So it does not seem to have been a topic of conversation. See Sebastian, *Journal 1935–44*, pp. 562–3.

## 10: Stalin Shows his Hand

1 Zhukov, *Reminiscences and Reflections*, Vol. 2, p. 180.

2 It is surprising that the Soviets did not have the ability to jam the Luftwaffe's Freya radar. British scientific intelligence under Dr R.V. Jones developed countermeasures from 1941 onwards. In his memoirs Jones makes no mention of sharing such techniques with Moscow.

3 Zhukov, *Marshal Zhukov's Greatest Battles*, p. 233.

4 Hastings, *The Secret War*, p. 188. Churchill also provided Stalin with a full German order of battle derived from Bletchley Park. Roberts, *Lorenz*, pp. 89 & 129.

5 It is impossible to judge just how important Cairncross' part in the Battle of Kursk was. He liked to think it was pivotal. Smith, *Station X*, p. 164.

6 The Red Air Force used similar tactics against the Japanese at Khalkhin Gol in the summer of 1939. Unfortunately this valuable combat experience did not save the Red Air Force from complete destruction in June 1941. It is unclear how much the Mongolian campaign influenced subsequent Soviet tactics and many of those involved by 1943 were dead, having either been killed in action or purged by Stalin. For more on this little-known battle see Vladimir Kotelnikov, *Air War over Khalkhin Gol: The Nomonhan Incident*, SAM Publications, 2010.

7 Bekker, *The Luftwaffe Diaries*, p. 381.

8 Boyd, *The Soviet Air Force Since 1918*, p. 175. The 17th Air Army under Lieutenant General V.A. Studets was from Malinovsky's South-western Front. This was deployed to the south of Konev's Steppe Front and was therefore nearest to Kharkov. Some sources, including Bekker p. 377, record the attack involved up to 500 aircraft, representing one-sixth of the Red Air Force's total strength at Kursk.

9 At the beginning of the war Kharkov was a major military industrial centre that produced, among other things, diesel engines, T-34/76 tanks, artillery tractors and Su-2 bombers. All these factories had been evacuated by the end of October 1941.

10 Clark, *Kursk*, pp. 235–6.

11 Khazanov, *Air War over Kursk*, p. 48.

12 Bekker, *The Luftwaffe War Diaries*, p. 377.

13 Bergström, *Kursk: The Air Battle*, pp. 28–9.

14 Zhukov, *Reminiscences and Reflections*,Vol. 2, p.183.

15 This dramatic opening air battle remains largely unknown and ignored. One of the reasons for this is that the Soviets subsequently underplayed their spoiling attacks because of the very disappointing results. Notably, the abridged English language version of the *Great Patriotic War of the Soviet Union* failed to mention it, focusing instead on the Red Army's initial shelling of German preparations. No one wanted to admit that Hitler's initial gains were thanks to the intact Luftwaffe blazing a trail for the Panzers, the cause of which was the initial failure of the Red Force.

Some limited coverage is provided by Bekker, *The Luftwaffe War Diaries*, Boyd, *The Soviet Air Force Since 1918*, Brookes, *Air War over Russia* and *Khazanov, Air War over Kursk*. Boyd says, 'Even Soviet military historians have been obliged to indicate the magnitude of this initial set back.' p.175. Only Zhukov though was initially prepared to own up to it being a complete disaster.

## 11: Ponyri or Bust

1 Zhukov, *Reminiscences and Reflections*,Vol. 2, p.182.

2 Zhukov, *Marshal Zhukov's Greatest Battles*, p.234.

3 Ibid., p.236. Zhukov changes his mind in *Reminiscences and Reflections*,Vol. 2, p.183, saying the German attack started thirty minutes after the artillery and air attacks. This would mean the German ground attack commenced at around 05.30, a good two hours after originally anticipated.

4 Eberle & Uhl, *The Hitler Book*, p.118.

5 Ibid.

6 Zhukov, *Reminiscences and Reflections*,Vol. 2, p.184.

7 Ibid.

8 Ibid.

9 Brookes, *Air War over Russia*, p.127.

10 Abdulin, *Red Road from Stalingrad*, p.99.

11 Ibid.

12 Zhukov, *Reminiscences and Reflections*,Vol. 2, p.185.

13 Sebastian, *Journal 1935–44*, pp.563–4.

14 Minasyan, *The Great Patriotic War of the Soviet Union*, p.183.

15 Zhukov, *Marshal Zhukov's Greatest Battles*, p.238.

16 Healy, *Kursk 1943*, p.71 cites the 10th Panzergrenadier Division supporting the 31st Infantry Division. In his subsequent *Zitadelle* he makes no reference to this unit. The 10th Panzergrenadiers came into being in June 1943 having been upgraded from an infantry division of the same number.

## 12: Prokhorovka Bloodbath

1  Khrushchev, *Khrushchev Remembers*, p.209. How accurate this dialogue is remains unclear as Khrushchev was clearly going from memory. He was not even sure which SS division the man was from, citing *Leibstanbdarte*, *Das Reich* and *Totenkopf* as his possible parent unit.

2  Zhukov, *Reminiscences and Reflections*, Vol. 2, p.186.

3  Mellenthin, *Panzer Battles*, p.265.

4  Fey, *Armor Battles of the Waffen-SS*, p.20.

5  Ibid.

6  Ibid., p.21.

7  Ibid., p.19.

8  Minasyan, *Great Patriotic War of the Soviet Union*, p.184.

9  Fey, *Armor Battles of the Waffen-SS*, p.24.

10  Mellenthin, *Panzer Battles*, p.267.

11  Ibid., p.269.

12  Eberle & Uhl, *The Hitler Book*, p.119. Günsche's memory may be faulty recalling this encounter, because Dietrich did not command *Leibstandarte* during Citadel. On 4 June 1943 he had handed the division over to Theodor Wisch, before heading off to Germany to command a new SS Panzer Corps. However, some accounts state that Dietrich did not leave *Leibstabdarte* until the end of July. Nonetheless, a two-month transition seems rather excessive. Günsche may have spoken with Wisch but it still seems odd that he would confuse the two men. Whoever Günsche saw, the message was the same: the Waffen-SS had failed to break through. See Messenger, *Hitler's Gladiator*, pp.117 & 225.

13  Ibid.

14  Ibid.

15  Kurowski, *Panzer Aces*, p.175.

16  Mellenthin, *Panzer Battles*, p.274.

17  Bryukhov, *Red Army Tank Commander*, p.28.

18  Abdulin, *Red Road From Stalingrad*, p.91.

19  Grossmann, *A Writer at War*, p.238.

20  Healey, *Kursk 1943*, p.81.

21  Kurowski, *Panzer Aces*, p.179.

22  Fey, *Armor Battles of the Waffen-SS*, p.25.

23  Kurowski, *Panzer Aces*, p.181.

24  Ibid., p.183.

25  Bryukhov, *Red Army Tank Commander*, p.28.

26  Ibid., p.29.

27  Axell, *Russia's Heroes*, p.166.

28  Fey, *Armor Battles of the Waffen-SS*, p.29.

29 Ibid.

30 Kurowski, *Panzer Aces*, p.179.

31 Ibid., p.181.

32 Abdulin, *Red Road from Stalingrad*, p.91.

33 Ibid., p.92. These Tigers were most probably Panzer III or IV as Soviet troops had a tendency to describe all German tanks as Tigers.

34 Ibid., p.93.

35 Ibid.

36 Chaney, *Zhukov*, p.255.

37 Axell, *Russia's Heroes*, p.166.

38 Healy, *Kursk 1943*, pp.86–7.

39 Ibid., p.87.

40 Khazanov, *Air War over Kursk*, p.70.

## 13: Flying Tank Busters

1 For failing to stop the Luftwaffe's bombers and ground attack aircraft Generals I.D. Klimov and A.B. Yumashev commanding the 5th and 6th Fighters Corps were immediately sacked and replaced by Ye Yerlykin and D.P. Galunov. The 5th Fighter Corps was to subsequently achieve impressive results during the battle in the Belgorod area. Boyd, *The Soviet Air Force Since 1918*, p.175.

2 Deichmann, *Spearhead for Blitzkrieg*, p.48.

3 Abdulin, *Red Road from Stalingrad*, p.115.

4 Healy, *Zitadelle*, p.259.

5 Weal, *Focke-Wulf Fw 190 Aces on the Eastern Front*, p.41.

6 Bekker, *The Luftwaffe War Diaries*, p.378.

7 Healy, *Zitadelle*, p.105.

8 Brookes, *Air War over Russia*, p.129.

9 The Fw 190A-6 was introduced in June 1943, incorporating a lighter-weight wing that could take four 20mm MG 151/20 cannon, and was the forerunner of the A-6/R1 with six 20mm cannon, R2 with two 30mm cannon, R3 with an additional cannon beneath each wing and the R6, the final A-6 variant armed with a 210mm WGr.21 rocket launch tube under each wing. For more on the development of the Focke-Wulf 190 see David Mondey, *Axis Aircraft of World War II*, London: Bounty, 2006, and Chris Chant, *Aircraft of World War II*, London: Amber, 2016.

10 Khazanov, *Air War over Kursk*, p.21.

11 From late 1941 Hubert Strassl clocked up thirty-seven kills. Weal, *Focke-Wulf Fw 190 Aces on the Eastern Front*, p.37.

12 Khazanov, *Air War over Kursk*, p.32.

13 Brookes, *Air War over Russia*, p.127.

14 Khazanov, *Air War over Kursk*, p.11.

15  Ibid.

16  Deichmann, *Spearhead for Blitzkrieg*, p.57.

17  Mellenthin, *Panzer Battles*, p.267.

18  These were SD-1 or SD-2 anti-personnel cluster bombs that scattered either 180 or 360 fragmentation bombs across a wide area.

19  Deichmann, *Spearhead for Blitzkrieg*, pp.131–2.

20  Mellenthin, *Panzer Battles*, p.364.

21  Zhukov, *Reminiscences and Reflections*, Vol. 2, p.183.

22  Mellenthin, *Panzer Battles*, pp.364–5.

## 14: The Zoo Disappoints

1   Clark, *Kursk*, p.237.

2   Ibid., pp.237–8.

3   Mellenthin, *Panzer Battles*, p.265.

4   Clark, *Kursk*, p.238.

5   Guderian, *Panzer Leader*, p.311.

6   Fey, *Armor Battles of the Waffen-SS*, p.22.

7   Ibid.

8   Guderian, *Panzer Leader*, p.311.

9   Mellenthin, *Panzer Battles*, pp.276–7.

10  Ibid., p.279.

11  Zhukov, *Reminiscences and Reflections*, Vol. 2, p.196.

12  Axell, *Russia's Heroes*, p.166.

13  Healy, *Kursk 1943*, p.81.

14  Hughes & Mann, *The T-34*, pp.70–1.

15  Churchill, *The Second World War*, Vol. V, p.229.

16  Eberle & Matthias, *The Hitler Book*, p.199. While Günsche's and Linge's interrogation dossier refers to the performance of the Ferdinand and Tiger at Kursk, surprisingly there is no mention of the Panther. There is no ready explanation for this as it seems unlikely that both men were completely unaware of the troubled development of the Panther.

## 15: Victory at Orel

1   Bryukhov, *Red Army Tank Commander*, p.29.

2   Werth, *Russia at War*, p.624.

3   Klemperer, *To the Bitter End*, pp.232–3.

4   Manstein, *Lost Victories*, p.449.

5   Ibid., p.448. Following the Axis surrender in Tunisia Hitler and his generals were anticipating an Allied landing in southern Europe. The key questions

were where and when? Allied deception plans helped convince Hitler that they were planning to attack Greece or Sardinia, whereas their goal was Sicily, followed by mainland Italy.

6  Cornish, *Images of Kursk*, p.190. After sacrificing the Afrika Korps and 5th Panzer Army in Tunisia, Hitler was not keen about strengthening German forces on Sicily. Nevertheless, he decided to reinforce the hastily reconstituted 15th Panzergrenadier Division, which had capitulated in Tunisia, with an additional division. By July the *Hermann Göring* Division, with a company of Tiger tanks, originally assigned to the 15th Panzergrenadier had joined them on the island. The German garrison amounted to some 75,000 men with about 160 tanks. See Eric Linklater, *The Campaign in Italy*, London: HMSO, 1977, and S.W.C. Pack, *Operation Husky: The Allied Invasion of Sicily*, New York: Hippocrene, 1977.

7  Manstein, *Lost Victories*, p.448.

8  Ibid.

9  Ibid.

10  Sebastian, *Journal 1935–44*, p.565.

11  Bialer, *Stalin & His Generals*, p.361.

12  Khazanov, *Air War over Kursk*, p.83. For some reason Lebedeva's squadron adjutant, Ivanovich Evgeniy, wrote to her father to say that she had survived and been taken by the Germans to a hospital in Orel. There he claimed she spat in the face of her interrogators. He also said she behaved like a Bolshevik and patriot. However, her remains including skull fragments and log books were found near Betovo in an unmarked grave in 1982 and Pestryakov refused to discuss the matter further. See http://airaces.narod.ru/woman/lebedeva.htm.

13  Lebedeva's and Blinova's 65th Guards Fighter Aviation Regiment formed part of the 4th Guards Fighter Aviation Division serving with the Soviet 15th Air Army assigned to the Bryansk Front. Their regiment was previously the 653rd Fighter Aviation Regiment until renamed on 21 March 1943.

14  The 4th Guards Fighter Aviation Division under the command of Colonel V.A. Kitaev flew Yak-1, Yak-7 and Yak-9 fighter aircraft.

15  Some twenty days later Lieutenant Blinova and seven other prisoners managed to escape and reach their own lines. It is possible that this is why Pestryakov assumed that Lebedeva was still alive. Other female pilots involved in the battle included Senior Lieutenant Z. Seid-Mamedova, who flew a Yak-9 with the 586th Fighter Regiment.

16  Brookes, *Air War over Russia*, p.130. Khazanov also quotes Model but with a slightly different translation, p.84.

17  Klemperer, *To the Bitter End*, pp.234–5. The first half of this quote is from an entry dated 19 July 1943, the second from 21 July 1943.

18  The Germans recorded 1,560 railway detonations in July, and another 2,121 in August. Werth, *Russia's War*, pp.647–8.

19  Stalin, *On the Great Patriotic War of the Soviet Union*, p.64.

20  Ibid., p.63 – Bialer's translation is slightly different but the sentiment is the same.

21  Bialer, *Stalin & His Generals*, p.361.

22  Klemperer, *To the Bitter End*, pp.236–7. 24 July 1943.

23  Wilmot, *The Struggle for Europe*, p.145.

24  Ibid.

25  Ibid. Hitler, fearing the worst, drafted War Directive 49 outlining the occupation of Italy and all her overseas possessions. The directive was never issued, but on 31 July a series of separate orders were sent out instructing commanders what they should do if the Italians dropped out of the war. Although Hitler was dissuaded from putting troops on to the streets of Rome, he swiftly secured the Alpine passes. Eight divisions were assembled from France and southern Germany as Army Group B, ready to rescue those German forces in Italy, some of which were fighting in Sicily. In early August forces including the 1st SS Panzergrenadier Division and the 44th Infantry Division rolled into northern Italy unopposed.

Rather than occupy all of Italy the Germans drew up plans for a defensive line in the Apennines well north of Rome. In August contingency planning was well under way to deal with the anticipated Italian defection. That month five infantry and two Panzer divisions crossed the frontier. In central Italy the German 10th Army was activated, able to call on five divisions and another two near Rome. Up until the end of the Sicilian campaign and the successful escape of four German divisions, Hitler only had two divisions covering the whole of southern Italy.

To fend off a German takeover of northern and central Italy in early September the Italian Army had eight infantry divisions and two motorised/armoured divisions, supported by another eight weak infantry divisions. Against these forces Hitler could field about sixteen highly experienced divisions. For more on the successful German occupation of Italy see B.H. Liddell Hart, *The Rommel Papers*, London: Collins, 1953.

26  Grossmann, *A Writer at War*, p.240.

27  Werth, *Russia at War*, p.622.

28  Bessonov, *Tank Rider*, p.40.

29  Merridale, *Ivan's War*, p.194.

30  Werth, *Russia at War*, p.625.

31  Grossmann, *A Writer at War*, p.240.

32  Werth, *Russia at War*, p.623.

33  Ibid., p.630.

34  Bessonov, *Tank Rider*, p.40.

35  Russian officials exhumed 200 corpses at the Orel prison, but Werth estimated the massed graves contained at least 5,000 bodies. Werth, *Russia at War*, p.626.

36  Seaton, *Stalin as Warlord*, p.190.

37  Zhukov, *Reminiscences and Reflections*, Vol. 2, p.208.

38  Ibid., p.209.

39  Bessonov, *Tank Rider*, p.36.

40  Ibid., p.38.

41  Ibid., p.39.

42  Bryukhov, *Red Army Tank Commander*, p.32.

43  Werth, *Russia at War*, p.625.

44  Of the sixteen casualties, twelve of them were platoon leaders. Bessonov, *Tank Rider*, p.43.

45  Deichmann, *Spearhead for Blitzkrieg*, p.130.

46  Ibid.

47  Ibid., p.131. These inflated figures are were undoubtedly based on pilot claims. It is hard to believe each German aircraft shot down almost thirty Soviet aircraft. Likewise, 1,100 Soviet tanks destroyed is nearly a third of their tanks and self-propelled guns committed to the battle. As the Red Army was left in possession of the battlefield there was no way the Luftwaffe could verify these alleged enemy losses.

# 16: Kharkov Liberated

1  Zhukov, *Reminiscences and Reflections*, Vol. 2, p.193.

2  Ibid., p.190.

3  Ibid., p.191.

4  Mellenthin, *Panzer Battles*, p.277.

5  Zhukov, *Reminiscences and Reflections*, Vol. 2, p.191.

6  It is interesting that Abdulin mistook the *Grossdeutschland* Panzergrenadier Division for a SS unit, when it was actually an army formation. The Red Army tended to lump all collaborationist units under the category of the Russian Liberation Army. The latter created for propaganda purposes never really existed as such, though two regular divisions were formed toward the end of the war. Abdulin, *Red Road from Stalingrad*, p.99.

7  Ibid., p.95.

8  This was the issue dated 28 July 1943. Werth, *Russia's War*, p.659. The Allies failure to immediately invade Calabria, the toe of Italy, and cut the Messina Straits to prevent the Germans and Italian troops escaping from Sicily sealed mainland Italy's fate. The Germans successfully evacuated almost 55,000 men during 1–7 August from the island. Despite this achievement they lost vital equipment, including seventy-eight tanks and armoured cars, 287 guns and 3,500 vehicles.

The Italian garrison left to their own devices evacuated 7,000 men the week before Rome finally authorised a full-scale evacuation on 11 August. By the time the evacuation had ended five days later they had managed to save 62,000 men, 227 vehicles and 41 artillery pieces. The American and British armies reached Messina on 17 August. Once Sicily had fallen a tremor ran through the Italian political elite in Rome. Pack, *Operation Husky*, p.161.

9  Bullock, *Hitler: A Study in Tyranny*, p.692.

10  Mellenthin, *Panzer Battles*, p.277.

11  Zhukov, *Reminiscences and Reflections*, Vol. 2, p.191.

12  Ibid.

13  Ibid., p.200.

14  Ibid., p.198.

15  Khazanov, *Air War over Kursk*, p.115.

16  Ibid., p.121.

17  Ibid.

18  Zhukov, *Marshal Zhukov's Greatest Battles*, p.252.

19  Minasyan, *Great Patriotic War of the Soviet Union*, p.190.

20  Werth, *Russia at War*, p.625.

21  Stalin, *On the Great Patriotic War of the Soviet Union*, p.65.

22  Bialer, *Stalin & His Generals*, p.362.

23  Ibid.

24  Ibid., p.598.

25  Zhukov, *Marshal Zhukov's Greatest Battles*, p.252.

26  Abdulin, *Red Road from Stalingrad*, p.98.

27  Günther Rall was promoted commander 3rd Gruppe, 52nd Fighter Group in early July. Khazanov, *Air War over Kursk*, p.121.

28  Minasyan, *Great Patriotic War of the Soviet Union*, p.190.

29  Egger's distraught wife, Traute Kaiser, and four children attended a memorial service for him on 26 September 1943 at Berlin's Kroll Opera House. In December 1943 the SS-Kriegsberichter battalion was expanded to a regiment. In recognition of Eggers contribution to war reporting the unit was renamed SS-Standarte Kurt Eggers.

30  Jones, *Most Secret War*, p.347.

31  Irving, *The Rise and Fall of the Luftwaffe*, p.233.

32  Zhukov, *Reminiscences and Reflections*, Vol. 2, p.206.

33  Khazanov, *Air War over Kursk*, p.123.

34  Ibid.

35  Weal, *Focke-Wulf Fw 190 Aces on the Eastern Front*, p.42.

36  Ibid.

37  Zhukov, *Marshal Zhukov's Greatest Battles*, p.255.

38  Ibid.

39  Bialer, *Stalin & His Generals*, p.363.
40  Werth, *Russia at War*, p.630.
41  Ibid.

## 17: Hitler's Bitter Harvest

1   Mellenthin, *Panzer Battles*, p.277.
2   Ibid., p.361.
3   Zhukov, *Reminiscences and Reflections*, Vol. 2, p.209.
4   Khrushchev, *Khrushchev Remembers*, p.208.
5   Shtemenko, *The Last Six Months*, p.343.
6   Zhukov, *Reminiscences and Reflections*, Vol. 2, p.209.
7   Between 5 and 20 July 1943 losses for the two German Army Groups were recorded as just under 50,000 men. See Cornish *Images of Kursk*, p.219. Successive historians have tied themselves in terrible knots trying to make sense of the casualties for the four phases of Kursk.

    Healy in *Zitadelle* quotes Soviet estimates of 70,000 losses for the Germans during the first two phases. So somewhere in the region of 60,000 would be a fair estimate. By the end of September, Army Groups Centre and South listed 445,871 men killed, wounded and missing, which gives some credence to Zhukov's figure.

    Regarding Soviet casualties, Manstein claimed that Army Group South by 13 July accounted for 24,000 prisoners, 1,800 tanks, 267 field guns and 1,080 anti-tank guns. Healy again quoting Soviet Sources says by 23 July total losses for the Soviet Central, Voronezh and Steppe fronts amounted to 177,847 (of which 70,330 were killed and missing). This though does not include losses incurred up to the end of August.
8   Khrushchev, *Khrushchev Remembers*, p.211.
9   Ibid.
10  Shirer, *The Rise and Fall of the Third Reich*, p.1011. The day before this meeting the Allies had invaded Italy with Operation Avalanche conducted at Salerno on the western coast, with two slightly earlier subsidiary operations taking place at Reggio di Calabria and Taranto. The Salerno invasion force consisted of 100,000 British troops and 69,000 Americans, with some 20,000 vehicles delivered by an armada of 450 vessels.
11  Ibid., p.1012.
12  Eberle & Uhl, *The Hitler Book*, p.119.
13  Liddel Hart, *The Other Side of the Hill*, p.321.
14  Liddell Hart, *The Rommel Papers*, p.428.
15  Guderian, *Panzer Leader*, p.312.
16  Mellenthin, *Panzer Battles*, p.278.
17  Gehlen, *The Gehlen Memoirs*, p.86.

18  Ibid.

19  Zhukov, *Reminiscences and Reflections*,Vol. 2, p.192.

20  Zhukov, *Marshal Zhukov's Greatest Battles*, p.257. For more on the partisan war see Matthew Cooper, *The Phantom War*, London: Macdonald & Jane's, 1979, Kenneth Slepyan, *Stalin's Guerrillas*, Lawrence: University Press of Kansas, 2006, and Nigel Thomas & Peter Abbot, *Partisan Warfare 1941–45*, London: Osprey, 1983. The latter offers a particularly useful overview, while Slepyan devotes a chapter to operations in 1943.

21  Zhukov, *Reminiscences and Reflections*,Vol. 2, p.192.

22  Zhukov, *Marshal Zhukov's Greatest Battle*, pp.246–7.

23  Ibid., p.247.

24  Roberts, *Lorenz*, p.135, also see pp.129–31. Throughout his memoirs Jerry Roberts emphasises that the three-month warning was vital in helping Soviet preparations and ensuring they secured victory.

25  Ibid., p.131. Enigma was declassified in the 1970s but Lorenz was not declassified until 2002. The latter cipher machine was more secure, complex and faster than Enigma.

26  Bullock, *Hitler: A Study in Tyranny*, pp.716–7.

27  Arnold-Forster, *The World at War*, p.143, citing Jacobsen & Dollinger, *Der zweite Weltkrieg in Bildern un Dokumenten*,Vol.VI, Munich: 1968, p.21.

28  Minasyan, *Great Patriotic War of the Soviet Union*, p.181.

## Epilogue

1  This presentation took place during the Tehran Conference. Montefiore, *Stalin The Court of the Red Tsar*, p.414.

2  Minasyan, *Great Patriotic War of the Soviet Union*, p.191.

3  Ibid., p.192.

4  Both commemorative scrolls were dated 17 May 1944, just three weeks before Britain and America finally opened their long-awaited second front in France with D-Day.

# NOTE ON SOURCES

Rather surprisingly, Kursk is largely neglected in many of the more accessible contemporary sources. This is perhaps in part a reflection of how the stature and significance of the battle has grown over time. For example, Khrushchev in his memoirs only briefly touches upon their victory. Bialer's collected senior Soviet military memoirs simply mentions it only in passing.

Zhukov, who took a leading role in planning and shaping the battle, has the most to say. It is worth noting, however, that his version of events varies slightly between the series of articles he had published in the late 1960s (which formed the basis of Zhukov's *Greatest Battles* published in English in 1969) and his subsequent memoirs published in 1974 (first published in English in 1985). Although similar the English translations are not exactly the same and there are a number of detailed disparities. This will be in part due to using different translators, but also shows that Zhukov's memory of events changed over the years. Even though his articles were published nearer to the battle there is no way of knowing which versions are the most accurate.

Likewise, on the German side Otto Günsche's memories collected for the Stalin dossier cannot be relied upon to be entirely accurate when dealing with Kursk. Guderian spent little time discussing Operation Citadel other than to point out his opposition and to highlight the poor performance of their newer tanks. Speer, who worked closely with Guderian to build up Hitler's depleted Panzer forces, references it just briefly despite the heavy loss of tanks. Manstein's coverage is very perfunctory and is understandably overshadowed by his much lauded victory beforehand at Kharkov in March 1943. Only Mellenthin offers much detailed analysis of the course of the battle.

German intelligence chief Gehlen largely took the opportunity to exonerate himself of any blame for the German defeat. His memoirs are characterised by a sense of frustration that no one would heed his intelligence warnings. Interestingly Rommel, who fought in North Africa, Italy and France, although a keen advocate of the Panzer, saw fit not to comment on Kursk or its ramifications. There is though intriguingly some indication from his memoirs that he was briefed on the plans and approved of them. In terms of Churchill and Bletchley Park's role, Roberts provides one of the clearest accounts of British assistance.

# BIBLIOGRAPHY

## Contemporary Sources

Abdulin, Mansur, translated from Russian by Denis Fedosov and edited by Artem Drabkin. *Red Road from Stalingrad: Recollections of a Soviet Infantryman*. Barnsley: Pen & Sword, 2004.

Bessonov, Evgeni, translated from Russian by Bair Irincheev and edited by Sergei Anisimov. *Tank Rider into the Reich with the Red Army*. London: Greenhill Books, 2003/Pennsylvania: Stackpole Books, 2003.

Bialer, Seweryn (ed.). *Stalin & His Generals: Soviet Military Memoirs of World War II*. New York: Pegasus 1969/London: Souvenir Press, 1970.

Bryukhov, Vasiliy, translated from Russian by Vladimir Kroupnik and edited by Steve Williamson. *Red Army Tank Commander: At War in a T-34 on the Eastern Front*. Barnsley: Pen & Sword Military, 2013.

Deichmann, General Paul, edited and with an introduction by Dr Alfred Price, *Spearhead for Blitzkrieg: Luftwaffe Operations in Support of the Army, 1939–1945*. London: Greenhill, 1996 (first published as *German Air Force Operations in Support of the Army*, USAF Historical Studies, No. 163, 1962).

Djilas, Milovan. *Wartime*. London: Martin Secker & Warburg, 1977.

Eberle, Henrik & Uhl, Mathias (ed.), translated from German by Giles MacDonogh. *The Hitler Book: The Street Dossier Prepared for Stalin*. London: John Murray, 2006.

Gehlen, General Reinhard, translated from German by David Irving. *The Gehlen Memoirs: The First Full Edition of the Memoirs of General Reinhard Gehlen 1942–1971*. London: Collins, 1972 (first published in a shorter edition in German, Mainz: V. Hase und Koehler Verlag, 1971).

Grossman, Vasily, translated from Russian and edited by Antony Beevor & Luba Vinogradova. *A Writer at War: With the Red Army 1941–1945.* London: Harvill Press, 2005.

Guderian, General Heinz, translated from German by Constantine Fitzgibbon and foreword by Captain B.H. Liddell Hart. *Panzer Leader.* London: Michael Joseph, 1952/London: Futura, 1982.

Kerr, Walter. *The Russian Army: Its Men, Its Leaders and Its Battles.* London: Victor Gollanz, 1944.

Khrushchev, Nikita, translated from Russian and edited by Strobe Talbott, introduction, commentary and notes by Edward Crankshaw. *Khrushchev Remembers.* London: André Deutsch, 1971.

Klemperer, Victor, abridged and translated from German by Martin Chalmers. *To The Bitter End: The Diaries of Victor Klemperer 1942–1945.* London: Weidenfeld & Nicolson, 1999 (first published in German as *Ich will Zeugnis ablegen bis zum letzten.* Berlin: Aufbau-Verlag GmbH, 1995).

Liddell Hart, B.H. *The Other Side of the Hill: Germany's Generals their Rise and Fall, with their own Account of Military Events, 1939–1945.* London: Cassel and Company 1948, revised and enlarged edition 1951.

Liddell Hart, B.H. (ed.), with the assistance of Lucie-Maria Rommel, Manfred Rommel and General Fritz Bayerlein, translated from German by Paul Findlay. *The Rommel Papers.* London: Collins, 1953.

Loringhoven, Bernd Freytag von, with François d'Alançon. *In the Bunker with Hitler.* London: Weidenfeld & Nicolson, 2006. First published as *Dans le bunker de Hitler.* Paris: Perrin, 2005.

Manstein, Field Marshal Erich von, translated from German and edited by Anthony G. Powell. *Lost Victories.* Elstree: Greenhill Books/Lionel Leventhal, 1987 (first published in German as *Verlorene Siege.* Bonn: Athenaum-Verlag, 1955).

Mellenthin, Major General F.W. von, translated from German by H. Betzler and edited by L.C.F. Turner. *Panzer Battles.* London: Cassell, 1955/London: Futura, 1984.

Ritgen, Colonel Helmut. *The 6th Panzer Division 1937–45.* Oxford: Osprey, 1982.

Roberts, Captain Jerry. *Lorenz: Breaking Hitler's Top Secret Code at Bletchley Park.* Stroud: The History Press, 2017.

Sebastian, Mihail. *Journal 1935–44.* London: William Heinemann, 2001.

Shtemenko, S.M. *The Soviet General Staff at War 1942–1945.* Moscow: Progress Press, 1970.

Speer, Albert, translated from German by Richard and Clara Winston, introduction by Eugene Davidson. *Inside the Third Reich*. London: Phoenix, 1995.

Stalin, Marshal J. *On the Great Patriotic War of the Soviet Union; Speeches, Orders of the Day, and Answers to Foreign Press Correspondents*. London: Hutchinson, 1943.

Trevor-Roper, H.R. (intro), translated from German by Noman Cameron and R.H. Stevens. *Hitler's Table-Talk: Hitler's Conversations Recorded by Martin Bormann*. London: Weidenfeld & Nicolson, 1953/ Oxford: Oxford University Press, 1988.

Trevor-Roper, H.R. (ed.). *Hitler's War Directives 1939–1945*. London: Sidgwick and Jackson, 1964/London: Pan, 1983 (first published in German as *Hitler's Weisungen für die Kriegführung 1939–45, Dokumente des Oberkommandos der Wehrmacht*. Edited by Walter Hubatsch. (Frankfurt am Main: Bernard und Graefe Verlag).

Werth, Alexander. *Russia at War 1941–1945*. London: Barrie & Rockliff, 1964.

Werth, Alexander. *The Year of Stalingrad*. London: Hamish Hamilton, 1946.

Zhukov, Georgi, translated from Russian by Theodore Shabad and edited by Harrison E. Salisbury. *Marshal Zhukov's Greatest Battles*. London: Macdonald, 1969 (first published in Russian in *Voyenno-Istoricheskii Zhurnal*. Moscow: Ministry of Defense, June 1965, August, September and October 1966 and August and September 1967; and in *Stalingradskaya Epopeya*. Moscow: Military Publishing House, 1968).

Zhukov, Georgi, Marshal of the Soviet Union, translated from Russian by Vic Schneierson. *Reminiscences and Reflections*, Volume 2. Moscow: Progress Publishers, 1985 (first published in Russian in 1974).

## Secondary Sources

Abbott, Peter & Eugene Pinak. *Ukrainian Armies 1914–55*. Oxford: Osprey, 2005.

Andrew, Christopher. *The Defence of the Realm: The Authorized History of MI5*. London: Allen Lane, 2009.

Applebaum, Anne. *Gulag: A History of the Soviet Camps*. London: Allen Lane, 2003.

Arnold-Forster, Mark. *The World at War*. London: William Collins, 1973.

Axell, Albert. *Russia's Heroes 1941–45*. London: Constable 2001.

Bean, Tim & Will Fowler. *Russian Tanks of World War II: Stalin's Armoured Might*. Hersham: Ian Allan, 2002.

Beevor, Antony. *The Second World War*. London: Weidenfeld & Nicolson, 2012.

Beevor, Antony. *Stalingrad*. London: Penguin, 1999.

Bekker, Cajus, translated and edited by Frank Ziegler. *The Luftwaffe War Diaries*. London: Macdonald, 1967/London: Corgi Books, 1972 (originally published in German as *Angriffshöhe 4000*. Hamburg: Gerhard Stalling Verlag, 1964).

Bellamy, Chris. *Absolute War Soviet Russia in the Second World War*. London: Macmillan, 2007.

Bergström, Christer. *Kursk: The Air Battle*. Hersham: Ian Allan, 2007.

Binns, Stewart & Adrian Wood. *The Second World War in Colour*. London: Pavilion, 1999.

Bonn, Keith E. *Slaughterhouse: The Handbook of the Eastern Front*. Bedford, USA: Aberjona Press, 2005.

Boyd, Alexander. *The Soviet Air Force Since 1918*. London: Macdonald and Jane's, 1977.

Brookes, Andrew. *Air War over Russia*. Hersham: Ian Allan, 2003.

Bruce, George. *Second Front Now! The Road to D-Day*. London: Macdonald and Jane's, 1979.

Bullock, Alan. *Hitler: A Study in Tyranny*. London: Odhams, 1952 (revised edition Pelican Books 1962).

Burleigh, Michael. *The Third Reich: A New History*. London: Pan, 2001.

Chaney Jr, Otto Preston. *Zhukov*. Newton Abbot: David & Charles, 1972.

Chant, Chris. *Aircraft of World War II*. London: Amber Books, 2016.

Chant, Chris. *The Encyclopaedia of Codenames of World War II*. London: Routledge & Kegan Paul, 1986.

Churchill, W.S. *The Second World War, Volume V Closing the Ring*. London: Cassell, 1965.

Clark, Alan. *Barbarossa: The Russian German Conflict 1941–1945*. London: Cassell, 2001.

Clark, Lloyd. *Kursk, The Greatest Battle: Eastern Front 1943*. London: Headline Review, 2011.

Collier, Richard. *The War That Stalin Won*. London: Hamish Hamilton, 1983.

Conley Ruffner, Kevin. *Luftwaffe Field Divisions 1941–45*. Oxford: Osprey, 1990.

Cooper, Matthew. *The Phantom War: The German Struggle against Soviet Partisans 1941–44*. London: Macdonald & Jane's, 1979.

Cornish, Nik. *Hitler versus Stalin: The Eastern Front 1943–1944: Kursk to Bagration*. Barnsley: Pen & Sword Military, 2017.

Cornish, Nik. *Images of Kursk: History's Greatest Tank Battle July 1943*. Staplehurst: Spellmount, 2002.

Cradock, Percy. *Know Your Enemy: How the Joint Intelligence Committee Saw the World*. London: John Murray, 2002.

Davies, Norman. *Europe at War 1939–1945: No Simple Victory*. London: Macmillan, 2006.

Drabkin, Artem & Oleg Sheremet. *T-34 in Action*. Barnsley: Pen & Sword, 2006.

Edwards, Bernard. *The Road to Russia: Arctic Convoys 1942*. Barnsley: Leo Cooper, 2002.

Einsiedel, Heinrich Graf von, translated from German by Arnold J. Pomerans. *The Onslaught: The German Drive to Stalingrad*. London: Sidgwick & Jackson, 1984. First published as *Der Überfall*. Hamburg: Hoffmann and Campe Verlag, 1984.

Erickson, John. *The Road to Berlin: Stalin's War with Germany Volume 2*. London: Weidenfeld & Nicolson, 1983.

Evans, Geoffrey. *Tannenberg 1410/1914*. London: Hamish Hamilton, 1970.

Farrell, Nicholas. *Mussolini: A New Life*. London: Weidenfeld & Nicolson, 2003.

Fey, W. *Armor Battles of the Waffen-SS 1943–45*. Mechanicsburg, PA: Stackpole, 2003.

Galante, Pierre. *Hitler Lives – and the Generals Die*. London: Sidgwick & Jackson, 1982.

Glantz, D.M. & J.M. House. *The Battle of Kursk*. Lawrence: University Press of Kansas, 1999.

Glantz, D.M. & H.S. Orenstein. *The Battle for Kursk 1943: The Soviet General Staff Study*. London: Frank Cass, 1999.

Hastings, Max. *All Hell Let Loose: The World at War 1939–1945*. London: Harper Press, 2011.

Hastings, Max. *Catastrophe Europe Goes to War 1914*. London: William Collins, 2014.

Hastings, Max. *The Secret War: Spies, Codes and Guerrillas 1939–1945*. William Collins, 2017.

Haupt, Werner. *Army Group Centre: The Wehrmacht in Russia 1941–1945*. Atglen, PA: Schiffer Military History, 1997 (originally published in German as *Heeresgruppe Mitte*. Friedberg: Podzun-Pallas Verlag).

Healy, Mark. *Kursk 1943: Tide Turns in the East*. Oxford: Osprey, 1993.

Healy, Mark. *Zitadelle: The German Offensive against the Kursk Salient 4–17 July 1943*. Stroud: The History Press, 2008.

Hilton, Stanley E. *Hitler's Secret War in South America 1939–1945*. Baton Rouge and London: Louisiana State University Press, 1981.

Hughes, Dr Matthew & Dr Chris Mann. *The T-34 Tank.* Staplehurst: Spellmount, 1999.

Humble, Richard. *Hitler's Generals.* London: Arthur Barker, 1973.

Irving, David. *The Rise and Fall of the Luftwaffe: The Life of Luftwaffe Marshal Erhard Milch.* London: Weidenfeld & Nicolson, 1973.

Jackson, Robert. *Aircraft of World War II.* Enderby: Silverdale Books, 2005.

Jukes, Geoffrey. *The Eastern Front 1941–1945.* Oxford: Osprey, 2002.

Jukes, Geoffrey. *Stalingrad to Kursk: Triumph of the Red Army.* Barnsley: Pen & Sword, 2011.

Kennedy, Paul. *Engineers of Victory: The Problem Solvers who Turned the Tide in the Second World War.* London: Penguin, 2014.

Khazanov, Dmitriy. *Air War over Kursk: Turning Point in the East.* Bedford: SAM Publications, 2010.

Kotelnikov, Vladimir R. *Air War over Khalkhin Gol: The Nomonhan Incident.* Bedford: SAM Publications, 2010.

Kurowski, Franz, translated from German by David Johnston. *Panzer Aces: German Tank Commanders of World War II.* Mechanicsburg, PA: Stackpole, 2004.

Liddell Hart, B.H. *History of the Second World War.* London: Cassell & Company, 1970.

Linklater, Eric. *The Campaign in Italy.* London: HMSO, 1997.

Lucas, James. *War on the Eastern Front 1941–1945: The German Soldier in Russia.* London: Jane's Publishing, 1979.

Mackintosh, Malcolm. *Juggernaught: A History of the Soviet Armed Forces.* London: Secker & Warburg, 1967.

Mathews, R. *Hitler Military Commander.* London: Arcturus, 2003.

McKay, Sinclair. *The Lost World of Bletchley Park.* London: Aurum, 2013.

McKay, Sinclair. *The Secret Life of Bletchley Park.* London: Aurum, 2011.

Melvin, Mungo. *Manstein: Hitler's Greatest General.* London: Orion, 2010.

Merridale, Catherine. *Ivan's War: The Red Army 1939–1945.* London: Faber & Faber, 2005.

Messenger, Charles. *The Art of Blitzkrieg.* Shepperton: Ian Allan, 1976 (second edition 1991).

Messenger, Charles. *Hitler's Gladiator: The Life and Times of Oberstgruppenführer and Panzergeneral-Oberst der Waffen-SS Sepp Dietrich.* London: Brassey's Defence Publishers, 1988.

Minasyan, M.M. (ed.-in-chief), translated from Russian by David Skvirsky and Vic Schneireson. *Great Patriotic War of the Soviet Union 1941–45.* Moscow: Progress Publishers, 1974.

Mitcham, Samuel W. Jr. *Hitler's Field Marshals and their Battles*. London: William Heinemann, 1988.

Mondey, David. *Axis Aircraft of World War II*. London: Bounty Books, 2006.

Montefiore, Simon, Sebag. *Stalin the Court of the Red Tsar*. London: Weidenfeld & Nicolson, 2003.

Morgan, Hugh. *Soviet Aces of World War 2*. Madrid: Del Prado, 1999.

Muñoz, Antonio J. (ed.). *Wehrmacht Rear Guard Security in the USSR 1941–1945*. Washington DC: Department of the Army Pamphlet 20-240, 1951.

O'Balance, Edgar. *The Red Army*. London: Faber & Faber, 1964.

Overy, Richard. *The Dictators: Hitler's Germany Stalin's Russia*. London: Allen Lane, 2004.

Overy, Richard. *Russia's War*. London: Allen Lane, 1998.

Pack, Captain S.W.C. *Operation Husky: The Allied Invasion of Sicily*. New York: Hippocrene, 1977.

Quarrie, Bruce. *Hitler's Samurai: The Waffen-SS in Action*. London: Patrick Stephens, 1985.

Quarrie, Bruce. *Hitler's Teutonic Knights: SS Panzers in Action*. London: Patrick Stephens, 1986.

Reitlinger, Gerald. *The SS Alibi of a Nation 1922–1945*. London: William Heinemann, 1956/ London: Arms and Armour Press, 1981.

Ripley, Tim. *Elite Units of the Third Reich: German Special Forces in World War II*. Lewis International: Miami, 2002.

Ripley, Tim. *Steel Storm: Waffen-SS Panzer Battles on the Eastern Front 1943–1945*. Stroud: Sutton Publishing, 2000.

Roberts, Geoffrey. *Stalin's General: The Life of Georgy Zhukov*. London: Icon, 2013.

Roland, Paul. *The Secret Lives of the Nazis: The Hidden History of the Third Reich*. London: Arcturus, 2017.

Rutherford, Ward. *Hitler's Propaganda Machine*. London: Bison Books, 1978.

Seaton, Albert. *The Fall of Fortress Europe 1943–1945*. London: B.T. Batsford, 1981.

Seaton, Albert. *The German Army 1933–45*. London: Weidenfeld & Nicolson, 1982.

Seaton, Albert. *Stalin as Warlord*. London: B.T. Batsford, 1976.

Service, Robert. *Stalin: A Biography*. London: Macmillan, 2004.

Sharpe, Michael & Davis, Brian L. *Das Reich: Waffen-SS Armoured Elite*. Hersham: Ian Allan, 2003.

Sharpe, Michael & Davis, Brian L. *Grossdeutschland: Guderian's Eastern Front Elite*. Hersham: Ian Allan, 2001.

Sharpe, Michael & Davis, Brian L. *Leibstandarte: Hitler's Elite Bodyguard*. Hersham: Ian Allan, 2002.

Shtemenko, General S.M. *The Last Six Months: Russia's Final Battles with Hitler's Armies in World War II*. London: William Kimber, 1978.

Slepyan, Kenneth. *Stalin's Guerrillas: Soviet Partisans in World War II*. Lawrence: University Press of Kansas, 2006.

Smith, Michael. *Bletchley Park the Code-Breakers of Station X*. Oxford: Shire, 2013.

Smith, Michael. *Station X: The Codebreakers of Bletchley Park*. London: Pan Books, 2004.

Suvorov, Viktor. *Inside the Soviet Army*. London: Hamish Hamilton, 1982.

Thomas, Nigel & Peter Abbott. *Partisan Warfare 1941–45*. London: Osprey, 1983.

Toland, John. *Adolf Hitler*. New York: Doubleday 1976/Ware: Wordsworth 1997.

Warner, Philip. *World War Two: The Untold Story*. London: Bodley Head, 1988/London: Cassell, 2002.

Weal, John. *Focke-Wulf Fw 190 Aces on the Eastern Front*. Madrid: Del Prado, 2000.

Weitz, John. *Hitler's Diplomat: The Life and Times of Joachim von Ribbentrop*. New York: Ticknor & Fields, 1992.

White, B.T. *German Tanks and Armoured Vehicles 1914–1945*. Shepperton: Ian Allan, 1966.

Williamson, Gordon. *German Military Police Units 1939–45*. Oxford: Osprey, 1989.

Williamson, Gordon. *The SS: Hitler's Instrument of Terror*. London: Sidgwick & Jackson, 1994.

Williamson, Gordon. *Waffen-SS Handbook 1933–1945*. Stroud: Sutton, 2003.

Wilmot, Chester. *The Struggle for Europe*. London: Collins, 1952.

# ACKNOWLEDGEMENTS

No book is written in complete isolation, so thanks are due to a number of people who kindly assisted in one way or another. Firstly, Chrissy McMorris at The History Press, who suggested this new study to mark the seventy-fifth anniversary of the battle with a very personalised approach. Chrissy wanted the human story from ground level and felt it worth telling. Forget the armies she said, what about the people, what was it like for them? In addition I am a great believer in battles being viewed in their wider context and how this affects the outcome. In this instance Britain's role should not be overlooked or underestimated. Behind the scenes at THP, I am indebted to the excellent team: project editor Jezz Palmer, copy editor Paul Middleton, proofreader Matilda Richards and cartographer Glad Stockdale.

I must thank Professor Lloyd Clark, author of a first-class study on Kursk, for his sage advice and encouragement. Lloyd was kind enough to highlight the pitfalls of dealing with the bureaucratic Red Army staff system. He also warned that writing a book on Kursk is no easy feat and he was certainly right. This project has been rewarding and frustrating in equal measure. Unravelling and clarifying its complexity was certainly an enormous challenge.

Professor Geoffrey Roberts, author of *Stalin's General*, charting Zhukov's career, also very kindly offered encouragement and advice on English language sources and Soviet perceptions of the role of Bletchley Park. Likewise I am beholden to Russian military historian Nik Cornish for his support. It was Nik who first got me writing and researching about the Eastern Front through a joint project.

This study draws on a number of years of very detailed research, and indeed assembling the source material was a military operation in itself. Therefore I am grateful to all those who helped with both out of print and still in print titles, in particular Katie Eaton, Mark Willey and Chrissy McMorris. Lastly, my heartfelt thanks go to my wife, Amelia, and daughters, Henrietta and Ophelia, for their unending patience.

# INDEX